THE IMPOSTER'S WAR

THE PRESS, PROPAGANDA, AND THE NEWSMAN WHO BATTLED FOR THE MINDS OF AMERICA

MARK ARSENAULT

PEGASUS BOOKS
NEW YORK LONDON

AUTHOR'S NOTE

This is a work of nonfiction. Nothing in this book has been made up or dramatized by me. The characters, scenes, and dialogue come from documented sources.

THE IMPOSTER'S WAR

Pegasus Books, Ltd.
148 W 37th Street, 13th Floor
New York, NY 10018

Copyright © 2022 by Mark Arsenault

First Pegasus Books cloth edition April 2022

Interior design by Maria Fernandez

Library of Congress Cataloging-in-Publication Data is available.

ISBN: 978-1-64313-936-4

10 9 8 7 6 5 4 3 2 1

Printed in the United States of America
Distributed by Simon & Schuster
www.pegasusbooks.com

For Jennifer, my wife, spreader of joy. How lucky am I?

CONTENTS

Author's Note   ii

1: The Imposter   1

2: Bombs, Bullets, and Bad Luck   17

3: Frostbite and Dynamite   31

4: Birth of a Sensation   46

5: The Creation of John Revelstoke Rathom, Part 1: From Thin Air   62

6: Spies, Lies, Allies   84

7: Transformation   96

8: Romancing the Dictator   110

9: The Creation of John Revelstoke Rathom, Part 2: Love, Sex, and Poison   121

10: Minister without Portfolio   135

11: "Idiotic Yankees"   153

12: Good Friends/High Places   170

13: The Creation of John Revelstoke Rathom, Part 3: Tried by Fire   187

14: Shock & Awe   199

15: Department of Judas   214

16: The Only Thing We Have to Smear   237

17: Kompromat   254

18: Out of Character   269

19: Genesis of a Lie   285

Acknowledgments   297

Notes   299

Index   321

CHAPTER ONE

The Imposter

Three days after Christmas in 1915, a New York City taxi bounced over streetcar tracks and weaved among the horse buggies, on its way out of the city. The cab carried a special fare to the 5th Street Pier in Hoboken, New Jersey, home of the Holland-America cruise line. Snug along a dock reaching hundreds of feet into the Hudson River, the grand Dutch ocean liner *Rotterdam* prepared for its Atlantic crossing to Europe. Coal smoke from the *Rotterdam*'s pair of tall orange funnels wafted through the busy waterfront. A dozen blocks away, in an apartment on Monroe Street, a two-week-old baby lay injured in his crib, recovering from wounds caused by a doctor's forceps during a difficult delivery. The baby was Frank Sinatra.

At 11:40 A.M. the taxi doors opened and out stepped a German diplomat, Captain Karl Boy-Ed, a career military man and the German embassy's naval attaché, one of the highest-ranking consular posts. On this chilly morning, Boy-Ed wore an immaculate gray suit with a matching fedora and decorative ankle gaiters, known as spats. The outfit was finished with a brown overcoat with a white carnation in the lapel. The captain's valet got busy unloading the bags.

After nearly four years stationed in America, Captain Boy-Ed was sailing home in disgrace. President Woodrow Wilson's administration had ejected Boy-Ed from the United States, along with his colleague in the German diplomatic corps, military attaché Franz von Papen. The president had asked Germany to recall them due to a rising pile of evidence, much of it in the newspapers, that the diplomats were engaged in sabotage and deceptive propaganda in brazen violation of America's policy of neutrality in World War I.

The war had been raging in Europe for a little over a year. As a neutral nation, the United States maintained diplomatic relations with each of the major combatants: Germany and its ally Austria-Hungary on one side, and England, France, and Russia on the other.

The expulsion of Boy-Ed and Papen was for Germany a humiliating setback in international relations. What made the day even worse for the intellectual and gentlemanly Boy-Ed was that he had been chased from America by a mysterious loudmouth who edited a small daily newspaper in, of all places, Providence, Rhode Island.

Over the previous six months, the *Providence Journal*—led by its flamboyant, Australian-born editor John Revelstoke Rathom—had printed dozens of exclusive stories exposing alleged German intrigue in America. German diplomats in the United States were scandalized by the onslaught of articles, which blamed them for plots from passport fraud to propaganda, to undermining US industry and labor, to outright sabotage.

In Rathom's most outrageous story, he had named Boy-Ed as the point man in a German conspiracy to return the exiled Mexican dictator Victoriano Huerta back to power in a coup, and to smuggle weapons to Huerta so Mexico could attack the southwestern United States. It sounded too crazy to be true. *Boy-Ed was trying to goad the United States and Mexico into a shooting war?* Boy-Ed denied every word of it.

But the Germans understood that many people in the United States believed Rathom—too many. If enough Americans came to see Germany as a menace, the United States might enter the war on the side of Britain and its allies.

The Hoboken pier was already borderline bedlam when Boy-Ed arrived. Hundreds of passengers, well-wishers, and sightseers crowded inside the narrow, covered dock. A cluster of news photographers and moviemakers

waited for Boy-Ed at the dock entrance. Cameras blazed. A brawny, 6'4"
Hoboken cop led Boy-Ed onto the pier like a bodyguard protecting a stage
star. Police officers and a "flying wedge" of beefy stevedores pressed their
way through the crowd, plowing a path for the German officer. Spectators
were roughly elbowed out of the way, some nearly toppled over. Boy-Ed
seemed shaken by the chaos and "looked wildly about him as if trying to
find something to climb," one writer observed.

At the end of a long walk to the gangway, another group of forty
reporters and photographers waited. The journalists fired questions and
demanded interviews. Boy-Ed reached inside his coat and produced copies
of a statement, each one written in red ink.

"I think there are enough to go around," he said, in a quivering voice,
"but I wish to make sure the Associated Press man gets one." The Associated Press was a premier newswire service. The story the AP filed that day
would appear the next morning in newspapers across the country.

Boy-Ed's hands shook as he passed out his statement. There were not, in
fact, enough copies to go around, and in the mad jostle to get one Boy-Ed's
hat was knocked off. The fedora's lip caught his right ear and the hat dangled
there, comically. Other transatlantic passengers mistook the commotion
as a sign the *Rotterdam* was about the leave and they rushed the gangway,
trying to push through. Holland-America security guards shoved people
away from Boy-Ed and shouted, "Make way!" The melee threatened to
break into a riot before the police restored the peace.

Boy-Ed shook hands with friends who had come to see him off, then
stormed up the gangway. "Good-bye," he announced. "I am gone."

He let his written statement settle the score with the journalist he blamed
for his expulsion:

"Of course I refrain at the hour of my departure from again reciting all
the stories which were told about me in the American papers and which,
like the silly Huerta tale, were invented by the *Providence Journal*," Boy-Ed's
statement raged. "This paper with its British-born Mr. Rathom, has done
its utmost to create an almost hysterical suspicion throughout the country
in order to prejudice public opinion against Germany."

Providence Journal editor John Rathom was a naturalized American, but Boy-Ed's inference was clear; Rathom's native Australia was a British dominion and Rathom had been born a British subject. At the time, German and British troops were slaughtering each other in trench warfare in France.

"We Germans do not understand what you call your free press," Boy-Ed's statement continued. "We do not permit the representatives of friendly governments to be insulted ad libitum or our government to be embarrassed in its dealing with friendly nations, nor men's reputations to be wantonly sacrificed by the wild and reckless utterances of irresponsible papers like the *Providence Journal*."

Rathom was far from the only journalist to publish damning stories about German espionage in the critical years the United States remained neutral before joining the war. The *New York World*, for instance, contributed several embassy-rattling stories about German propaganda and economic sabotage. But Rathom's *Providence Journal* became the go-to source for German plots and intrigue. It earned the reputation as "a paper that has brought to light and proved story after story of the very essence of this war that is shaking the world," as one Canadian reporter put it in 1916.

Rathom's stories distinguished his newspaper, despite a circulation barely one-tenth the size of the major New York rags. He did it through syndication deals, under which his scoops were published simultaneously in other newspapers, most notably the *New York Times*, one of two New York newspapers that President Woodrow Wilson scoured cover-to-cover every day, along with the *World*.

The stories Rathom published confounded his readers' imagination—and at first many of his scoops were dismissed as fantasies. He exposed German plots to corner the US weapons market, to falsify evidence against President Wilson, and to illegally broadcast coded messages to Berlin in violation of US neutrality. He alleged that German diplomats had spent $40 million on propaganda (more than $1 billion today) to sway America to Germany's side, and that German sailors planned to scuttle one of their own ocean liners in the Hudson River to trap visiting US warships upstream.

His allegations of the so-called Huerta plot with Mexico contributed to Boy-Ed and Papen's ejection from the United States.

These sensations and dozens more almost overnight built a national reputation for the combative news editor, even if Rathom never explained in print how a modest, conservative newspaper in Rhode Island was getting all these explosive scoops. Rathom's stories were reprinted in national, regional, and local newspapers and magazines, delivered to front stoops and coffee counters in every state in the country, each story starting with what would become a famous opening line: "The *Providence Journal* will say today . . . "

Most Americans wanted the United States to stay far away from the European conflict, but each blockbuster story about German scheming in America weakened the country's resistance to war, eroding it, slowly, over time, like the wind wearing down a mountain.

"His news stories on those German intrigues were not only among the most sensational of all newspaper feats," an editor of the prestigious *World's Work* magazine wrote of Rathom in 1918, "but they had such a profound effect on American opinion that they were among the potent causes of the entry of the United States into the world war. . . . Nothing did more to create a state of public opinion favorable to military action against Germany."

With the expulsion of Boy-Ed and Papen from the United States in 1915, German propagandists were desperate to dig up some dirt to discredit Rathom, so nobody would believe his articles. The pro-German press found his background to be a dark forest full of fog, getting thicker the deeper they looked. They unearthed an embarrassing love triangle and bizarre poisoning plot from Rathom's West Coast days, as well as a few questionable claims in Rathom's résumé, but not even Rathom's most fearsome enemies could have imagined the breadth of his deception.

John Rathom was an imposter.

His identity was an invention, built on a biography of lies. John Revelstoke Rathom was a character, created and embodied by a remarkable actor playing the role of a lifetime, all to hide the secret he feared would destroy him.

By 1917 Rathom was the most famous newsman in the United States, a confidant of the president, trusted by millions of Americans, and there is no evidence he ever spoke his real name on this continent.

❖

The man who called himself John Rathom was 6'2", a rotund 260 pounds, with an enormous booming voice, and no obvious Aussie accent after a quarter century in the United States. He turned forty-seven in 1915, the year he launched himself into a propaganda fight against the Germans. He had a gigantic, round head, gray eyes on a chubby baby face, and in the few photos of him that exist, a puckish half-smile. There was usually a cigar between his fingers, flecks of ash on his shirt, the scent of tobacco around him like his own atmosphere. He wore a flashy diamond and sapphire ring on his left hand and worked in shirtsleeves and open collar with a necktie swinging loose. Brash and bossy, he barked orders and often lost himself to floor-stomping tantrums. His first secretary in Providence had to be replaced after fainting at her desk over Rathom's rages. Three things bothered him in the newsroom: any whiff of laziness, reporters who put their feet on their desks, and wishy-washy editorial writers who tried to pee down both legs, as the saying goes, instead of taking a stand.

When Rathom got genuinely mad, he broke out in mottled red blotches, like the pattern on a giraffe. His meaty fists would slam down on a desk and he'd scream, "This is the way I want it, dammit, and this is the way it's going to be!"

At other times, Rathom was capable of sugary sentiment and deep tenderness. He wrote quiet poems and essays about love and nature, which were published in national magazines such as *Scribner's*. He was an exquisite writer and a mesmerizing storyteller, known for the ability to make any person laugh at any time. "He could be deeply serious one moment and brilliantly jocose the next," his colleagues wrote of him. Reporters who worked themselves to the bone might find themselves brusquely summoned to the editor's office, but instead of the ass-kicking they expected, walked out with a surprise pay raise or with extra time off and complementary train tickets to visit family out of state.

John Rathom was a made-up identity, so naturally most of his personal biography was fake. A bio he submitted in 1920 to a *Who's Who*–type publication was an extraordinary salad of hyperbole, misdirection, and lies. He claimed to have been educated at Scotch College, Melbourne; Whinham College, Adelaide, Australia; and Harrow School in England. None of those institutions had any record of him. He said he was a war correspondent for the Melbourne *Argus* in the Sudan campaign in 1886, but the company that holds the records of the newspaper has confirmed nobody named Rathom ever wrote for the paper. Rathom boasted that he accompanied the explorer Frederick Schwatka on an Alaska expedition in 1890: there was no such expedition. He said he was wounded in the shoulder as a correspondent in the Spanish-American War; in truth he contracted yellow fever, became delirious, and was sidelined soon after setting foot in Cuba. He insisted he was twice wounded in the Boer War in 1900–1901, during which time he became chums with British field marshal Horatio Kitchener. In fact, Rathom was working in Chicago during those years.

Rathom's lies could be oddly specific. Among his most cherished possessions, he said, was a congratulatory telegram from William McKinley on the day Rathom became a US citizen. That's unlikely, unless McKinley sent it by Ouija board—the twenty-fifth president had been dead five years by the time Rathom took the oath of citizenship in 1906.

It almost feels like piling on to point out that the Melbourne couple Rathom named as his parents in fact never lived. Or that the woman he introduced as his wife, Florence Mildred Campbell, was not his legal spouse.

Of course, Australia has no records of Rathom's birth. Nor any immigration records in his name. Because "John Revelstoke Rathom" *did not exist*.

The imposter was undeniably brilliant. He was also a grifter, a con man, and an extortionist. He was one of the most gifted liars of his era and immune to shame. Under ordinary circumstances, someone of his dark talents would have been best suited for a career fleecing marks at a crooked carnival.

But in the midst of an unprecedented global conflict this ink-stained rogue found redemption in dedicating his unusual skill set to a cause bigger than himself—the defeat of the Central Powers and allied victory in the First World War. He hurled himself fully into the effort, at enormous personal and professional risk.

Then, almost immediately after seeing his goal to bring the United States into the conflict on the side of Great Britain, Rathom flew too close to the sun. His personal weakness for lies and self-indulgent bombast led to his crashing public downfall:

- When Rathom became too big to control, the US government betrayed him, and blackmailed him into silence.
- When Rathom fought back, federal agents destroyed his reputation to protect a rising Democratic politician by the name of Franklin Delano Roosevelt. Rathom's public standing fell into ruins, and the writers of history punished him with the ultimate sentence: they left him out. The influence he wielded before and during World War I was forgotten.

Rathom is difficult to write about. Piercing his cocoon of lies is one problem—the other is the fact that he left almost no evidence of his unguarded thoughts. He wrote miles of news copy, and thousands of letters, but tested every word through his mental self-censor for possible minefields. The imposter was always *on*, never showing his inner self. I don't know what he liked for breakfast. Or whether he cared when the Boston Red Sox sold Babe Ruth. To profile Rathom largely requires writing about the space around him, and the spaces between the lines that flowed from his pen.

I don't even know how he pronounced his name, since it appears no one of his time bothered to make a record of it. I say RAY-thum because that's how I first heard it as a reporter at the *Providence Journal*, where I worked for a decade, seventy-five years after the imposter last stalked the newsroom. Rathom's contemporary, Adolph Ochs, publisher of the *New York Times*, once wrote a poem that rhymed his friend's name with *fathom*. So was that the correct pronunciation? RATH-um? Or just the shaky work of an amateur poet?

❖

At the time of his ejection from the United States in late 1915, Captain Boy-Ed was forty-three years old, solidly built, and with a ridiculously grim resting face. Photographs of him look like they were taken the instant before he started yelling at children to get off his lawn. His somber looks didn't fit with his genial personality. People who knew him liked him a lot. Boy-Ed thoroughly charmed the Washington political and military establishments during his station in America, despite his severe affliction with two mental disorders: Insomnia wrecked his nights, and phagomania, the manic desire to eat, tortured him by day. Controlling these problems took extreme personal discipline.

Boy-Ed grew up in Lubeck, a German city on the Baltic Sea, in an educated and affluent family. His grandfather was a journalist, a newspaper publisher, and a politician who served in the German Parliament. Boy-Ed's father, Karl Boy, was a well-to-do merchant; his mother, Ida Ed, an accomplished essayist, novelist, and women's rights crusader. Ida Ed was a patron of the arts, and in Boy-Ed's youth it was common in his household to find musicians, composers, and writers lounging around, drinking, arguing, and solving the world's problems.

Boy-Ed joined the German Navy at age nineteen, seeing the world from the decks of German ships. He was an excellent sailor and flew up the ranks. In 1912 he was assigned to be German naval attaché to the United States and Mexico, and the next year took a full-time station in Washington, DC. The year after that, 1914, the First World War began in Europe.

At the outbreak of war, German diplomats in the United States were no longer just representatives of the empire. Germany expected them to help win the fight. The German government funneled great sums of money through its US staff for propaganda to manipulate American public opinion. On top of the psychological warfare, in January 1915 the chief of the political section of the Imperial German General Staff transmitted authorization to German diplomats in the United States for sabotage against "factories for military supplies; railroads, dams, [and] bridges" in the United States and Canada, largely to interrupt the shipment of war supplies to Great Britain and its allies.

The diplomats who carried out these orders thought of themselves not as saboteurs but patriots. They were assigned the impossible task of stopping American munition exports by any means necessary, while at the same time deploying agile diplomacy to keep the United States out of the war. This mission was made infinitely harder by German submarine policy controlled by Berlin, which was costing the lives of Americans on the high seas, creating one diplomatic crisis after another, and enflaming US public opinion.

These diplomats were not trained spies, and they made mistakes, sometimes head-slappingly stupid ones. They could not imagine how their every misstep ended up in the headlines.

❖

Most Americans don't think much about World War I.

It took more than a century for the United States to build a major memorial in Washington, DC, to the 117,000 Americans who died to "make the world safe for democracy." Maybe we don't think about World War I because its history is so complicated. It involves some counties that no longer exist, as well as about a thousand years of preamble.

Rathom's story is intertwined with America's in World War I. The battlefields were in Europe, but the war was fought here, too, with printer's ink, propaganda, and bombs. I have edited away all but the bare essentials to explain what caused the war, and to argue that many threads of the story never really ended. The things German agents did to manipulate the United States in 1915, the Russians copied in 2016, and continue today. During the First World War, people in power used the press to spread a fear of foreigners. Some still do, though now the fear radiates digitally. In Rathom's day, the US government ruined the lives of people who dared to say unpopular things; now civilians do this to each other on social media. John Rathom is a human Rorschach test for whether a collection of lies can tell a larger truth, an argument that carries over from his era to ours.

I'm not much interested in history written as the movement of armies. History is what happens to individuals, each of whom is a fiber bound up with many others in a story tethered between their time and now. Sometimes a single individual pulls this braid hard in one direction. The murder of one man, Archduke Franz Ferdinand, heir presumptive to the throne of Austria-Hungary, ignited the First World War and set the rest of the twentieth century on a bloody course.

But even the most minuscule vibrations resonate forever. Consider a New Brunswick farm boy named Henry Arsenault, born in 1896, and drafted at age twenty-one in 1917 into the Canadian Expeditionary Force. He was a skinny kid, 5'7", 135 pounds, with blue eyes, and a wiry strength from barn chores.

Henry was shipped out to Europe and attached to the 44th Canadian Infantry Battalion. He arrived at the Western Front, in northern France, on September 18, 1918, and was wounded just ten days later, while his unit fought at the Battle of Canal du Nord, about a hundred miles northeast of Paris. On Henry's medical report, the doctor scribbled "GSW R leg," abbreviating a familiar diagnosis: gunshot wound. There is a simple line drawing of a human figure in Henry's records; on it the doctor marked with two black pencil dots where the bullet entered and exited his right leg. Move those dots ever slightly, to, say, the femoral artery, and that's a fatal battlefield wound in 1918.

Henry was evacuated to a military field hospital. He would survive the war, marry an Irish girl, and raise five sons, all of whom he named Joseph, for reasons never credibly explained to me. The youngest Joseph is my father. Four generations of descendants followed after Henry, so far, and all these people came to be because some German rifleman aimed a few inches low and saved our family's story. I think of Rathom in these same terms—by how much he bent the braid of history.

❖

Eighteen months after Captain Boy-Ed's humiliating exit from the United States, members and guests of the Canadian Press Association assembled in downtown Toronto, on June 14, 1917, for the group's annual meeting. The event stirred more buzz than usual, for the crowd was scheduled to hear from the famous American journalist John R. Rathom.

Rathom's talk was titled "Some Inside History." With the United States now involved and committed to victory in World War I, the conference crackled with speculation that Rathom would for the first time reveal how the *Providence Journal* had broken so many exclusive stories about German espionage. "No other man in the world has done more to defeat the plots of the German conspirators and spies in the United States than Mr. Rathom," one Canadian newspaper wrote, "the secret of which has never been disclosed."

Rathom's Toronto trip had already been a smash. He had arrived by train the day before like a returning conqueror, greeted personally by the mayor and city dignitaries. They whisked Rathom by car to city hall, a sandstone palace with a 340-foot clock tower, where officials feted him in a ceremony in the ornate City Council Chambers. The president of the Canadian Press Association introduced Rathom by declaring, "No journalist on this continent has done better service in the cause of humanity than Mr. Rathom."

Officials honored Rathom with the key to their city and a three-cheer salute. *Hip-hip-hurrah!*

The imposter once thought himself an outcast. Now he was a hero.

But that was just the beginning.

Rathom was about to shock the world.

His address was scheduled for the new Central Technical School, a blocky four-story building of brown limestone that looked more like a troop garrison than a place of learning. Rathom climbed the school's stone steps and entered between two tall columns. On each column sat the decorative figure of a gnome carved from stone. The figures were perfect for the coming-out party of John R. Rathom—one of the gnomes was writing; the other swung a hammer.

❖

Under a shower of applause, Rathom stepped up to the podium on the tall wooden stage, looked out over the rows of journalists sitting before him, and in the balconies above, and proceeded to drop every jaw in the house.

How did he break all those exclusive stories?

By turning his staff of thirty Rhode Island newspaper reporters into America's most effective counterspy operation, he said. Those condescending German diplomats never knew it, but Rathom placed a reporter undercover in the German embassy for seventeen months, as personal assistant to the ambassador. This man eavesdropped. He swiped documents. He snooped into ledgers and letters and diplomatic cables.

The Huerta plot with Mexico? *Providence Journal* reporters tricked German spies into holding their clandestine talks with Victoriano Huerta in a hotel room riddled with hidden *Journal* microphones.

They got a trove of evidence after reporters faked a fistfight on a New York train, and then swapped identical briefcases with a distracted German diplomat.

Rathom shared that the *Providence Journal*'s wireless stations had intercepted years' worth of German messages, and the paper had broken German codes.

The swagger practically dripped from Rathom: "We have been aided in this work by a certain degree of fatuity—by green blubber, taking place of grey matter in the brain, which the Lord has seen fit to deposit in the head of every German diplomat. We have always found that if we looked long enough into any German scheme, we should find a hole big enough in it for a schoolboy to crawl through."

It was on this night Rathom debuted the "hearts story." This amazing nugget would become his "Freebird"—that greatest hit no fan wanted to miss.

The setup: Rathom had placed a young woman undercover as a stenographer in the Austrian consulate in New York City. This *Providence Journal* employee learned that at the consulate the Germans had filled a packing crate with secret documents to be shipped to Europe and smuggled to Berlin. At the time, the British Royal Navy enforced a policy that neutral shipping to Europe had to detour to British ports, such as Falmouth, to be searched for contraband war supplies. But in the giant hold of a cargo ship, what was one more anonymous crate?

We pick up with Rathom's words, verbatim, from a stenographic transcript of his retelling of the story the next day:

> The day this box was to be finally nailed up, this young woman, under instructions, stayed late and ate her luncheon at the office. There were only two or three people left in the office during the lunch hour. One of them was Captain von Papen, the German military attaché, a man with a weakness like a good many of us for beauty and talent in feminine form. This young lady answered that description and Captain von Papen proceeded to make love to her, sitting on this box, a packing case some three or four feet square.
>
> We could not possibly stop the box on this side, so the only thing we cared about was to identify the box by marking it so that the British officers in the first port of call could get it from among the hundreds of other articles in the hold of that ship. This young lady, taking out a heavy red crayon pencil, and listening to Papen's advances, drew sentimentally two large red hearts on the top of that box—and it was Captain von Papen himself who took the pencil and put the arrow through the hearts.

This is where a showman would pause for the story to sink in. He would wait for the gathering laughter as the listeners began to figure out what came next.

Then the punchline: "The British authorities informed us and we have their word for it, that *that* was the method of identification of that box when it reached Falmouth."

The imposter did not just mesmerize the audience, he dominated it, making his listeners laugh on his cue, or shout and clap, or fight back tears. His speech was packed with humor, danger, and thrills, all unfolded in a spirit of joy. The subtext never wavered: *We are brave and clever and our enemy underestimates us. How can we lose?* Rathom's remarks were not only shocking in detail, they were uncut, medical-grade optimism, which was powerful stuff in a frightening time.

To close, Rathom carried his listeners to an emotional peak. With its soldiers fighting and dying, Canada had "won her destiny as a nation," he said.

To England, he paid poetic tribute:

> So small a shield to bear so great a sign,
> So small a shield to hold so great a blade.
> England, but in this darkest hour of thine,
> 'Tis those who know thee best are least afraid.

"God bless Canada," Rathom concluded, and sat down.

As one reporter who was there described, "The large audience, held spellbound for an hour, again broke into a storm of applause which lasted for minutes."

Rathom's revelations were genuinely astounding. Amateur detectives working for a *newspaper* had defeated Germany's spies at their own game?

The *Toronto Star* blew out its front page for Rathom's feats. "One of the most amazing stories ever related to a Toronto audience," the paper raved. "Fiction never created stranger happenings."

Rathom and his wife, Florence, were shepherded among luncheons and celebrations. Florence spoke a few words of thanks to the Canadian Press

Association, and the crowd was so moved it rose as one and burst into a spontaneous singing of "My Country, 'Tis of Thee."

News reports summarizing Rathom's incredible address raced around the world over the newswires. These stories were reprinted hundreds of times in papers across the country. The Providence newsman shot into national stardom. A sold-out speaking tour that autumn swept Rathom through New York, Philadelphia, Boston, Detroit, and Chicago, drawing huge crowds and armies of reporters begging for his time at every stop.

And none of them suspected—not yet—that Rathom's astonishing spy tales were *not true*. At least, not true as he told them.

As Rathom's reputation grew, the lies got bigger and more dangerous, until they consumed him. Through the lies is the way to the imposter's truth.

CHAPTER 2
Bombs, Bullets, and Bad Luck

I t was a festive, sunny Sunday, June 28, 1914, in Sarajevo, a Bosnian city on the outer boondocks of Austria-Hungary, one of the great powers of Central Europe. It was the day for which Nedeljko Cabrinovic had planned and trained and long imagined. He was nineteen, skinny and sickly, a radical Bosnian Serb, and an aspiring terrorist. And he was about to assassinate Archduke Franz Ferdinand, heir presumptive to the throne of Austria-Hungary, during the archduke's motorcade. Cabrinovic carried a grenade for Ferdinand, and a capsule of prussic acid, what we now call hydrogen cyanide, for himself. This was a suicide mission; the police must not take him alive.

The city was dressed up for the visit by the archduke and his wife, Sophie, the Duchess of Hohenberg. Buildings were draped with bunting and flags. Garlands of flowers drooped over the streets. The people of Sarajevo had become Austro-Hungarians when their region was annexed six years earlier, not that anyone had asked them. They poured outside to see the man who would someday, probably soon, become their emperor.

As a city, Sarajevo was "a curious mixture of East and West: streets crowded with officers in uniform, Turks in fezzes, Muslims in turbans, and mysteriously veiled women," wrote Ferdinand biographers Greg King and Sue Woolmans. "All moved at a frenetic pace between narrow alleys lined by red-roofed shops and beneath a forest of church spires and the thin minarets of mosques."

The assassin mingled in the crowd lining the motorcade route along the Appel Quay, a wide, flat avenue that hugged the north bank of the Miljacka, the narrow river that flowed east to west and split the city in half. Immediately behind Cabrinovic, a retaining wall of cut stone sloped almost vertically to the languid river below. Across the avenue, the opposite sidewalk was crammed with people waiting to catch a glimpse of the archduke. They stood before a charming streetscape of three- and four-story buildings, brick and stone, ornamented with awnings and rounded windows. Artillery guns in the distance sounded a thunderous salute.

There! About ten minutes past ten o'clock in the morning, the archduke's seven-car convoy came into view from the west, on its way to city hall.

And *there* was fifty-year-old Archduke Franz Ferdinand, riding in the third car. He looked, frankly, a little clownish in a high-collared blue cavalry tunic and a gleaming silver helmet blooming with a shock of green peacock feathers. Sophie, the Duchess of Hohenberg, forty-six, the mother of their three children, sat beside her husband, clutching a dainty parasol, dressed in a long-sleeved white gown with a red sash and flower corsage, a wide-brimmed white hat sprouting ostrich feathers, and a near-invisible veil decorated with polka dots. It happened to be the week of the royal couple's thirteenth wedding anniversary. They rode in the back of a 1910 Gräf & Stift Bois open-top touring car, with the driver up front and the ragtop folded back so the masses could see the archduke and duchess. The car was lavish for the time, with spoked rims, a spare tire strapped above the running board, and a protruding set of round brass headlamps that looked like the car was wearing glasses. The crowd clapped and cheered politely. Some voices shouted "Zivio!"—*long may he live!*

Cabrinovic was part of a team of assassins targeting Ferdinand that day to punish Austria for annexing Bosnia. While the car putt-putted slowly through the crowd, Cabrinovic decided it would be *his* name in the history books. What he could not have known was that murdering the archduke would spark an unprecedented worldwide war.

Cabrinovic struck the bomb's percussion cap on a lamppost with a *bang* to start the internal timer, took aim, and hurled the grenade at Ferdinand's open car. He had to think as he let it go . . . *what could be easier?*

Whoops. Threw it too far.

The grenade bounced off the folded fabric car top and trampolined into the street. It rolled beneath the next car in the convoy and exploded in a dragon's cough of fire and smoke. Shrapnel shot sideways from under the car, a few inches off the ground, slicing ankles in the crowd. A dozen or more innocent people went down shrieking, though no one was mortally wounded; certainly not the intended target, Archduke Franz Ferdinand, who suffered not a scratch.

Having bungled the murder, Cabrinovic ran away. His frantic fingers fumbled for his cyanide. He popped it in his mouth, gulped it down, and waited for the world to fade to black . . . waited . . . waited . . . nope, it was painful, but definitely not working.

The poison was old and had expired. It only burned Cabrinovic's throat and made him gag. He vaulted a stone wall and hurled himself into the Miljacka River. Alas, a summer drought had lowered the river to four inches deep. He splashed around on the slimy river bottom, dry heaving from the old cyanide, trying to drown himself in barely enough water to wet his pant cuffs. An angry crowd jumped him. Fists pounded him tender. Then the police manhandled him to jail.

After the explosion, the convoy sped away. Co-conspirators lurking along the route had heard the blast and figured Archduke Franz Ferdinand was dead. By the time they saw he had escaped, the car had zoomed by, and it was too late to take another shot.

Ferdinand was alive! The archduke had eluded assassination on the streets of Sarajevo.

❖

European history in the years immediately before World War I is a cascade of mistakes and calamities, with scenes of forbidden love, stunning betrayal, murder, vengeance, and more murder. In the summer of 1914, at the time of Ferdinand's motorcade in Sarajevo, Europe contained five great powers: Germany, Austria-Hungary, France, Britain, and Russia. With so many rivalries and crisscrossing concerns, each power sought to protect its national interests by signing alliances and by spending enormous sums on its military.

Central Europe was dominated by the German Empire and Austria-Hungary, the major nations in an alliance known as the Central Powers.

This is a simplified description, but imagine the German Empire of the time as essentially the land of modern Germany, about half of modern Poland, and the area running along the Baltic coast to where Lithuania is today. Germany was led by fifty-five-year-old Kaiser Wilhelm II. In June 1914, he celebrated twenty-six years of ruling the empire. Kaiser Wilhelm had hard, serious features—handsome if you could get past the aggressive moustache, which looked like a pair of hairy Christmas stockings with the toes laid up on his lip, waxed into shape daily by his barber. Kaiser Wilhelm nearly died at birth. The delivery left him with nerve damage in his left arm, which developed short and withered. He was often photographed with his left hand behind his back or stuffed in a pocket. Kaiser Wilhelm was known as unpredictable, belligerent, and overly competitive. Historians have wondered if he developed those traits to compensate for his physical disability. Doctors have also speculated that the kaiser's erratic personality may have been related to brain damage from a lack of oxygen at birth.

Whatever the reason, Kaiser Wilhelm was vain, incurious, easily distracted, and a habitual liar. He was known for giving insulting nicknames to other world leaders, and for his personal weakness for flattery. He enjoyed attention and talking about himself. These shortcomings may have been manageable were he not so lazy. "He wanted the power and the glory and the applause without the hard work," wrote the Canadian historian Margaret MacMillan. The kaiser whined about what a bear it was to run an empire, yet "refused to read newspapers and tossed long documents aside in irritation." He thought of himself as "a master of diplomacy and insisted on dealing with his fellow monarchs, often with unfortunate results."

"Sadly, he had no clear policies beyond a vague sense to make Germany, and himself, important and, if possible, avoid war," MacMillan wrote.

Unusual hair? Self-indulgent? Changed positions as readily as changing a hat? The resemblance is uncanny: Kaiser Wilhelm is the original Donald Trump, a likeness noted by historian Miranda Carter in 2018.

The comparison, though, is not entirely fair to either of them. Trump came to power not by inheritance but a democratic election. And Kaiser Wilhelm actually served in the military.

Bordering Germany to the south was the massive Austro-Hungarian Empire. It spread from Switzerland in the west, all the way east to well into what is now Ukraine and Romania. The empire was a "cobbled-together assortment" of thirteen nationalities speaking sixteen languages and following five religions. When the empire shattered after the war, it seeded modern Europe. The nations of Austria, Hungary, Slovakia, Slovenia, the Czech Republic, Bosnia, Croatia, a slice of Poland, and a chunk of Serbia were once folded into Austria-Hungary.

For an astounding sixty-six years, Emperor Franz Josef I—the uncle of Archduke Franz Ferdinand—had ruled Austria-Hungary. In the summer of 1914 no one figured he would be for much longer. The emperor was eighty-three years old. His reign began in 1848, during the Polk administration in the United States, when Abraham Lincoln was a backbench Illinois congressman. The emperor was a balding man with stinging blue eyes and bushy white muttonchops that blended into a robust mustache, all sculpted around a shaved chin. Emperor Franz Josef was obsessed with formalities and arcane rules, and would work himself to exhaustion on the bland minutia of his massive empire. His wife, Empress Elisabeth, was murdered in 1898, stabbed in the heart by an anarchist who just wanted to kill a royal.

The Central Powers were pinched between another alliance, signed between France and Russia. In the summer of 1914 the Russian Empire extended deep into Europe, stretching from modern Finland through Belarus and Ukraine, and controlling a substantial cutout of what is now Poland. The prewar borders of France and the rest of Western Europe, from Spain and Portugal to Britain and Italy, would mostly be recognizable now. Belgium was wedged uncomfortably between Germany and France.

In the early twentieth century Great Britain and Germany were strategic rivals engaged in an arms race on the seas; Germany aggressively built ships to challenge the dominance of the British Navy. An ascending Germany pushed Britain closer to Russia and France, and the three nations became known as the Triple Entente, or sometimes just the Allies. The great powers of Europe drew up plans for how to defeat each other in war, while aggressively building their armies. By 1914, "France could call upon about 700,000 soldiers; Germany had 850,000 and the Russians at least 1.3 million."

South of Austria-Hungary were the nations of Serbia, Bulgaria, Romania, and the remnants of the shrinking Ottoman Empire, which included what is now Turkey. This region became the flashpoint for war. We could go back ten centuries in search of the first event in a chain of consequences that led to World War I. In this greatly abridged version, we pick up in Serbia in 1903, when rebellious army officials staged a coup and assassinated King Alexander I, whom they considered too friendly to Austria-Hungary. There are differing accounts of how the coup went down. In the worst version of the story, the king and queen are hunted throughout a darkened palace until discovered huddling in a saferoom. They are riddled with bullets, their corpses then hacked with sabers, the chunks thrown off a balcony into a compost pile. In the nice version, they are only riddled with bullets. The coup established a pro-Russia rule in Serbia, bringing those nations closer.

One of the participants in the coup was Dragutin Dimitrijević, a bulky army man nicknamed Apis, after the bull god worshiped by the ancient Egyptians. Dimitrijević cofounded a secret military society in Serbia called Union or Death, but known to its members by the more enigmatic name, the Black Hand. The group would provide logistical support to the disillusioned young men who would later attack Archduke Franz Ferdinand in Sarajevo.

In 1908 Austria-Hungary caused a crisis in the region by seizing Bosnia and the little neighboring region of Herzegovina. For thirty years, the territory had been administered by Austria-Hungary, though technically it was still part of the Ottoman Empire. The annexation turned the occupants of the region into Austro-Hungarians, whether they liked it or not. Many did not. About 45 percent of the population of the annexed region identified as Bosnian Serbs, many of whom wanted their region to become part of a Greater Serbia. Austria-Hungary got the land, but at the price of provoking hatred within this population and in Serbia. We can draw a straight line from the annexation, through Archduke Franz Ferdinand, to war.

❖

Nineteen-year-old Gavrilo Princip was a "passionate Serbian nationalist," who grew up poor in Bosnia, as the "slight, introverted, and sensitive son of a hardworking farmer." Physically weak and tubercular, Princip "idolized Nietzsche and clung to a black view of humanity." In the coffeehouses of Belgrade, he mingled with like-minded young radicals, including Cabrinovic, who would later chuck the bomb at Archduke Franz Ferdinand. They were part of a terror cell willing to kill government officials and any innocents who happened to wander into the way, in order to "serve the larger goal of undermining Austria-Hungary as a force in the Balkans." Princip was their leader.

The terror group was inexperienced and sometimes bumbling, combining the brutal intentions of Al-Qaeda with the logistical execution of a first grade soccer game. One member, Muhamed Mehmedbašić, was chosen in early 1914 to assassinate the military governor of Bosnia with a dagger. The plot was scotched when he panicked at seeing a policeman on his train and threw the weapon out a window.

Princip read in the newspaper about Archduke Franz Ferdinand's upcoming trip to Sarajevo. Raging at Austria-Hungary's annexation of Bosnia, the men agreed to "sacrifice their lives for the cause of unifying the southern Slavs." They would kill Archduke Franz Ferdinand. They trained with the Black Hand, the secret military organization with Serbian ties, then made their circuitous way to Sarajevo.

On the morning of Archduke Franz Ferdinand's motorcade, seven assassins spread out along the route.

❖

At his birth in 1863, nobody would have predicted that Franz Ferdinand would become presumptive heir to the Austro-Hungarian throne. He was too low in the pecking order. But then the royals ahead of Ferdinand in the line of succession began to die under odd and violent circumstances, like dinner guests in an Agatha Christie novel.

First to go was Emperor Franz Josef's younger brother, Archduke Maximilian. In 1864 Maximillian was talked into accepting a bizarre offer engineered by France to become the emperor of Mexico.

Though this episode is largely now forgotten in the United States, in 1861 French troops sailed some six thousand miles and attacked Mexico, on the pretense of collecting bad debts. When modern Americans clink margarita glasses on Cinco de Mayo, they commemorate a Mexican victory over French troops in the Battle of Puebla, May 5, 1862. With the United States distracted by the Civil War, the French fought their way to an occupation of Mexico, intending to create a French client state in North America.

The French thought it would be a good idea to install a calming, European-style monarchy in Mexico. And who better for the job than the little brother of a real European monarch? They recruited Archduke Maximilian.

US reporters could smell disaster the moment Archduke Maximillian landed in Mexico. "In no [way] did the subjects of Maximillian demonstrate any joy at his arrival," the *New York Herald* observed. "The Mexicans are evidently averse to the ruler forced upon them by the bayonets of the French." The locals never did get on board. After French troops withdrew in 1866, Mexican opposition forces roared back. In 1867 the opposition captured Emperor Maximillian I, stood him on a hill in Querétaro City, in Central Mexico, and shot him.

The next potential Austrian ruler to perish was Rudolf, Crown Prince of Austria, Emperor Franz Josef's only son. Crown Prince Rudolf was well-liked internationally and legitimately qualified to rule. "He was not in the least a comic-opera prince, but a high-minded, sensible, serious man who spoke four or five languages, wrote books that still can be read with pleasure, and was deeply aware of his responsibilities," the *New York Times* wrote of Crown Prince Rudolf in 1964, on the seventy-fifth anniversary of his death.

In 1881, at age twenty-two, Crown Prince Rudolf did his duty and married the fifteen-year-old daughter of Leopold II, the king of Belgium. The political marriage did not interfere with Crown Prince Rudolf's affairs with other women. In 1889, during a stay with friends at a hunting lodge outside Vienna, Crown Prince Rudolf seemed to be having a grand time. The next morning, he was discovered shot to death in his room. With him was the naked body of a young baroness, also dead. Their deaths appeared to have been the result of a suicide pact or a murder-suicide. Authorities slapped together a sloppy cover-up, announcing that Crown Prince Rudolf had died of "apoplexy of the heart," which doctors today might call an aortic aneurysm. Reporters soon picked the lie apart, and officials reluctantly acknowledged that Crown Prince Rudolf died from an apparent self-inflicted gunshot wound. Within a couple weeks, news of the dead baroness also leaked, and the crown prince's death erupted into a global scandal.

The cursed line of succession fell to Archduke Franz Ferdinand's father, Archduke Karl Ludwig, the emperor's brother. Ferdinand was the oldest of Archduke Karl's four children with his second wife, the daughter of an Italian king. Archduke Karl was a devoted Roman Catholic. Maybe too devoted. On a pilgrimage to the Holy Land, he visited the River Jordan and was so deeply moved that he drank from it. By imbibing water polluted with sewage, he contracted typhoid fever and died in 1896.

As a young man, Ferdinand was unmarried and unhealthy. Sick with tuberculosis in his twenties and early thirties, he was mocked as the "heir consumptive." In early 1896 American newspapers reported that Archduke Franz Ferdinand was near death and unlikely to survive. Some printed his premature obituary, with a Berlin dateline and attributed to "rumor" that Ferdinand had expired. He eventually licked the disease and his sickly frame filled out.

The emperor-in-waiting had a large square skull and tiny ears that belonged on a smaller head. He wore his hair brushed straight back and cultivated a hefty mustache that curled up at the ends. Photographers often caught him with a vacant look in his eyes, like it had just occurred to him he might have left the stove on. He was described in US news reports as "a very big man," standing 6'2", with "a pink and white skin, as fair as a woman's." Personally, he was aloof and often bad-tempered. Politically, he was seen as a reformer and more likely than his uncle, the sitting emperor, to expand the rights of the empire's many nationalities. He was a passionate hunter and scoured the planet for new game. Archduke Franz Ferdinand was a one-man extinction event, who claimed to have bagged nearly three hundred thousand animals: deer by the herd, elk, kangaroo, tiger, elephant—if it walked, loped, or hopped, Archduke Franz was there to shoot it.

Unlike many royals of the time, Ferdinand married for love. We know it because of the hardship he endured to marry. The woman who took his heart, Sophie Chotek, came from an aristocratic family, but not one high enough on the social ladder to yield the wife of an archduke. Sophie had been lady-in-waiting, a sort of noblewoman's valet, to Princess Isabella of Croÿ. Princess Isabella had nearly enough eligible daughters for a softball team, and hoped to pair one off with the archduke. Ferdinand didn't want any of the daughters; he wanted Sophie. But the emperor said no. Sophie, by the conventions of the day, was beneath him.

Ferdinand stood his ground with his uncle in a battle of wills. He begged for permission to marry Sophie. He suggested he would go mad if he could not make her his wife. The emperor held the power, but time favored Ferdinand. He could wait for Emperor Franz Josef I to die, take the throne, and marry whomever he wanted. Under a grudging compromise in 1900, the emperor permitted the marriage, with the understanding that the union would be morganatic, meaning Sophie could never be empress and none of their children would be eligible for the crown. The line of succession would jump to the children of Ferdinand's brother. To ensure that Ferdinand would not weasel out of the terms later, he was forced to swear on a Bible in a formal ceremony that he would abide by the conditions, forever.

Newspapers around the world printed romantic stories about the archduke who forfeited the line of succession for love. Most of Ferdinand's family boycotted the wedding. Sophie was a second-class citizen throughout the marriage, generally forbidden to appear with her husband. "The morganatic wife may live in her husband's house," a British newspaper explained on the eve of the wedding, "but she must not sit in the same box with him at the opera nor be seen with him at the Imperial stand at the races. . . . Trifles, no doubt—but what is life but the sum of an infinite series of trivialities?"

Their trip to Sarajevo in June 1914 was a break from the oppressive rules. That month, the emperor dispatched Ferdinand to Bosnia to view military exercises and pay the region some attention. In the far reaches of the empire nobody cared about the social protocols of royalty. Sophie could join him in public. It was the week of their wedding anniversary, so they left their three kids behind and went away.

They arrived separately on Thursday, June 25, to the resort town of Ilidze, and checked into the Hotel Bosna, a ten-minute train ride from Sarajevo. That evening they shopped the public markets, feeling encouraged by the friendly reception they received. On Friday and Saturday, Ferdinand watched some twenty thousand soldiers in war games in the mountains outside the city. On Saturday evening, the couple enjoyed dinner at their hotel, believing that the trip was already a success.

The archduke's public schedule for Sunday morning, June 28, the day that changed history, began humbly enough, with a brief train ride into Sarajevo and a walk-through inspection of a military barracks. Then Ferdinand and Sophie got into a car for a motorcade to city hall, through the gathered crowds and a gauntlet of would-be killers.

The first plotter along their route was Muhamed Mehmedbašić, the man who had already ruined one assassination plan by throwing his dagger off a train. He let the convoy pass. He later said a police officer was standing too close to make a move.

The next was Cabrinovic, whose grenade pitch was high and outside.

The motorcade raced away after the explosion, and within minutes arrived at Sarajevo City Hall, a spectacular Moorish-style, layer cake of a building, cheerfully striped in orange and yellow, like a municipal office in a cartoon city. The city's mayor stood on the steps of the building and tried to deliver his prepared speech as if nothing had happened.

Ferdinand was a ball of rage. "I come to Sarajevo and am greeted with bombs?" he interrupted. "It is outrageous!"

Sophie whispered to her husband, and he piped down. The speeches wrapped up quickly, and the dignitaries poured inside city hall to figure out what to do. The next items on the schedule were a visit to the National Museum and then lunch at the governor's house. Ferdinand insisted on visiting the hospital to see one of his officers gashed by shrapnel in the bombing.

The mistakes made in Sarajevo City Hall over the next few minutes would shape the rest of the century. These errors led directly to one world war, which in turn set up another, along with the Holocaust, the Soviet domination of Eastern Europe, the nuclear age, and the Cold War. Everyone on the planet today lives with the consequences of a few hurried decisions by a small group of men, on a sunny Sunday in Sarajevo.

The safest course, presuming more plotters were waiting for Ferdinand, was to call the nearby military barracks and flood the streets with troops. Oskar Potiorek, the region's military governor, said no; the troops had been in the field and did not have formal uniforms to serve as honor guard. It was a stupid reason not to guarantee the future monarch's safety.

The governor did have a helpful thought about the route out of city hall. The motorcade's planned course was back down the Appel Quay, and then a right turn onto Franz Josef Street, which was narrow and seemed dangerous. Potiorek suggested a new route: back the way they had come, all the way down the Appel Quay, which was wide and could be driven at higher speeds, and then onto another route to the hospital. His instinct was sound. Princip had stationed himself in front of Moritz Schiller's deli at the corner of Franz Josef Street. He loitered there, in a dark suit jacket, white shirt, buttoned vest, and a pistol in his pocket, on the unlikely chance that Ferdinand kept to his published itinerary after the bombing.

Barely half an hour after arriving at city hall, Ferdinand and Sophie walked out and got back in the car, now the second vehicle in the motorcade.

In the haste and confusion of the moment, nobody told the drivers the route had changed.

The convoy pulled out, speeding down the Appel Quay. Suddenly, the chauffeur in the lead vehicle turned right, following the old route onto Franz Josef Street. The driver of Ferdinand's car followed. Governor Potiorek, riding with Ferdinand, shouted that they were going the wrong damn way. Had he kept his mouth shut, Ferdinand may have escaped again.

The driver braked to a hard stop, to change gears into reverse. For a few surreal seconds, the car held still in the street, in front of Schiller's deli and maybe three steps from an utterly dumbfounded Princip. Princip shook off the shock, drew his pistol, and fired. Two shots at least, possibly three.

Ferdinand and Sophie sat upright for a few moments, while the shooter was wrestled to the ground. Then blood began to seep from Ferdinand's mouth. Sophie collapsed into his lap. Each had been fatally hit; he in the neck and she in the abdomen.

"It is nothing, it is nothing," Ferdinand softly repeated, as he bled to death.

With Cabrinovic and Princip in custody, police soon rounded up most of the assassins. Within a week, Austrian officials knew that "high-ranking Serb nationalist officers" had aided the plot. Hawks in the Austro-Hungarian government pushed for a military reprisal. Kaiser Wilhelm assured his ally that Germany would support Austria's response to the murders. That guarantee became known as the "blank check," and it made it a certainty that Austria would use its military against Serbia.

Three weeks after the murders, on July 23, Austria-Hungary gave Serbia a list of demands, most of which had to do with suppressing anti-Austrian activities in Serbia. In response, Serbia, on July 25, mobilized its military, a provocative move in that era. Three days later, Austria-Hungary declared war on Serbia. With its Serbian ally going to war, Russia mobilized its forces.

And so it began. The other great powers honored their alliances and cascaded into the conflict like cars sliding on an icy road into an expanding pileup. Beginning August 1: Germany declared war on Russia and then on France; German troops invaded neutral Belgium on their way toward Paris; Britain declared war on Germany; Austria-Hungary declared war on Russia; Serbia declared war on Germany; France and then Britain declared war on Austria-Hungary. In late August, Japan declared war on Germany and then on Austria-Hungary. More than thirty nations would ultimately become involved.

Watching these dizzying events from Washington, DC, President Woodrow Wilson issued a proclamation on August 4 that said the United States would not takes sides. Every American had "the duty of an impartial neutrality during the existence of the contest," Wilson said. The policy would not interfere with the "free expression of opinion and sympathy" toward any nation in the conflict, naturally, nor with "the commercial manufacturing or sale of arms and munitions of war." This was America: Free speech and guns were protected.

A covert battle for the control of American hearts and minds began at once, largely fought in the pages of America's newspapers.

CHAPTER 3
Frostbite and Dynamite

Shortly after midnight, on February 2, 1915, in the dark, frozen hamlet of Vanceboro, Maine, inside a whistling gale whipping great curtains of fallen snow, a solitary figure hefted a heavy suitcase through the empty streets. His name was Werner Horn. He was an Oberleutnant, a junior officer, on the inactive list in the German Army, called back to duty with his homeland at war. Horn was an imposing man: thirty-seven years old, 6'2", 180 pounds, blue-eyed, clean-shaven with blonde hair buzzed short.

Horn had tried to dress for the weather, in a brown suit, heavy gray socks, chunky black boots, a cap, and overcoat. Still, after waiting two hours in the woods before launching his plan, the unforgiving cold of −30 degrees Fahrenheit had numbed his hands and feet. The wind made his eyes water and pelted his face with snow. At least he was unlikely to be spotted. No one in their right mind would be out on a night like this. Horn himself may not have been entirely in his right mind. He may have already been in the early stages of mental decline and dementia, caused by a case of syphilis he had contracted in his twenties.

Horn's cheap brown suitcase weighed eighty pounds. It contained sixty sticks of dynamite, each about a foot long and an inch and a half in diameter, packed like cigars in a box. Horn had a gun on him, too, a .38 caliber, five-shot revolver. He had matches, blasting caps, rubber tape, and wire cutters. He wore cuffs over his arms with the black-white-red stripes of the German flag.

At the outbreak of war the previous summer, Horn had been half a world away from home, hanging around Guatemala and working at a coffee plantation.

Now, as he lugged the heavy bomb toward the Maine Central Railroad yard, he was a soldier again, operating on secret orders from one of the highest-ranking German officials in the United States. These orders had brought Horn to Vanceboro, a secluded railroad and lumber town of several hundred hearty souls on the eastern edge of Maine. It was the site of the most vulnerable point along the rail line, a bridge that carried the tracks over the St. Croix River, the border between the United States and Canada. The bridge linked the Maine Central and Canadian Pacific railroads, as well as the towns of Vanceboro on the US side and Saint Croix, New Brunswick, across the river. The completion of the rail line in 1871 had been widely celebrated in both countries; President Ulysses S. Grant had visited Maine for the line's opening ceremonies.

And now it was Horn's job to blow it up. His mission was to stop Canadian trains from transporting war supplies to the ice-free seaport at Saint John, New Brunswick, for transport to England.

Horn carried the dynamite onto the steel truss bridge, which was about 150 feet long and quite narrow, with just enough room for a single train. The St. Croix River, flowing south toward the Bay of Fundy, was an icy mess below. Horn slipped twice on ice on the bridge, managing to avoid a fall into water too cold to survive.

Horn's superior had told him no trains used the bridge between midnight and early morning. But as he picked his way over railroad ties on feet deadened by the cold, he heard an unmistakable rumble from the American side. *There were not supposed to be any trains*, he thought. Horn stepped to the side of the bridge, grabbed a steel beam with one hand, and leaned out into empty space, out of the way, while dangling the heavy case of dynamite above the river with his other hand. He held on for his life as the train clattered past.

Horn waited until all was quiet again but for the howling wind, lit a cigar, and got to work setting the explosives. He took care to place his bomb on the Canadian side of the bridge, well over the international border in the middle of the river. Germany was at peace with the United States but at war with Britain, and therefore with Canada, which was then a dominion of Great Britain. Attacking the bridge in Canada, Horn reasoned, would be a valid act of war; not a crime, as it would be on the American side.

Horn's frozen hands were clumsy claws. He struggled in the fearsome wind to strap the bomb to a girder and then attach the fuse. The long fuse was designed to burn for about fifty minutes, to give Horn time to skip town before the boom. Half an hour into the work, though, another train interrupted, this time from the Canadian side. Horn edged out over the water again and hung on. He realized the earlier train was no fluke. The bridge was not quiet all night. Werner Horn was a soldier, not a mass murderer. "I never wanted nor intended to destroy life," he later said, "only to destroy the bridge and communications so supplies, food, ammunition and war supplies could not pass."

Horn could not chance that a train would be on the bridge when the bomb went off. He made sure the rails were quiet, then clipped off most of the wick and flung the excess over the side. He left just enough wick to burn for three minutes, knowing he would not have time to escape the town before the explosion.

The saboteur lit the wick with his cigar and ran for America.

❖

The circumstances that brought Werner Horn to that darkened bridge in the middle of a winter gale dated to the earliest hours of the war.

On August 4, 1914, the day Great Britain declared war on Germany, and the day after Germany declared war on France, hundreds of German-born men gathered in Battery Park at the southern tip of Manhattan to profess their loyalty to their fatherland. Within sight of the Statue of Liberty, they chanted German songs, while their representatives delivered a list of seven hundred names to the nearby German consulate—the names of men who wanted to go home to fight for Germany.

The gathering transformed into a parade. The men marched up Broadway, waving German and American flags, and singing at the top of their lungs "Die Wacht am Rhine," a patriotic German song.

> *The cry resounds like thunder's peal,*
> *Like crashing waves and clang of steel:*
> *The Rhine, the Rhine, our German Rhine,*
> *Who will defend our stream, divine?*

With news reporters in tow, the march grew bigger as it snaked through the city. By the time the parade reached the Twenty-Third Street ferry docks, it numbered close to two thousand people. Several hundred of them piled onto a ferry, crossed the Hudson, and picked up their march in Hoboken, heading along River Street to the piers of the North German Lloyd, a German shipping line.

There, the gathering morphed into a raucous pep rally, with patriotic speeches and songs. A tricolor white-blue-red Russian flag was slowly shredded, to wild cheers and waving hats.

These men were itching to fight.

Their problem was they could not get to Europe. Not while Great Britain's massive navy controlled the Atlantic. England clamped a naval blockade around Germany at the start of the war. And to prevent Germany from importing war materials through neutral ports, British warships intercepted incoming neutral cargo steamers, including US ships, forcing them into British harbors, where the ships would be searched for "war contraband." German nationals of fighting age discovered on any liner could expect to spend the war in an internment camp.

The British prevented the import of anything that could conceivably support the German war effort—weapons, ammunition, and fuel, certainly, but also cars and machine parts, tools and chemicals, metal ore and rubber, textiles, horses and other livestock. And to sap the energy of the German public, the British declared imported food to be contraband. By the winter of 1916–1917, the food blockade turned Germany into a nation of breadlines and foragers. The German national health office estimated after the war that 763,000 Germans died as a result of the blockade.

Of course, control of the ocean meant the British could freely import things from the United States, including superior US-made artillery shells. This was the critical problem facing German diplomats in America. It motivated nearly every covert act by German agents during the period of American neutrality: black propaganda, economic vandalism, outright sabotage, attempts to push the United States and Mexico into a war—all of it flowed from the fact that the British could import American munitions and supplies, and Germany, for the most part, could not.

❖

This was Germany's situation, broadly speaking, at the outbreak of war in August 1914:

Germany was sandwiched between enemies on two fronts, fighting the Russians in the east and the French and British, primarily, in the west. Germany had a plan for a two-front war, named for Alfred von Schlieffen, a military planner credited with the general strategy. The plan was to invade France by storming through the neutral country of Belgium, to outflank French border defenses, and then roll into Paris in a matter of weeks—before the Russian army had time to fully mobilize. With France defeated, German troops would be free to concentrate on Russia.

But by mid-September 1914, the plan had already failed. Allied soldiers stopped the Germans before Paris, and both sides burrowed into trenches for a long and grotesque war of attrition.

Meanwhile, on the oceans, Germany's merchant fleet promptly got out of harm's way. More than six hundred German steamers at sea when the war broke out took refuge, or "interned," at docks in neutral harbors, including Baltimore, Philadelphia, and New York, to wait out the fighting safe from British warships.

Communication between Berlin and its US-based diplomatic team was tricky. The British dragged the ocean floor, fished up Germany's transatlantic telegraph cables, and cut them. This forced the Germans to rely on human couriers, who could be exposed or caught, and coded wireless broadcasts, which could be plucked from the air and possibly decrypted.

The problem of getting German-born men home from the United States to fight fell to Captain Franz von Papen, the German government's military attaché to the United States, a colleague of Karl Boy-Ed. Under Papen's direction, Germany organized and funded a passport-forging operation based in New York, illegal under US law, to provide Germans heading to Europe with bogus paperwork to fool the British.

Papen was a career soldier, unblinkingly loyal to his government. He was thirty-four years old in the summer of 1914. He was fit and handsome, with a narrow oval face and a wedge-shaped mustache the width of his lips. He was a disciple of the philosophy of Friedrich von Bernhardi, a German military commander and historian, who wrote lovingly—creepily?—about the nobility of human warfare. Bernhardi believed that war was "the great civilizing influence of the world."

Papen was from the German town of Werl, about eighty miles northeast of Cologne. His family were aristocrats and devoted Roman Catholics. Papen was educated in military schools and followed his love of horses into the cavalry. He was an excellent rider who competed in steeplechase races in Germany, and galloped through fox hunt adventures in England. He believed horse racing enhanced self-discipline, endurance, and decision-making, and provided, in his words, "a fine contempt for broken bones—by no means a bad training for a politician."

Papen arrived in the United States in January 1914, to begin his post as military attaché. In peacetime, the job could hardly be easier. He schmoozed at dinner parties, while collecting observations about the US military to pass to Berlin. Papen was witty and well-mannered. Yet at his core he was a blunt instrument, a soldier first, and he would make a clumsy spy.

Stationed in the United States, a vast land of farms and factories, Papen foresaw that American industry possessed the power to tip the outcome of the war.

"When the war broke out, it was obvious that the time it would last would depend very materially upon the extent to which the [Triple] Entente would succeed in increasing its resources in the way of war material," Papen said in 1920, in a hearing in Germany. "The only country which could be considered in this regard was the United States."

Papen had many ideas to prevent Germany's enemies from benefitting from America's industrial might. At the outbreak of war, the US arms industry was "ridiculously small." Papen recommended that Germany "tie up" the United States's weapons output by buying whatever America's munitions factories could produce. He estimated that for less than $30 million (about $800 million today), Germany could corner the American market. Even if the British blockade prevented the weapons from being shipped to Germany, denying munitions to the Triple Entente was the next best outcome.

The German War Department declined to put up the money, thinking the war would be over before the investment yielded a benefit. So instead, in March or April 1915, Papen took steps to establish Germany's own weapons plant in the United States. It was called the Bridgeport Projectile Company, and it manufactured chaos. Under the disguise of an ostensibly American munitions maker, Papen sought to buy every specialized hydraulic press he could find, robbing the market of machinery needed to produce artillery shells, to slow the growth of the US weapons industry. He did the same thing with gunpowder, with chemicals needed to make explosives, and the acid-proof containers to hold the chemicals. Meanwhile, German and Austrian diplomats tried to undermine the labor force of the US munitions industry by provoking strikes and pressuring workers of German and Austrian backgrounds to quit.

Ultimately, German agents employed direct sabotage against shipping and industry to slow the export of US munitions to the Allies.

Papen and his colleagues devoted a lot of attention to attacking Canada. Papen funded a plot to dynamite the locks along the Welland Canal, a shipping channel between Lakes Ontario and Erie, to prevent Canadian troops from moving along the St. Lawrence Seaway on their way to eastern ports, and the ships that would take them to Europe. The plot ended with several Papen flunkies under arrest and no damage to Canada.*

In December 1914 the German government sent its embassy in the United States secret instructions to stop troops and supplies flowing across the Canadian Pacific Railway. "The General Staff is anxious that vigorous measures should be taken to destroy the Canadian Pacific in several places for the purpose of causing a lengthy interruption of traffic," the order stated. "Acquaint the Military Attaché [Papen] with the above and furnish the sums required for the enterprise."

Wrecking the railroad became Papen's problem.

He needed a loyal man for this dangerous, sensitive mission.

By coincidence, a loyal man was already on his way.

❖

Werner Horn was born in October 1877, in Stettin, a city now called Szczecin, about ninety miles northeast of Berlin. The city is just inside the borders of Poland now; in Horn's time it was part of the German Empire.

Not much is known about Horn's early life. His own story is that he was a ten-year veteran of the German Army, who around 1910 traveled to Guatemala. He worked two years on a coffee plantation, and then became the plantation's manager for two years. He spoke Spanish reasonably well, and English with a heavy accent. At the outbreak of fighting in the summer of 1914, inactive soldiers such as Horn were called back to Germany to join the war. Horn sailed from Guatemala to Galveston, Texas, in August 1914, and then traveled to New York City, where he spent a fruitless month trying to get passage on a liner to bring him home.

Horn gave up and started back to Guatemala. He made it as far as Mexico City when he learned that some other guy had his old job at the

---

* Papen would be among those indicted for the canal plot by a US grand jury in 1916. He was never prosecuted; he had already been sent home to Germany.

coffee plantation. He checked in with the German consulate in Mexico, and was directed back to New York to find some other way to fulfil his duty. Horn returned to Manhattan in the first week of January 1915, and offered his service to Papen.

For the tricky job of destroying the international railroad bridge at Vanceboro, Papen chose this enthusiastic stranger, a man who had literally just walked in off the street, who was neither a spy nor a munitions expert. Papen gave Horn some crude maps, railroad schedules, and eighty pounds of dynamite, then pointed him toward Canada and sent him on his way.

"I admit that this was not a particularly intelligent piece of work on my part," Papen later wrote, referring to Horn's effort as well as the failed plot to blow up the Welland Canal, "and it must be put down to the confusion of those early days and my lack of experience in this particular field."

Horn stayed several weeks in a Staten Island hotel while preparing his attack. He bought a $12 suit to go with an overcoat he had picked up at Wanamaker's in Manhattan. He departed on his mission at 1:00 A.M. on Saturday, January 30, in a sleeper car on the New York, New Haven, and Hartford Railroad. He slept in the upper berth. The dynamite was tucked under the lower bunk, beneath some unwitting traveler, lost to history, who slept an inch above it. At 7:00 A.M., Horn got off the train in Boston's South Station, a lovely neoclassical revival building with a curved granite edifice facing Atlantic Avenue in downtown Boston. Horn would not let a porter touch his bag—not that he was afraid of it blowing up; he didn't want to pay any tips. Horn lugged his heavy cargo to the cab stand and took a taxi about a mile and a half across town to Boston's other major train hub, North Station.* The connection was tight, but Horn made it. He bought a first-class ticket for Vanceboro, and departed at 8:00 A.M. on the Maine Central Railroad. The train chugged into Vanceboro well after dark, at about 6:40 P.M. Horn hid the suitcase in a woodpile near the rail

---

* North and South Stations were not directly connected by commuter rail in Horn's day, and are still not connected today. This infuriating gap in the rail line has been irritating German spies and Boston commuters for more than one hundred years.

yard, then walked the neighborhood to scout the bridge. If all went well, he'd blow it up that very night.

All did not go well. A local spotted Horn casing the area and reported "a man acting strangely" to the Vanceboro office of US Immigration Services. An immigration officer, by great coincidence also named Horn, responded. Officer Carr G. Horn caught up with the stranger and questioned him.

The saboteur had to think fast. He spat out what had to be the first fake name that popped into his head. He was Olaf Hoorn, he said, masking his surname with a single redundant vowel. He was Danish, fresh from the train from New York, through Boston, here scouting for property he might want to buy.

Officer Horn tested Mr. Hoorn. What time was the train?

The visitor knew the answer, so it seemed he had indeed come from Boston, not from across the border. The immigration officer was satisfied.

Shaken by the close call, Horn decided not to attack the bridge that night. He asked for directions to a hotel and got a recommendation for the Vanceboro Exchange Hotel, a three-story, whitewashed rooming house with a big front porch within sight of the railyard. Horn collected his hidden suitcase and checked into the hotel around 8:30 P.M.

He holed up in the hotel the next day, making only quick dashes to the dining room to eat. Once while he was out, a chambermaid entered his room to tidy up. She tried to move Horn's suitcase but found it too heavy to lift.

On Monday, February 1, Horn checked out, setting up an alibi by conspicuously telling the staff he was leaving on the evening train for Boston.

Instead, Horn hid in the woods, waiting until midnight to make his move.

❖

A thunderous boom woke the innkeeper in his bed. Aubrey Tague, proprietor of the Vanceboro Exchange Hotel, dashed to the window, threw it open, and poked his head out into the cold night.

Was that a boiler explosion? Was his hotel on fire?

Tague listened for a minute or two. His watch said 1:10 A.M. It was February 2, 1915. He left his room and checked the hallway. To his surprise, in the hall bathroom he saw the big German who had checked in a few days before. Werner Horn was in a cap and heavy coat. He was out of breath and looked wind-whipped and cold. He rubbed his hands together.

"Good morning," Tague said.

"Good morning," Horn said.

Tague retreated back to his room. The German had clearly just been outside. There had obviously been an explosion somewhere nearby. Tague recalled that the housekeeper had been unable to lift Horn's suitcase. Tague began to put it together. He jumped into his clothes, then went back to the hall.

"I freeze my hands," Horn told him, in a heavy accent.

They were frozen, all right. Frostbitten. People lose fingers to frostbite sometimes. Tague told Horn to put snow on his hands, a first aid treatment for frostbite at the time. Horn opened the bathroom window and scooped some snow from the ledge.

Tague ran down the stairs and outside into the night. He found footprints in the snow, leading from the railyard toward the hotel. Fresh prints—they would have to be; the wind and drifting snow would erase any tracks in minutes. He bumped into a neighbor, who told him someone had detonated a bomb on the railroad bridge. Tague ran toward the bridge. Dozens of windows were shattered among fifteen homes near the railyard. The bridge still stood. Railroad ties had been splintered. Some were gone. A section of steel beam was shredded, the metal curled back like the lid of a sardine can. The rails looked intact, but Tague couldn't be sure they were safe. He hurried to the railroad station, explained what he had seen, and then went back to his hotel. Horn was still in the bathroom. He asked to check into a room for the night. Tague found him space on the third floor.

The exhausted, frostbitten saboteur shrugged off his overcoat and collapsed into bed.

❖

Horn had planned a nocturnal getaway from Vanceboro, though his so-called escape plan was suicidal. He had intended to plant the bomb and then bushwhack on foot about six miles to the village of Lambert Lake, then walk fifteen miles southwest to Topsfield, and then sixteen more miles south to Princeton, where he could catch the train. He did not understand how far apart these towns were, nor the brutal topography of rural Maine in February. Had he tried his escape plan, we might still be looking for his skeleton.

In the end, Horn was too frozen to flee. He had frostbite on his ears, nose, and fingers. The lure of a warm bed was too strong.

While Horn slept, Deputy County Sheriff George Ross, who also ran a local fruit store, began his investigation of the bombing. Ross lived a few hundred feet from the bridge and had been awakened by the blast, thinking it might be an earthquake. Ross was a plump man with thick jowls. His hair and short moustache were white. Around 7:00 A.M., Ross had the inspired idea to check the hotel for any suspicious persons. On the way he bumped into two uniformed railroad security officers, who tagged along.

Tague led Ross and his party to the room of the suspicious German, Werner Horn.

Ross knocked.

A voice asked, "What do you want?"

"Unlock the door," Ross ordered.

Horn opened the door and the men poured in. At the sight of the uniformed railroad officers, Horn lunged for his coat, where he had left his pistol. Ross pushed him back. "I'm an American officer," he announced.

Horn said, "I thought you were all Canadians. I am a German officer. I would not harm anyone over here."

Horn had blasting caps in his room. It was clear Ross had his man. He handcuffed Horn and marched him out. By the next day, the damaged bridge was already repaired and back in use. The beaming deputy sheriff posed for photographs with his prisoner, like a hunter with a ten-point buck. A teenaged newsreel photographer from Massachusetts, Louis de

Rochemont, persuaded Ross to reenact Horn's arrest for film.* Horn gamely went along. Ross clearly became fond of Horn in the few days the German was his prisoner. Ross rebuffed officers of the Canadian Pacific Railway who wanted the lawman to take his prisoner to the bridge so Canadian authorities could grab him. One Canadian constable hinted at a bribe if Ross gave up Horn to Canada. Another wanted Ross to allow an undercover agent in the cell with Horn to pump him for information. "I will do no such goddam thing," Ross insisted.

Justice was swift in Vanceboro. Two days after the bombing, Horn pleaded guilty to malicious destruction of a hundred or more windows. He was sentenced to thirty days in jail, and taken to the county jug in Machias, Maine, while the federal government figured out what to do with him. He would ultimately be indicted by a Boston grand jury for transporting explosives on a passenger train.**

❖

A few days into Horn's jail sentence in Maine, he received an important visitor from the US Department of Justice.

The guest was A. Bruce Bielaski, director of the department's Bureau of Investigation, a new agency, which we now call the FBI.

Bielaski was tall, athletic, and young—just thirty-one. He was clean-shaven and boyish, and wore a conservative haircut. He looked like the gentle sort of man who enjoyed gardening in the morning—and in fact, he did. But his mild looks were a weapon that hid a cunning mind and a ruthless streak.

Bielaski, who went by his middle name, Bruce, was born just north of Washington, DC, in Montgomery County, Maryland. His paternal

---

* Louis de Rochemont became one of the great filmmakers of the era, won two Academy Awards, and is known as the father of the docudrama. He died in 1978.

** Horn spent the war in US jails, then was extradited to Canada. In 1919 he was sentenced to ten years of incarceration in New Brunswick. He was diagnosed as insane in 1921, and repatriated to Germany. What happened to him there, to my great frustration, is unknown.

grandfather, Alexander Bielaski, was a Polish military officer wounded in 1831 in a revolt against the Russian Empire. He escaped to the United States, and died fighting for the Union in the Civil War.

Bruce Bielaski's father was a Methodist minister in Maryland. Under his father's roof, Bruce grew up deeply religious, with a "powerful streak of morality." He graduated from the George Washington University Law School in 1904, and went into public service. Bielaski was a Republican, uncommon for Polish Americans at the time, and his politics may have helped him land a job in Teddy Roosevelt's Department of Justice. He was assigned to help organize the court system in Oklahoma, before the US territory leveled up to statehood.

In 1908 the Department of Justice established its own internal force of detectives, so it no longer had to borrow them from the Treasury Department's Secret Service. Bielaski became one of the first special agents of the Bureau of Investigation. By 1912 he was the bureau's chief. With the outbreak of war in Europe, the agency took on counterintelligence duties and investigations into violations of America's neutrality in the war.

Which was how Bielaski came to sit across Werner Horn on February 6, 1915, in a county lockup in eastern Maine. They spoke for three hours. Bielaski took careful notes. He found Horn intelligent, educated, and "extremely patriotic" for his German homeland. He also deduced that Horn possessed a natural inclination for truth and honor. The man was just not built for lies.

Horn confessed to the bombing plot and answered every question but one: He refused to say who ordered him to bomb the bridge. "This would be impossible, at least until after the war is over," Horn told Bielaski. He'd rather swing from a Canadian gallows than give up the name of his superior.

Bielaski also sensed that Horn had told him one thing—and only one—that was untrue. Horn claimed he had come from New York without dynamite, and had received the explosives on the Canadian end of the bridge from a mysterious man known only as "Tommy." Bielaski didn't believe it, and he knew how to expose the lie. This was Bielaski's superpower: He had the ability to size up a person and identify a weak spot, the place to squeeze to get what he wanted. With Horn, it was his sense of honor.

Bielaski typed up Horn's statement, including the tall tale about the mysterious "Tommy," then reviewed the confession with him. Horn agreed it was accurate. Then Bielaski took a pencil and wrote at the bottom of the last page: "I certify on my honor as a German officer that the foregoing statements are true."

He slid the paper to Horn to sign. The prisoner studied the handwritten addition for several minutes with a wrinkled brow. He shook his head, seemed disturbed, then smiled at Bielaski and said, "Tommy."

"All true except as to Tommy?" Bielaski asked.

Yes. Horn admitted there was no Tommy; he had received the dynamite in New York from the superior who ordered him to destroy the bridge. Horn still refused to give up the name, and Bielaski had to return to Washington without it.

It would fall to John Rathom to finger Franz von Papen for ordering the attack on the international railroad bridge. That sensational scoop, and many others, would make Rathom famous, and would bring Bielaski and Rathom together. The lawman and the imposter developed a secret collaboration and a warm friendship, both of which would end in betrayal.

CHAPTER 4
Birth of a Sensation

It is likely John Rathom wrote the story personally, either by hand or dictation. He would have noted corrections and edits on the paper draft, and struck superfluous words with blue pencil. No copyeditor would be permitted to muck with the prose of the editor in chief, though one may have been recruited as a second pair of eyes to proof for clarity and grammar. When Rathom was satisfied with the text, the headline, and the subheads, sometime in the evening of April 6, 1915, the pages of the draft were rolled up, slid into a narrow cylinder, and inserted into the *Providence Journal*'s pneumatic tube system. With a hiss of air and a satisfying *thoomp*, the news story that would launch Rathom's climb to national stardom shot into the copy flow, part of the daily miracle of putting out a newspaper.

The *Providence Journal* was not yet known for original World War I reporting. Rathom published wire stories in every edition on the major developments in Europe. Rhode Islanders are famously provincial, but Rathom had grown up on the other side of the world, and he brought an international perspective to the job. His front pages often paired news about naval attacks in the Atlantic or troop movements in France, with breaking stories about local house fires and the political circus at the Rhode Island State House. Much of the war news he published was datelined from London, written by American wire service correspondents.

The *Journal* published two daily editions. The morning paper, the *Providence Daily Journal*, was considered the more erudite and worldly. The afternoon edition, the *Evening Bulletin*, founded in 1863 to report Civil War news arriving by telegraph, was the more locally minded, blue-collar paper, read by factory workers over dinner. Circulation was modest: in 1915 the *Daily Journal* had about 20,300 daily readers and 33,000 on Sundays. The *Evening Bulletin*'s circulation was 48,565. For comparison, the *New York Times* reached about 260,000 readers a day; the *New York Telegram*, about 220,000; and the *New York Herald* about 220,000.

With such a small direct audience, Rathom could only increase his reach if other newspapers reprinted his stories. Going viral in 1915 meant that your words, properly credited to you, were rolling off printing presses in other cities across the country.

The *Providence Journal* newsroom was on Westminster Street, back-to-back with city hall in the commercial and social heart of Providence, what the locals call Downcity. The paper was in a gorgeous Beaux Arts–style low-rise, made from gray stone and plate glass, with green copper trim, tasteful columns and ledges, and a row of ornamented dormers along the roofline that offered nooks for nesting pigeons and starling. Canvas awnings and American flags on the building flapped in the breeze.

It was much more than an office building. It was a rowdy, steam-snorting, Industrial Age factory, which manufactured new product every day and could never shut down. Much of the action happened underground, in a two-story basement bunker dug from soggy soil and lined with up to seven feet of concrete. A steam system turned two main engines, which cranked electric generators in the newspaper's private power plant. Fires in the sweltering boiler room burned bituminous and anthracite coal by the ton, a fuel mix designed to minimize exhaust. The coal smoke wafted through downtown streets crowded with office workers and shop patrons, many of them pouring through the massive Liggett's Pharmacy occupying the street-level floor of the *Journal* Building. The surrounding blocks were thick with banks, financial and real estate firms, clothing stores and cobblers.

The written draft of Rathom's story landed in the third-floor composing room, a large and frenetic space, where the air was warm and smelled like hot oil. More than ten typesetting Linotype machines stood in a line, a tribe of hulking metal monsters, each weighing a couple tons. The Linotypes' electric motors whirred, their mechanical parts clattered. They were absurdly complicated, with some eighteen thousand moving pieces, once lovingly described as "a gloriously complicated love affair between a Singer sewing machine, a loom, and an oom-pah band." The Linotype threw a lot of heat, too; an asbestos-wrapped crucible inside each one held 40 pounds of hot type metal—a molten stew of lead, tin, and antimony—heated to 535 degrees Fahrenheit.

Racing against the clock—perhaps perspiring from heat, an impending deadline, and the job of typesetting the boss's copy—a Linotype operator clipped the pages of Rathom's story to an easel, sat at the machine, and began to enter the text, letter by letter, at a peculiar keyboard. The keys were not arranged like a typewriter, but by how frequently the letters appeared in the English language. First vertical column: E-T-A-O-I-N.[*]

At each tap, a chip of brass—the mold for a single letter—dropped jangling from an overhead magazine into a carriage. When the molds for the first line of type were all in place, the operator threw a lever, and the Linotype performed a complex mechanical ballet. In seconds, the machine cast from liquefied lead a rectangular wafer imprinted along its narrow edge with the line of text, written backward. The solidified slug dropped into a tray, still hot to the touch. As more lines dropped, a worker collected the slugs and fit them like jigsaw pieces into a wooden form, creating a fifty-pound mirror image of the front page of the next day's paper, a template done entirely in shiny gray metal.

Next door in the stereotyping room, workers made a mold of the template and through a second hot metal process created a curved plate, from which the newspaper would be printed. A counterweighted elevator

---

[*] The Linotype was invented in the 1880s by the German American Ottmar Mergenthaler. Thomas Edison called the machine the "eighth wonder of the world." It was the dominant typesetting technology for the newspaper industry from the Victorian era to Watergate.

lowered the plate to the basement press room, where it was affixed to a drum on one of the paper's twin printing presses. The presses were turn-of-the-century models from R. Hoe & Company and the size of mobile homes, each capable of printing forty-eight thousand newspapers an hour. Together they filled their windowless underground tomb with an unholy roar. Workers close enough to bump elbows had to shout to communicate.

The printed, folded copies of the April 7 edition of the *Providence Journal* came off the line still warm. Rathom's story appeared beneath a heavy black headline on page 1:

FLAGRANT VIOLATIONS OF NEUTRALITY
DISCOVERED IN MANY AMERICAN PORTS

BRITISH CRUISERS CONSTANTLY
GET SUPPLIES FROM NEW YORK HARBOR

The story reported sensational revelations:

> Evidence in possession of the Journal shows that neutrality laws have been broken brazenly for several months past in the ports of New York, Charlestown, Wilmington, Norfolk, San Francisco and Seattle, with the aid of tugboats and lighters, backed by men of large wealth and with the connivance of Government officials.

In essence, the story alleged that tugboat captains were ferrying supplies from US ports to beyond the three-mile limit of US territorial waters, and illegally delivering the goods to British warships.

The story charged that the local officer in charge of enforcing neutrality at the Port of New York had for months turned a blind eye to the violations, and the activity only became public because Captain Boy-Ed and the German ambassador to the United States, Count Johann Heinrich von Bernstorff, had collected signed affidavits from tugboat captains admitting to the scheme.

The *Providence Journal* transmitted a copy of Rathom's blockbuster to the *New York Times*, which published a long extract of the story the same day it appeared in the *Journal*, a model of simultaneous publication that would exponentially expand Rathom's reach and influence.

Violating American neutrality was a big deal. And a conspiracy to do so would be an international scandal for the British—had it been true.

Rathom's first original World War I report of national scope was entirely wrong.

He had been duped by a German agent into printing black propaganda on behalf of the fatherland.

❖

But how did Rathom succumb to this journalistic hoodwink?

In early 1915 German naval attaché Boy-Ed hired a shady private detective in New York City for the job of unscrupulous propagandist and dabbler in the occasional underhanded black-bag operation for the German Empire.

The detective's name was Gaston Bullock Means, and he would become one of the most famous criminals of his generation. At the time of his hiring by Boy-Ed, Means was thirty-five years old, and still in the embryonic phase of his infamous career as thief, con artist, crooked lawman, bootlegger, blackmailer, and murder suspect. In the Roaring Twenties, Means became "the symbol of American criminality and corruption in the gaudiest and most lawless era in the nation's history," wrote biographer Edwin P. Hoyt, in a brilliant 1963 book about Means.

Gaston Means, often called Bud, was a North Carolinian and a husky man, nearly six feet tall and some two hundred pounds. Though he had a street fighter's body, Means was blessed with sweet blue eyes and an angelic smile pinned between deep dimples. He oozed Southern charm, and with "the hypnotic influence of that cherub-face," he was a gifted manipulator. Means loved intrigue, plotting, and pulling something over on somebody—on anybody. Though he worked for the Germans, he was not really pro-German. Who should win the war? Who gave a goddam? Means liked money, and the German checks always cleared.

In 1917 Means would be charged with the murder of a wealthy socialite, Maude King, with whom Means had ingratiated himself as a financial advisor. He drained King's fortune. Then she wound up dead from a gunshot wound to the head while rabbit hunting with Means. Despite a strong circumstantial case, Means was acquitted of King's murder.

Means repeatedly sidestepped justice with the flamboyance of a matador, and always with a smile, until he went too far even for him. In 1932 Means cooked up a scam to profit from the abduction of the Lindbergh baby. He convinced another rich acquaintance, Evalyn Walsh McLean, the owner of the Hope Diamond, that he was in touch with the kidnappers and could save the baby—for $100,000 in ransom, plus a few thou in walking-around money. Means was convicted of grand larceny for the hoax. He died while serving his fifteen-year sentence at the federal penitentiary in Leavenworth, Kansas, in 1938.

If we back up a bit, to early 1915, Means was not yet a killer—that we know of. He was a largely unknown private dick, working as a political mercenary for German diplomats/spies in the United States. In dealing with his German handlers, Means, ever the showman, adopted the goofy code name of Agent E-13.

Agent E-13 unwittingly opened the door for Rathom to become Germany's most destructive enemy in the American press. Rathom's rise to national prominence as a spy hunter, a celebrity journalist, and a confidant of the Wilson administration can be traced to the spring of 1915, and to a black propaganda plot orchestrated by Gaston B. Means.

❖

From the moment the fighting began in Europe in August 1914, Germany lagged in the propaganda war to shape public opinion in the United States.

This public relations battle was fought mainly in the US press. And in that arena, the British had home court advantage. It began with a common language, which meant no need for time-consuming translations. London was also the newspaper capital of Europe. For years, "the American public had received its day-by-day picture of Europe through a distinctly British perspective," wrote journalist Walter Millis in *Road to War*, his 1935 analysis of America's slide into World War I. US newspapers with bureaus overseas "tended to cover European politics from London," where their correspondents were steeped in British civic life and could not help but absorb a British perspective.

Germany, to compound its disadvantages, had no experienced communication professionals on the ground in the United States when the war began. The German ambassador to the United States was on a badly timed summer vacation in Europe when war broke out, and did not make it back to the United States for several weeks.

That left initial German propaganda efforts in the hands of disorganized laypersons, mostly pointy-headed German American professors and intellectuals, who "utterly botched the task of balancing British influence on American dailies and magazines" with esoteric philosophical arguments that sailed over the heads of most American readers.

The British, meanwhile, got tremendous mileage in the US press by fanning outrage over Germany's incursion into neutral Belgium. "Reports of unspeakable atrocities graced the headlines of American dailies," wrote author Heribert von Feilitzsch, who studies the period. "The invasion presented a clear breach of international law and Germany appeared to the public as a despotic bully pouncing on a weak neighbor."

After a six-week pounding in the press, Germany finally put a team on the field. German officials in New York organized a propaganda bureau, the German Information Service. It was led by a former German government administrator, Bernhard Dernburg, a forty-nine-year-old barrel-chested man with a thick black beard that tapered into a sharp point beneath his chin. Dernburg took an office at 1123 Broadway. The editorial staff of the pro-German magazine the *Fatherland* moved in to help him.

Dernburg's press office created tons of content and got a significant proportion of the propaganda published in American newspapers, as the

German point of view. In November 1914, for instance, Dernburg placed a long op-ed under his own name in the *Saturday Evening Post*, a national magazine with a circulation of more than one million.

"We do not believe in incorporating in our empire any parts of nations that are not of our own language and race," Dernburg assured skittish Americans. He continued:

> I have read in your papers statements to the effect that probably the next thing Germany would do after the close of the present war would be to invade the United States or take Brazil. Why not say the same of England? She has always had a navy twice the size of that of any other nation; she is now creating a big army; she has always been aggressive; she has conquered half the world.

❖

Let's take a quick side tour through the different flavors of propaganda deployed in America during the period of neutrality before the United States joined the First World War. Dernburg's article in the *Saturday Evening Post* was typical of the white propaganda produced by the German Information Service; *white* refers not to the content but how it is presented. *White propaganda* is standard public relations—it is information with the true name of the source attached, and could include op-ed columns and press releases, public speeches, signed political pamphlets, or tweets from a verified blue checkmark account. This sort of propaganda might still be a lie, but as readers we know who supplied the information and we can make informed judgments about the material's veracity and how much weight to give it.

Both sides of the conflict employed this kind of public relations in the United States, along with more sinister varieties.

Gray propaganda refers to information with no identifiable origin, such as newspaper articles with unnamed sources. This was Rathom's specialty. Gray propaganda can also include anonymous clickbait formatted to look like news, which Facebook users pass among themselves like an STD. Without knowing the source, we lack the context to know how much weight to give the information.

Black propaganda is material presented with a fake source. Readers trying to make sense of it are working with false context about its origin, and might be tricked into giving the information more credibility than it deserves.

A modern example: In November 2016, a purported grassroots political group called United Muslims of America posted on its social media accounts: "American Muslims [are] boycotting elections today, most of the American Muslim voters refuse to vote for Hillary Clinton because she wants to continue the war on Muslims in the Middle East."

Who were the United Muslims of America? Neither Muslim nor American. They were Russian internet hackers in an office building in St. Petersburg, trying to depress Muslim voter turnout in the United States to help the Donald Trump presidential campaign.

Fake source + intention to deceive = black propaganda.

❖

Dernburg stabilized Germany's propaganda effort in the United States, but German officials decided their press shop needed a local touch. They hired a prominent American journalist named William Bayard Hale, an Indiana native schooled at Boston University, Harvard, and Cambridge Divinity School. He had been a magazine editor and then a staffer for the *New York Times*.

The German press operation improved, but still lagged behind that of the British. German diplomats decided to pursue a "gray" path. From the beginning of the war, the German ambassador, Count von Bernstorff, had mused about Germany supercharging its propaganda by buying an American newspaper. "In the spring of 1915, with the propaganda effort starting to show better results, with Hale and others pushing for more 'mainstream' efforts, Count Bernstorff's idea resurfaced," Feilitzsch wrote.

Count von Bernstorff was the official face of Germany in America. He was fifty-one when the war started in 1914. He was tall and broad-shouldered, though slender. His hairline had made a great retreat, exposing a massive forehead that gave him a big-brained look. The hair that remained was blonde, as was his thin moustache, which he wore with the ends curled up in a modest copy of Kaiser Wilhelm's aggressive facial hair.

When Bernstorff wasn't speaking, his lips pressed into thin lines, giving him an unintentionally mean or hard-boiled look. In reality, he was impeccably cultured, educated, charming, and smooth. He spoke English with a slight accent and extremely fast, as if he were in a big rush. He had served in the United States since 1908, and was broadly liked. Brown University, the school down the street from John Rathom's house in Providence, gave Bernstorff an honorary Doctor of Laws in 1910.

In March 1915 Bernstorff cabled the German Foreign Office for permission to buy a newspaper. He argued, "Entire press here, as well as all telegraph agencies, in hands of money interests allied with England. Therefore, although best possible news bureau organized here under Dernburg's direction, news gets only scant circulation, as long as we do not control an important newspaper here which will force other papers to accept German news for sake of their journalistic reputation."

Working through a front man, Germany struck a deal to buy the *New York Evening Mail*, a newspaper headquartered at Broadway and Fulton Street, in a lovely 1890s stone building with a striking narrow tower. The paper's best-known employee was cartoonist Rube Goldberg, remembered even now for his schematic drawings of fantastically complicated machines designed to perform simple tasks.*

Using the code name Operation Perez, the German government made several covert payments totaling $943,000 for the newspaper, about $24 million in today's money.

Under secret German control, the news pages generally played stories fairly to preserve the paper's credibility. Its editorial page, however,

---

* The Linotype has often been called a real-life "Rube Goldberg machine."

criticized the British naval blockade, defended Germany's use of submarines against Atlantic shipping, and agitated for the United States to intervene militarily in the ongoing Mexican Revolution, which would have required the United States to hoard munitions that otherwise would be sold to the Allies. It was the finest German-engineered gray propaganda.

❖

How private detective Gaston Bullock Means came to work for the Germans is unclear. One story says the Germans tried to hire Means's boss, William J. Burns, who owned the detective company that employed Means. Burns had already agreed to work for the British, so he gave the job to his associate, Means, and together they cheerfully milked fees from both sides of the conflict.

Boy-Ed assigned Means to plant informers as workmen inside US shipbuilding companies suspected of building submarine parts for the Triple Entente, in the hope of catching the British violating US neutrality.

This seemed lazily inefficient to Means. Why wait to catch the British in a violation? Just invent one.

At the time, British warships were lurking behind Fire Island, off the coast of Long Island, waiting like spiders in international waters to attack any interned German ship that might steam out of New York and dash for open ocean. It was illegal for anyone in the neutral United States to supply these waiting warships with necessities, such as food or coal. If the Germans could show that the British ships were in fact being resupplied from the United States, that would be a blow to the Triple Entente and a public relations victory for the Central Powers.

Means developed a plan to manufacture just such an international scandal. He cleared the plan with Boy-Ed, and in March 1915—at Germany's expense—Means moved into his new headquarters in a suite of rooms at the Hotel Manhattan, an exquisite fourteen-story tower of white limestone at Madison Avenue and Forty-Second Street. Means scoured the city's waterfront for underemployed tugboat crews willing to consider carrying supplies to British warships for generous monthly pay. Not that Means ever intended to pay them.

When he finally found a willing skipper, Means delivered the bad news: the Brits were picky about whom they hired. They preferred seamen they knew. Not to worry, though. If the skipper would sign an affidavit swearing *he had previously supplied* a British warship, he'd likely get the job. Means had taken the liberty of preparing such an affidavit, stating that the skipper had ferried supplies in February to the British cruiser HMS *Essex*, a few miles off Sandy Hook. It was a big lie, of course, but times were tough and the tug needed the work. Means got his first signature.

Means tried to leverage that initial affidavit into more fake evidence, by showing it to other skippers and asking them to sign similar documents attesting to past deliveries that never actually took place. One captain caught the strong odor of rat, and spilled what he knew to the man in charge of enforcing neutrality rules in the harbor, the collector of the Port of New York, Dudley Field Malone.

Malone was a clean-shaven baby-faced lawyer of thirty-two. The collector's job was a patronage post, a reward for service as a loyal Democrat and a Woodrow Wilson campaign organizer. Malone had his own political ambitions, and saw in the harbor plot an opportunity to emerge as a public hero.*

Malone roped the Secret Services and the US military into his investigation. A torpedo boat and a US Navy destroyer hunted for tugs ferrying coal to British warships. Some poor Secret Service agent was ordered to be at the Navesink lighthouse station, in Highlands, New Jersey, at first light every morning to scour the sea by telescope.

The sudden heat forced Means to accelerate his plan. He wished there had been more time to fatten his dossier of fake affidavits, but it was either

---

* In 1920 Malone lost a run for governor of New York. He is better known as Clarence Darrow's co-counsel in the 1925 Scopes Monkey Trial, in which he eloquently defended Tennessee high school teacher John T. Scopes against criminal charges for teaching human evolution. The prosecuting lawyer in the case, by coincidence, was William Jennings Bryan, who was US secretary of state when World War I broke out in 1914.

strike now or lose the whole plot. Around April 1, Means claimed to be a whistleblower and met with Malone. He turned over the manufactured evidence of the British "plot" to violate US neutrality. Means told Malone that an unnamed "detective agency" working out of a downtown hotel had masterminded the scheme to aid the British, a story that braided fiction and just enough fact into a golden lasso of deceit.

The dossier was meager, but Means was a persuasive liar. Malone was impressed enough to bring the fabrications to H. Snowden Marshall, the US attorney for the Southern District of New York, for a possible grand jury review.

That was when the New York press discovered the story. Well, not *the* story, but the alternate truth invented by Agent E-13, which was that Malone had unearthed evidence that tug skippers had been supplying British warships.

The newswires led the story this way:

> New York, April 5—Dudley Field Malone, collector of the port, charged tonight that British cruisers patrolling the waters along the coast of the United States had been violating the neutrality law by coaling and taking on supplies from vessels putting out from the port of New York.

Means would not have changed a word. This was black propaganda of the highest order. Means had tricked Malone into becoming the source of a falsified revelation about the British. Means's name was nowhere in the story. And without knowing that a German agent had supplied the evidence, the public lacked the context to properly weigh the information.

Rathom ran the newswire story in the *Providence Journal* on page 3, under the headline BRITISH NEUTRALITY VIOLATION CHARGED.

The very next edition of the *Providence Journal* contained Rathom's first original World War I story, the much more detailed and inflammatory "scoop" about the vast conspiracy to evade neutrality laws. The opening lines of Rathom's story flecked at the fact that the first inklings of the scandal had leaked the day before:

The widespread conspiracy creating continuous breaches of neutrality in favor of both the Allies and the Germans, which was hinted at in the Journal yesterday morning in connection with statements made by Dudley Field Malone, Collector of the Port of New York, is assuming grave proportion.

The handiwork of Agent E-13 is threaded throughout Rathom's exposé. Rathom's widow, Florence Campbell, confirmed after Rathom's death that Means was the source of the story. In an unpublished 1938 interview with a Stanford University master's candidate, Florence said Means had called Rathom unsolicited with a tip that "British cruisers were being coaled and supplied by American vessels at secret rendezvous."

According to Florence, Means brought the story to Rathom because the *Providence Journal* had a good reputation and was strategically located between New York and Boston. It may also have been that Means chose Rathom through a family connection. Means's brother Frank, an electrician, lived in Providence. It is certainly possible that Rathom and Frank Means had become acquainted in the nine years since Rathom arrived in the city. At the very least, Means had a compelling family reason to visit Providence and get to know its most influential newspaper.

Florence claimed that Rathom vetted the "secret rendezvous" story as best he could, and found at least "some" of what Means claimed credible. That suggests Means was feeding Rathom information before the story broke in New York, perhaps weeks before. When Malone revealed part of the story on April 5, Rathom would have felt immense pressure to publish the full account from Means, or take a chance that his world-breaking scoop would be pecked to death by incremental revelations in other newspapers. For months, Rathom had published the work of other journalists on the biggest news story in the world. For a man who had taken on the fake identity of a swashbuckling war correspondent, this was intolerable. No personal recognition? No glory? It was too much for his invented self to bear.

Something else is notable about Rathom's initial World War I story: Yes, he was bamboozled by his source, and he was reckless to publish before trying harder to vet the information, but the story was an honest attempt to commit journalism—the pursuit of the facts, no matter where they led. Rathom published a story embarrassing to the British, whom he personally favored in the war.

Within days, Agent E-13's operation began to unravel in New York. A tugboat captain publicly confessed that his affidavit was fraudulent. The British consul general denied any secret supply rendezvous and suggested that Malone had been pantsed by a German propaganda scheme. Malone, in turn, claimed that *of course* he knew all the while the plot was a German hoax and had only pretended to go along to expose it. The New York press found Means at the Hotel Manhattan. Means offered some obtuse lies about his membership in a secret organization dedicated to preserving neutrality in US ports. He was an early proprietor of Trump adviser Steve Bannon's media strategy: "Flood the zone with shit." Make the truth unknowable, and people will eventually shrug and give up trying to find it.

Five days after Rathom's "scoop," on April 12, he corrected course. He published another sensation, which was essentially a long correction for the previous story. It was headlined: GERMAN EMBASSY'S PLOT TO DISCREDIT WASHINGTON ADMINISTRATION REVEALED.

The story alleged that figures in the German embassy in Washington had cooked up the fake harbor plot to discredit the Wilson administration.

"The Journal is now in a position to make public the exact facts with regard to the alleged violations of neutrality by the Allies in New York harbor and off Sandy Hook," the story reported, without mentioning the paper's prior account of these events. With perhaps one minor exception, the story insisted, "all the stories of breaches of neutrality of this character are willful falsehoods concocted and put together for the purpose of making the American people believe that the Administration was dishonorably permitting such breaches of neutrality to go unchecked."

The story gave a fairly accurate account of Agent E-13's affidavit-harvesting scheme, without mentioning Means. Who was at fault? Rathom accused German diplomats.

Again, the story was published simultaneously by the *New York Times*, with what would become a famous opening line: "The *Providence Journal* will say tomorrow . . . "*

What happened between the two stories? Rathom acquired new sources. They were deeply placed, rabidly anti-German, and they would come to see Rathom as a friend and collaborator. Were it not for the false story planted by Means, these sources may never have connected with Rathom. For all the migraines Rathom ultimately caused Germany over the next two years, the irony is that a paid German agent unwittingly invented "John Rathom, spy hunter." And the German government was billed for it.

---

*   The word *tomorrow* needs clarification. News stories of the era often carried datelines indicating when they were written, usually the day before publication. "The *Providence Journal* will say tomorrow . . ." refers to the day after the dateline. From the reader's point of view, that is today. Am I clarifying or making it worse? Later, some newspapers simultaneously printing Rathom's stories would be more straightforward: "The *Providence Journal* will say *today* . . ."

CHAPTER 5

The Creation of John Revelstoke Rathom, Part 1: From Thin Air

In early 1889 the ocean liner *Abyssinia* prepared to leave British Hong Kong, chartered by Canadian Pacific Railway, as one leg of the firm's new transglobal shipping enterprise. Goods and passengers from Asia could cross the Pacific by ship, Canada by rail, and then the Atlantic by steamer, to reach England in less than thirty days, cutting two weeks off the all-sea route.

The *Abyssinia* was a coal-burning liner, nineteen years old, more than 350 feet long; a narrow iron wedge with a dark paint job that gave it a sinister look. Black smoke poured from a single funnel. Its three masts could be rigged with sails. On this trip from Hong Kong, passengers were divided into first class, second class, European steerage, and Asiatic steerage.

Among those passengers holding a ticket for the dank space below deck, in European steerage, was a twenty-year-old Australian traveling alone. He had a bit of journalism experience, some talent as a writer, loads of personal charm, and a deep brazen streak.

The ship departed Hong Kong on January 10, sailing northeast for Amoy, now known as Xiamen, a city on the southeastern coast of China near Taiwan, where it transferred cargo and passengers. The *Abyssinia* stopped next in Shanghai, and then sailed about five hundred nautical miles to Japan, where it made port calls in Nagasaki, Kobe, and Yokohama, before beginning its transpacific crossing on January 24. The ship carried thirty-six passengers, including our young Australian, plus a cargo of three hundred bales of silk and thirty-five thousand chests of Asian tea and produce.

It was a brutal voyage, filled with headwinds, storms, and high seas. A Royal Navy Reserve officer onboard died during the trip of a preexisting case of malaria. After a sixteen-day crossing, the ship reached its final destination, Vancouver, British Columbia, in the black of night on February 9, and disgorged its exhausted passengers, finally, into North America.

As he lugged his bag down the gangway into Canada, the young Aussie left behind his former life, along with the secret that would have prevented him from achieving his dreams, here, on the other side of the world.

He became someone new.

This is where John R. Rathom suddenly pops into history, as if by magic, as an Australian immigrant in British Columbia, with no birth records in his name, no emigration records left behind in his native country; in fact, with no prior documented history of ever existing. He introduced himself as John Robert Rathom at first, and when he realized, perhaps, that the alias lacked flair, his middle name evolved to the more interesting Revelstoke, probably borrowed from the mountain town of the same name located halfway between Vancouver and Calgary.

From almost the moment he inhabited his new identity, and for the rest of his life, the imposter would show an uncanny knack for being in the middle of important events in history, as well as a talent for getting himself out of trouble, and then just as quickly back into it.

From Vancouver, Rathom made his way to Victoria, a port city on the southern tip of Vancouver Island, and a ferry ride from Washington State.

He was powerfully built in his youth, 6'2", handsome, broad-shouldered, and athletic. The first known reported mention of Rathom is an item about a boat race, published on June 7, 1889, in the *Daily Colonist*, a Victoria newspaper where Rathom would soon find work:

Articles have been signed by G. A. Richardson of Victoria, and J. R. Rathom of Melbourne, Australia, for a 2-1/4 mile race, with turn, in outrigged skiff, for a $200 trophy.

Victoria, then a city of about seventeen thousand, was Rathom's first real home in North America. The city grew up around a serpentine bay, which in the late nineteenth century was cluttered with a forest of ship masts. Downtown Victoria consisted of about a dozen blocks of brownstones and mid-rise office buildings, many of them lovingly designed with bay windows and turrets, built along wide dirt streets.

The city had a thriving Chinatown, full of immigrants fresh off the boats and the families of Chinese laborers who came for work building Canada's railroads. Beyond the business district, wooden homes seemed scattered at random, like hundreds of Monopoly houses thrown like chickenfeed over farmland and forest. Half a dozen church steeples poked above the houses; there was a synagogue in town, a convent, a skating rink, and an opera house. The city hosted an annual regatta on May 24th to celebrate the birthday of its namesake, Queen Victoria.

Rathom immediately sought work as a journalist. He wrote stories for the *Daily Colonist*, which was printed out of a three-story brick office downtown. It is hard to identify Rathom's early articles; few stories were bylined in those days and none of the paper's employment records exist from that era. What is clear is he made a good first impression. Six months after Rathom arrived, the competing *Victoria Daily Times* tipped its hat, saying the young Aussie was "a clever journalist, a real good fellow and popular wherever he goes."

Rathom also developed a darker reputation. He was always broke and eager to borrow money from anyone reckless enough to lend it. Rathom's boss, city editor Charles Gibbons, later recalled:

Rathom had many creditors and I well remember how the boys in *The Colonist* office had a great laugh on him one day when Rathom, seeing a creditor coming, made a flying exit by way of the fire escape only to run right into the arms of a man waiting to serve papers on him in a suit for money due.[*]

In August 1889 Rathom got a plum freelance assignment for the *New York Herald*, sailing out of Victoria on an Alaskan seal hunt aboard the schooner *Black Diamond*. Having just turned twenty-one, Rathom had persuaded the *Herald* to trust him to cover a tense international controversy over seal-hunting rights off Alaska. He became a regular contributor to the *Herald* in Victoria.

By the next year, Rathom landed another job in the Victoria assessor's office. The work put Rathom in close contact with the city's mayor, John Grant, a mellow, Scottish-born gold miner. Grant was so impressed by Rathom's energy and abilities, he hired him as his personal secretary. Rathom moved into workspace in the mayor's office in city hall, a two-and-a-half-story redbrick building with round-headed windows and a high clock tower. The building is still Victoria's city hall today.

It soon became known around town that when Rathom ran short of money, he would forge a check in some small amount from Mayor Grant's account and cash it. The easygoing Grant would eventually discover the bad checks, scold Rathom, and remind him he *promised* to stop forging the mayor's name.

"Rathom would be very contrite and that would be the end of it until the next bad cheque came along when there would be the same remonstrance and the same contriteness," a former *Colonist* employee named Ed Wright later explained to investigators. Wright recalled Rathom as a versatile and brilliant writer, but a slippery character. "He was a smooth article, and while he did not set like a regular grafter, he got the money just the same."

---

[*] The quote from Gibbons dates to about 1914, some twenty-five years after he edited John Rathom. Gibbons gave the statement to private investigators scrubbing Rathom's background for an angry Rhode Island businessman who was preparing to sue Rathom for libel. The investigation, conducted by a New York law firm, unfolds like an unflattering map of Rathom's early career in North America. It contains dozens of sworn statements from people who knew and worked with Rathom in the 1890s. The dossier was secret for decades after Rathom's death, and has never been made widely public.

Mayor Grant eventually tired of Rathom's skimming and fired him. Grant chose not to prosecute, which may have saved Rathom's career. It was the first of many career-ending catastrophes that Rathom would duck.

The chief owner of the *Colonist* was L. H. Ellis, a civic-minded printer, who in addition to publishing a newspaper, printed maps and guidebooks promoting the city he loved. He owned a purebred greyhound that hung around the news office, and would follow the paper's employees around town like a cub reporter learning the beat. Twenty years after employing John Rathom, Ellis recalled his former reporter as "about as unscrupulous and unreliable as anyone I ever met or heard of."

Rathom had barely started work at the *Colonist* when he misquoted a judge, who sued. The newspaper lost the case in court. Damages were small, but Ellis had to pay the costs of defending his publication.

More sinister stories about Rathom began to filter back to the publisher, including whispers that Rathom was using his position to extort wealthy residents of Victoria. Rathom would visit affluent people, show them a draft of an unflattering story he had written about them, and offer to smooth the harsher edges for a fee, or, for some larger sum, to squash the piece.

The allegations mortified Ellis. His newspaper used for blackmail? It was criminal—if true. Ellis was a newsman. He operated in the realm of fact. So when a complaint about Rathom came to Ellis directly, he decided to dig out the truth. A Victoria entrepreneur named May Fox told Ellis that Rathom was trying to extort her. Fox was a local businesswoman, in the business of managing prostitutes—"nymphs of the pave," as newspapers of the time euphemistically referred to them.

Ellis brought his city editor, Gibbons, into his plan. They told Fox to arrange a 1:00 A.M. meeting with Rathom at her place to discuss the reporter's illicit demands. Gibbons got there early and hid in the next room so he could eavesdrop on the discussion and trap Rathom hot in the act of blackmail. It was a simple sting, just about foolproof. At 1:00, right on time, Gibbons spied Rathom approaching on foot.

Was Gibbons finally going to nail him?

Nope. At the last moment, Rathom turned and hustled off. He didn't come back.

The plan failed. But how?

Gibbons walked out into the night, defeated. And there, on the stoop of May Fox's place, was Ellis's greyhound. The publisher's dog known to every *Colonist* employee had followed the city editor to the clandestine meeting and had been waiting like a good boy for Gibbons to come out.

Rathom had dodged another career-ending threat, saved by a dog.

For all the problems Rathom caused, why would the *Colonist* keep him around? The answer is in the work. When Rathom was not harassing coworkers for loans or squeezing some rich Victorian for cash, his thunderous journalism hit readers like a punch to the solar plexus.

Rathom wrote the sort of stories that got people talking. The stories that sold papers. And made enemies.

On December 4, 1891, Victoria police arrested Rathom on a warrant. The charge was obtaining goods under false pretenses, related to an unpaid bill from a Victoria clothing store. The cops hauled Rathom to jail. Reporters heard about the arrest and hurried over. They asked the jailer if it was really necessary to lock Rathom in a cell over a piddling misdemeanor. In fact, it was. The directive had come straight from police chief Henry Sheppard, who ordered that Rathom receive "no privileges whatsoever," the *Colonist* reported.

Rathom's editors were livid—not at Rathom, for once, but at the police. The *Colonist* alleged that the bust was political payback for one of Rathom's explosive stories.

In Rathom's coat pocket at the time of his arrest was a draft of a news story he had just written about a court appearance of defendants charged with selling young Asian girls into sexual slavery. Chief Sheppard, a slim, severe-looking man with light eyes and a short Vandyke, reviewed the story before permitting it to be taken to the *Colonist* to be typeset for print. The story was a follow-up to an exposé Rathom and another reporter, whose identity is unknown, had recently written. That story had shocked the community and embarrassed the police.

Following tips that girls were being sold as sex slaves, Rathom and his colleague had stormed into the city's Chinatown, hunting for interviews and evidence, pleasantries and property laws be damned. They physically bulled their way into apartments and bullied suspects for answers. Their discoveries ran on the front page in late November under the headlines: THIS IS SHAMEFUL CRIME; A HIDEOUS UNDERCURRENT OF INHUMAN PRACTICES IN THE HEART OF OUR FAIR CITY.

The story reported that six Chinese girls, ages eleven to fourteen, having arrived in October on a steamer from Asia, had been sold to local men as sex slaves, for up to $1,400 each. The story openly questioned how the practice could go on under the noses of the police chief and city officials. Rathom wrote it with caustic outrage:

> On Friday night, Lo Leet, a low, repulsive looking man, besotted with opium smoking, but dressed in a manner that at once proclaimed him wealthy, opened his door to two Colonist reporters and regretted it the moment afterwards. Though every effort was made to stop their effecting an entrance, they were quickly inside, and it took only a moment to discover what they were in search of. In the first room entered were seen huddled up in native bed two young girls, beautifully dressed, but pale and with eyes like those of hunted animals. Questioned minutely, they both told their tale in a plain, straightforward manner. To put it briefly, they are living in fear and dread of their owner, and are slaves, forced to prostitution with all whom their captor chooses to name—children being dragged to the depth of degradation by the sordid wretch who has bought them, soul and body. And this on the principal street of this city, two hundred yards from our City Hall and within hail of the heart of the town.

Rathom was twenty-three when he wrote this. The story works as he intended, even now across time; it stirs pity and rage. The story also goes right to the contradictions in Rathom's personality. He was a criminal *and* a crime fighter. He saw injustice in the world with uncompromising moral clarity, but either did not look inward or found his own heart opaque or too complicated to parse. It is a trait he would exhibit throughout his career, acting as though he could be permitted to lie, extort, or serve his personal ambition at the expense of others, so long as he paid for his reckless dishonesty with crusading good works. Rathom filled both baskets of the scales of justice with equal evidence of good and evil. If the scales stayed roughly in balance, he could live with the results. The costume of a fake identity granted the imposter just enough distance from the actions of the character he had created.

After the story was published, police raids on "the houses of ill-fame in Chinatown" resulted in at least one arrest and the recovery of a "little girl," who was placed in the city refuge home.

Rathom's editors claimed the police chief had turned "his little brief authority" against a journalist who had embarrassed him for not doing his job.

At Rathom's trial, Jacob Isaacs, a tailor, testified that Rathom bought a suit from him on credit in June, saying that he was working at the city assessor's office, and that Isaacs could present the $15 invoice to Rathom's boss, who would pay it out of Rathom's accrued wages. Rathom asked the tailor not to collect the debt until July 2, when Rathom's pay was due. Isaacs was sick in July and unable to present the invoice. Several weeks later, he ran into the assessor and asked him to pay Rathom's bill, and the assessor declined.

Rathom's lawyer argued that had the invoice been presented on time, it would have been paid.

Chief Sheppard argued otherwise, but produced no evidence. The chief felt the conviction slipping away. "Your Honor," he said of Rathom, "this young man has been here some time. I know him. His doings have been brought to my notice a good many times, by men who say—"

"Bring on your charges," Rathom's lawyer objected, "we are ready to meet them."

The objection was sustained. The tailor had acknowledged he sold the suit on credit. The judge saw no false pretense and dismissed the charge.

Rathom escaped again, though the police were getting closer.

❖

A few months after Rathom arrived in Victoria, he met a charming high school girl named Mary Harriet Crockford. She was seventeen, not quite four years younger than he, about 5'5", slim and pretty, with dirty-blonde hair. She was highly intelligent, often earning honors in school, and, like Rathom, a gifted writer. Mary fell in love. She would love Rathom through his crimes and misadventures, standing by him while he raced to stay ahead of the law. And when her devotion was ultimately betrayed, Mary would never love another.

Mary Crockford was born in Victoria in December 1871, and grew up in Nanaimo, a coal town about seventy miles northwest of the city, connected to Victoria by ferry and rail. Her father, William Crockford, died in 1884, when Mary was twelve. Her mother remarried in 1888, to a Victoria businessman named William De Veulle. Mary moved from Nanaimo to her stepfather's home on Fort Street in Victoria. De Veulle died suddenly eight months later, in January 1889, just as the imposter was beginning his long overseas journey to North America.

Mary's mother, Jane De Veulle, did not like the vibe coming from the smooth-talking newsman sniffing around her daughter. "I never had any respect for John R. Rathom and always discouraged his attention to Mary," De Veulle recalled later. But what is the only thing more exciting than love? Forbidden love. Mary and Rathom kept up their relationship through letters after Mary graduated and moved back to Nanaimo to work as a schoolteacher.

The couple announced plans to marry in the summer of 1890, over the better judgement of Mary's mother, who "greatly opposed" the union. Mrs. De Veulle reluctantly relented, on the condition that the ceremony take place at her home. Two days before the scheduled date, Rathom and

Mary eloped. They married on July 5, officiated by an Episcopal priest in a small ceremony in Nanaimo at the home of Mary's landlord. On their wedding license Rathom and Mary both listed the Church of England as their religion. Rathom listed his place of birth as Australia, which was true, and identified his parents as Harold Robert Rathom and Adela Pechard, which was not true. Those people never existed. He also lied about his age for some reason, saying he was twenty-four; he had in fact turned twenty-two the day before the wedding. Mary gave her true age, eighteen.

There is no indication Mary was aware that her husband's identity was phony. She had to know of his proclivity for lies, bombast, and corner-cutting. How could she not? But who imagines marrying an imposter? She would have known only if Rathom told her. There is no evidence Rathom ever trusted his hidden past with another soul.

The newlyweds moved to the James Bay neighborhood, on a peninsula at the southern tip of Victoria. Mrs. De Veulle seldom saw her married daughter, though she did visit once to berate her son-in-law about gossip that he tried to blackmail May Fox, the woman who ran the brothel. Mary took her husband's side in the argument, "as she always has," her mother later bemoaned.

❖

The law began to catch up to Rathom in 1892. That June, Police Chief Sheppard prosecuted Rathom for assault. Rathom was accused of forcing his way into a home while looking for information, shoving a woman, and then wrestling with a man who tried to throw him out. Rathom contested nearly every fact but was convicted and fined $20. The competing *Victoria Daily Times* headlined its trial coverage A RECKLESS REPORTER.

Soon after, Rathom pushed a scheme too far. A Chinese court interpreter in Victoria, Yip Wing, complained to Gibbons that Rathom had represented himself as a police inspector from Vancouver, and had accused Wing of running illegal gambling houses. Wing claimed Rathom demanded a $450 bribe or he would "make a hell of a stink."

Wing also called Rathom's nemesis, Chief Sheppard, to demand that Rathom be arrested. But it was too late. Gibbons had fired Rathom. And Rathom was gone.

It was just a ferry ride to Port Angeles, Washington, where John and Mary Rathom set foot in the United States.

Rathom had decided to start over, again. In time, his three years in British Columbia would be snipped from his biography and the myth of John R. Rathom edited to say he had journeyed across the world directly to the United States, to become an American.

❖

Rathom settled in Oregon that summer and worked a short-lived stint for several months on the telegraph desk of the *Portland Oregonian*. It was a dull job for his big brain—nitpicking somebody else's copy rather than writing his own—and Rathom was fired for dozing off.

Later in 1892, probably November, John and Mary Rathom moved to Astoria, Oregon, a city of about seven thousand crammed onto a tooth of land in the yawning mouth of the Columbia River, where Lewis and Clark had met the Pacific Ocean. It was an old sea town, full of fishermen and sailors, trappers, and immigrants, many of whom worked in salmon canneries. Rathom and his wife lived two blocks from Swilltown, a rowdy, bawdy neighborhood where a man could drink himself blind in a brothel, gamble away his wages in a saloon, and wake up hungover at sea, shanghaied into serving on a ship that was short a crewman. Rathom became editor of the *Astorian*, a newspaper with offices downtown.

Six weeks into the job Rathom wrote a scorching editorial, trashing a local lawyer as "a liar and a low-mannered coward." And in February 1893 Rathom was indicted for criminal libel. This was serious. Just the year before, another editor in Astoria had been sentenced to a year in jail for libel. Rathom was defended by C. G. Fulton and his brother Charles. Charles would later represent Oregon in the US Senate. After a two-day trial, the jury deadlocked, eight to four, in Rathom's favor. The judge discharged the jury, and Rathom went free, skating through another potential career-killer.

Rathom became a prominent member of Astoria civic society. He narrated events for the photography club. He performed in plays. He played in a men's soccer league. And, it appears, he frequently ran up debts, hit up his colleagues for loans, and liberally employed his blackmail scheme—preparing derogatory stories and offering to modify or suppress them for money.

"He was capable of doing almost anything for pay," a former Astoria newspaper colleague later said of Rathom.

C. G. Fulton heard the stories about Rathom's blackmail. Putting those rumors together with his own sense of the man, "I am satisfied in my own mind, while not prepared to swear it, that he was a goddamn crook," he said.

Rathom left Astoria suddenly, probably in 1896—the *Astorian*, which is still published, does not have records that could pinpoint the date.

Several years later, a cashier at Astoria Savings Bank said he heard that Rathom had tried to take his own life after being fired. There is no way to confirm whether Rathom attempted suicide, though he left a clue he may have considered it. Three years after leaving Astoria, Rathom contributed ten lines of text to go with a drawing by an artist for the *San Francisco Call*. Titled "The Suicide," the drawing showed a despairing man staring down from a cliff into a raging sea. With it was a short poem by Rathom:

> Dull on the sea, no hope for me,
> And the fog beats in to the water's edge;
> Rise the waves and they fall, sorrow comes to us all;
> What mystery lies neath the kelp and the sedge?
> Shall I plunge and see?
>
> Ay, why not, go to the depths below
> Under the quiet wash of the tide?
> Sorrow's balm may lie here, on this shore dark and drear,

Splash, and an eddy, an outcast has died;
Read my epitaph so.

Not all poetry is biographical, of course, but I cannot get over the image of a tombstone engraved with the words *an outcast has died*. What was the imposter if not an outcast? He was a solitary soul cut off from the world by lies that could never be untold.

❖

By 1897 Rathom and Mary were in San Francisco. Rathom bounced back yet again, and had found work as a correspondent for the *San Francisco Chronicle*, one of three prominent dailies in the city. Again, the exact dates are a mystery; the *Chronicle*'s employment records did not survive the 1906 San Francisco earthquake and fire.

Rathom became a favorite of *Chronicle* editors and scored choice assignments. In February 1897 the paper sent him to Carson City, Nevada, to cover a prizefight between the gentlemanly James J. Corbett and the prickly Australian Bob Fitzsimmons. The fight was the Ali-Frazier of its day, made even more famous because it was filmed and turned into a feature-length film, *The Corbett-Fitzsimmons Title Fight*, which drew eager audiences to theaters for months after the match, even though everyone knew Fitzsimmons had won. Clips of the silent movie are in the care of the Library of Congress and easily found online; they mostly show two pasty guys poking at each other. For three weeks, Rathom whipped up pre-fight hype, reporting on the training and sparring of the combatants. He listed the celebrities in attendance, including the writer Bat Masterson and the lawman and gambler Wyatt Earp, who fifteen years earlier had been in the gunfight at the O.K. Corral.

Rathom also proved to be an excellent crime reporter. In 1898 he exposed a bribery scheme aimed at state legislators. At the time, California was looking to buy automatic voting machines for its polling places. An inventor named C. W. Pike entered his machine in a competition for the

state contract but soon learned a public commission was going to rec-
ommend another model. Pike asked a lobbyist named George Baker for
advice. Baker told him a bribe should do the trick, and offered to buy
off a sufficient number of legislators for $25,000, including his fee. Pike
said he would think about it, but instead spilled the details to editors at
the *Chronicle*.

The editors assigned Rathom to investigate with a sting operation.
Rathom assumed a fake name—a different fake name—and posed as one
of Pike's financial backers to get the lobbyist to incriminate himself and
others.

I have to pause a second here and rewind. John R. Rathom was assigned
to create a false identity as part of a con. No surprise, he was good at it.
He met Baker in a boarding house, hid an eavesdropping stenographer in
the next room to create a transcript of the meeting, then plied the crooked
lobbyist with brandy and cigars and meticulously led him through a long
confession.

"What will it cost to buy the men in the legislature?" asked Rathom,
who was going by the name John Roberts.

"Four or five thousand dollars, I think, would make a good showing,"
Baker replied.

It was a sensational news story, perhaps Rathom's best—until he went
to war, and found inspiration not in the victory of US troops, but in their
mourning.

❖

On the evening of February 15, 1898, the USS *Maine* was anchored
in Havana Harbor, Cuba. The battleship was not supposed to become
famous. It wasn't supposed to do much of anything. Rebels on the island
were fighting for independence from Spain. Riots in Havana had spooked
US officials, who worried about the welfare of Americans in the city. The
Maine was ordered to Cuba to sit there, look tough, and protect American
interests.

Around 9:40 that night, the ship blew up. What probably happened, though has never been proved, was that a spontaneous fire began to smolder in the *Maine*'s coal bunker. Heat built up until the steel bulkhead walls would have been too hot to touch. Heat transfer ignited munitions stored in another compartment, and the internal explosion tore off the ship's bow. As a result, 266 American sailors were killed.

Hawkish US newspaper publishers, such as William Randolph Hearst, immediately blamed a Spanish undersea mine, and called for war. Within days, Americans were shouting the slogan "Remember the *Maine*, to hell with Spain!"

Spain denied doing anything to the ship. At the time, Spain was struggling to knock down a poorly armed rebellion in its own colony. Instigating a war with the United States would have been profoundly dumb. But when a US review panel studied the wreckage and concluded several weeks later that the ship had indeed been destroyed by a mine, calls for war against Spain grew deafening. Pro-war newspapers predicted the fight would be easy, and waxed enthusiastically about the United States slapping around a declining Old World power and freeing Cuba while in the neighborhood. Subsequent studies using better technology, including a review in 1974, concluded that a coal fire was more likely the cause, but that came a little too late for Spain.

On April 20, Congress demanded that Spain withdraw from Cuba, and authorized President William McKinley to use military force to make it happen.

Three days later the *San Francisco Chronicle* dispatched John Rathom and two other journalists to cover the upcoming war firsthand.

For this story of a lifetime, the *Chronicle* feted its war correspondents with a full-page sendoff, which included biographies and head-and-shoulder sketches. The drawing, published on April 23, 1898, is the earliest known likeness of Rathom. Still fit and athletic in youth, he is clean-shaven and movie-star handsome in that tough-guy sort of way, with a hint of world weariness around the eyes. His accompanying "biography" is a risible collection of fabrications: He began as a humble political reporter in

Australia, then suddenly found himself joining explorers on a six-month expedition to the country's untamed interior, where Rathom lived with two Aboriginal tribes. Next, he was a war reporter in Sudan, until being shot in the leg. Then he toured Europe, seeing every capital city on the continent, before departing for three years in Asia, where he spent half the time at sea serving as an honorary officer on a Chinese naval cruiser. None of those things are true. His real experience in British Columbia and Oregon was compressed in the bio, and Rathom shoehorned into that time period a fantastical adventure with the renowned Arctic explorer Frederick Schwatka. It is a wonder the *Chronicle* never questioned how anyone could have accomplished all these things by the age of twenty-nine.

The true part of the biography was this: "He has an unusual aptitude for gathering news."

Rathom joined US troops in New Orleans, where he attached to the First Infantry Regiment. On April 29, the army, and Rathom, left for a staging area in Tampa, all anticipating a swift invasion of Cuba.

But once in Florida it was hurry up and wait. For five weeks, Rathom and some seventy other reporters were stuck in Tampa, a city of about fifteen thousand, many working in the cigar factories. Bored soldiers from the military encampments wandered the town like tourists, buying snacks and supplies and cleaning out the shops of carved orangewood trinkets, machetes, and live baby alligators. The Rough Riders, the First US Volunteer Cavalry, strutted through town. Teddy Roosevelt had famously resigned his post as assistant secretary of the navy to join the Rough Riders for the war. They were media sensations even then. Rathom wrote about them:

> They are an interesting crowd of men, one of the most wonderful social mixtures ever brought into a regiment in this or any other war. Half-breed Indians, Arizona-bred men, Eastern millionaires in search of a sensation, long-haired college students, New Mexico cow-punchers and flotsam and jetsam from pretty near all over the world. These are the people who call Theodore Roosevelt "Colonel!" and "Sunny Boy." Individually

they are splendid fellows, most of them hard as nails, with good
physical frames, good revolver shots and brave.

Waiting around in Tampa, Rathom hunted for stories to file nearly every
day. He interviewed the US commander, General William Shafter, an
abdominous, gout-ridden, three-hundred-pound man. Shafter bragged to
Rathom that US artillery would negate any numerical advantage Spanish
troops enjoyed in Cuba. On another day, Rathom covered a two-hour
lecture on yellow fever, which would soon become painfully relevant for
him. And when Rathom ran out of news and got bored, he wrote features
saying there was no news, and everyone was bored. "Everything in Tampa
is now in a state of stagnation and we have had no news," read the opening
of one piece.

The center of the encampment was the Tampa Bay Hotel, headquarters
for the military officers planning the invasion, where a scribe could run
into Teddy Roosevelt or Clara Barton, founder of the American Red Cross.
The enormous hotel, now part of the University of Tampa, was a five-story
redbrick palace ornamented with tall minarets, like a cross between an
old New England textile mill and a mosque. Rathom was popular among
the scribes. They elected him "chairman" of the correspondents, making
him the one to lead them to the transports when the invasion began. One
morning a bunch of reporters were sitting around in the heat waiting for
news, probably on the hotel's veranda. Rathom was in a rocking chair,
fanning himself with his hat. He suddenly bolted up and said, "Say boys,
I can't stand this any longer. I'm going out somewhere to do something."
He marched off. An hour or two later he came back, flushed and dusty.
"I've been for a ride," he said.

"On the trolley car?" someone asked.

"Trolley car be hanged," Rathom said. "I've bought a horse."

The other reporters were intrigued. A horse? That *would* be conve-
nient. Soon there was a collection of reporter-owned horses tied up outside the hotel, and demand for more. "After the surplus supply had been
exhausted," one reporter wrote, "they began to fetch horses out of the milk

carts—gentle, contemplative charges, which, when you were riding them would stop from force of habit whenever they came to a house."

On May 15, Rathom finally found some excitement to cover. Soldiers mustered to fight a brush fire in the palmetto forest that threatened the encampment. The hardest work was done by Black troops, in the segregated US Army. "The Ninth, the Negro cavalry, was camped nearest to the blaze," Rathom wrote. "The bugles sounded fire call, and the regiment, though totally unprepared for an order of the kind, made a magnificent showing."

Rathom believed plenty of racial stereotypes. Years later, in the First World War, he would demonize foreigners as disloyal and dangerous, but in this piece about the fire, and in another later about Black troops in combat, he had no hesitation in the days of Jim Crow portraying Black Americans heroically: "After working nearly an hour, with the perspiration streaming down their faces, many of them burned and in pain from the terrible heat, they subdued the fire and gradually conquered, saving the camp from what looked like certain destruction."

❖

At last, on June 14, the order sounded for troops and scribes to make for the boats. The invasion of Cuba was to begin.

Rathom climbed aboard the steamer *Olivette*, a ship that had carried survivors of the USS *Maine*. The skies were clear above the convoy. With his field glasses, Rathom spotted General Shafter on another transport. The general listened to an infantry band playing "My Country, 'Tis of Thee" from his ship's top deck. The music carried across the water.

"Every man that hears it knows what it means," Rathom wrote of the song. He had not witnessed real bloodshed, and still saw the conflict as a thrilling adventure. "In each body beats a heart that responds with a thrill of enthusiasm to this hymn that seems today to be at once a benediction and an inspiration. We are off to the war."

Rathom came ashore with US troops in southern Cuba, and sent a short cable to the *Chronicle* confirming the landing. Then his byline disappeared from the paper for weeks while the troops skirmished toward Santiago. The *Chronicle* printed daily battle reports from other sources, probably due to transmission delays in getting Rathom's original material. It is clear from later stories that Rathom witnessed the decisive Battle of San Juan Hill on July 1. Yet his brilliant, mournful account of the battle's aftermath, written the night of July 3, the day before his thirtieth birthday, was not published until three weeks later. It is Rathom's best work of the war. He was sobered by what he had seen, his writing raw and beautiful, stripped of jingoism, infused with sorrow and anger.

It is bare honesty from an imposter, and worth quoting at length:

> Overhead is the typical Cuban sky, black as jet; studded with thousands of stars. The full moon floods everything with its soft light making the hills and valleys round our trenches as bright as they were at noon, and throwing back the white glitter of the roofs of Santiago like long beacon gleams, right in front of us. Below at the bottom of the ridge constant dull sounds and the flash of picks through the air tell us that our men are engaged in burying their comrades.
>
> I want to write tonight of our wounded, the Red Cross hospitals and the methods that have so far in this campaign characterized the medical arm of the service.
>
> This "picnic war," this "summer holiday" as some of our all-seeing legislators characterized it before the Army left Tampa, has already brought death and desolation to many American homes. I wish some of these men who for months reviled our President for his refusal to rush into battle, who talked of taking Havana with 5000 men, could see what I have seen in the past three days. Is there any sight, I wonder, more depressing in its effect, more lasting in its memories or more heartrending than a field hospital hastily erected in the wake of an army? Men strong, full of young manhood, bunches of vitality and enthusiasm, march along a winding bog to where the enemy waits

for them. The crack of Gatlings, the whistle of Mauser bullets, the shriek of the devilish shell and shrapnel fill the air and the grave-faced doctors and Red Cross nurses make ready quietly but with business-like activity for what they know will come back by that country road.

. . .

Our dead are buried all along the line of march and tenderly indeed they have been laid in their last resting place. In little clearings by the side of beautiful streams, where the coconut palms hang over and almost touch the water. I have seen these sad ceremonies performed twenty times since the month began, and never once, though the shells have been bursting about our ears, has the burial of a comrade been hurried or the solemn service slurred. Each little raised heap has at its head a board—generally a piece of cracker box, containing in roughly penciled letters the name and number of the regiment of him who sleeps beneath, and no soldier passes that way but brings his hand to the salute and lets his thoughts rest for a moment on more solemn things than generally occupy the mind of a man at arms.

It was Rathom's last substantial story of the war.

By mid-July, American troops and the reporters embedded with them began getting sick. First the reporter from the *Chicago Journal*, then one from the *National Journal*. Then an actor, Burr McIntosh, later to become a silent film star, who had joined the scribes to research a role. And then Rathom.

The early symptoms were flu-like: fever, chills, nausea. "It came so stealthily no one but the surgeons seemed aware of its presence until it was ditching the survivors of San Juan, El Poso, and El Caney by the hundreds," wrote a reporter for the *Arizona Republican*. Doctors knew yellow fever when they saw it. Infected men were ordered to quarantine in a fever hospital in the mountains, and when heavy rains forced the hospital closed, fever patients were transferred to the coastal town of Siboney, under the flag of the Red Cross in an encampment of tents and staked-out tarps.

Yellow fever is a viral disease transmitted by infected mosquitos. The initial flu-like symptoms go away in a few days, and most patients recover. But in about 15 percent of cases the disease snaps back ferociously with high fever; liver damage that turns the skin yellow; nosebleeds, mouth-bleeds, and even eye-bleeds; black vomit; and delirium. As many as half of the people who develop severe symptoms die. There is a vaccine now, but not in Rathom's day.

As others recovered, Rathom's case progressed to the dangerous second stage.

The *Arizona Republican* reported that Rathom ran off into the woods when stewards first tried to take him to the fever camp. While the stewards were standing around bemoaning that they had lost him, Rathom returned, "tottering up the path, dragging his blanket after him."

"There he is!" a steward shouted. They grabbed him. Rathom tried to get away. He was a big man, but "as weak as a child" from the disease, and easily overpowered.

"They want to take me off to the yellow fever camp," Rathom screamed to the scribes watching. "Won't some of you fellows help me?"

It was obvious to the reporter who witnessed the scene: "The fever was then in his brain."

The stewards begged Rathom to come along. They said he would die otherwise.

"That satisfies me," Rathom said.

"Do you want to die here?"

"Yes, if you will go away from me."

The stewards finally carried Rathom away by force.

On July 26, a wire story published across the country reported that Rathom of the *San Francisco Chronicle* was the last journalist in the fever camp. "He is in a very bad way," the story said.

In August, a correspondent from the *New York Sun*, identified as "Arm-strong," possibly Collin Armstrong, a *Sun* journalist at the time, hopped a filthy boxcar near Santiago for the train ride to Siboney, in search of his friend John Rathom. It was a brutally hot Cuban day with a blazing sun. "What a forlorn, repulsive place it was," he wrote of Siboney, "all ruins and soiled tents, the air impregnated with sickening hospital odors." Surf smashed on the beach and a buzzard glided across the cloudless sky.

Armstrong had just checked in with a doctor, when "a specter appeared" and grabbed his hand. It was Rathom, "the man himself—wasted, yellow, feeble, with dim eyes and a straggling beard. He had been in the shadow of death."

Rathom said, "The doctors told me one evening that I would die before midnight, and I dictated some farewell letters. I gave myself up but it was to be otherwise."

The *Sun* reporter filed a story about his search for John Rathom, head-lined THE LAST MAN ON THE BEACH: LOST TO THE WORLD, HE WAS FOUND AT SIBONEY, THE PLAGUE CITY.

The conflict with Spain effectively ended in August; by September Rathom was back home in San Francisco, convalescing. "He was a physical wreck when he returned from the war," recalled a *Chronicle* editor, years later.

Did war and pestilence change John Rathom? Well, his editors wanted to know what happened to the money they had advanced him for reporting expenses.

Rathom told them the money had burned up in a fire.

"In view of his marked ability and his offer to make restitution we over-looked it," *Chronicle* managing editor John Young said later. "He never did repay the money however."

Rathom was still one major scandal away from his editorship in Providence. The next time his name appeared in print across the land, it would be for a salacious story of love, sex, and poison.

CHAPTER 6
Spies, Lies, Allies

The door was unlocked, precisely as the source had promised. Emanuel Voska let himself into a furnished room on the fourth floor of an apartment building on New York's Upper West Side. No one else was there. His nerves fluttered.

Voska was eager—desperate, even—to affect the outcome of the war in Europe, to tip it toward the Allies. That was why he had come to this strange apartment for this covert appointment, in early autumn 1914.

But was he *too* eager? He knew that if this meeting was a trap, he was as good as dead, and his dirty bones might one day wash up on the banks of the Hudson.

He sat down to wait.

For whom? He had no idea.

❖

Emanuel Voska was a stocky man with arresting amber-blue eyes. He spoke English with a heavy Eastern European accent.

He was forty years old when he stumbled into becoming a spy.

Voska was born in 1875, in the town of Kutna Hora, in a region of Europe known as Bohemia, which is now roughly the western half of the

Czech Republic. At the beginning of the First World War, Bohemia was part of Austria-Hungary. Voska's father, a Bohemian nationalist who had owned a marble quarry, had been killed in a cave-in when Emanuel was six years old. At age fourteen, Emanuel Voska ran away from home because his uncle insisted he become a priest. Voska wanted to be an artist—a great sculptor. He worked his way through art school as a tombstone engraver. Politically, he was a young hothead who believed Bohemia should be a free nation. When someone reported him to the government as a radical, Voska fled to the United States.

He arrived in New York City in 1894, "without a word of English and with only four dollars in his pocket," according to the journalist Will Irvin, who collaborated with Voska on a memoir published in 1940. Voska couldn't make rent as a sculptor, so he tried his father's business, rock quarries, did very well, and became modestly rich. He married another Czech immigrant and fathered six children. He followed Czech politics closely, and was an early supporter of Tomáš Masaryk, the Czech-born college professor who would become Voska's mentor. In 1910 and 1912 Voska arranged lecture tours for Masaryk before Czech social organizations in the United States. Masaryk would go on to lead the Czech independence movement, and then after the war became a political leader. He is the George Washington of Czechoslovakia.

In June 1914 Voska and his daughter Villa visited Masaryk on a trip to Prague. Voska was relaxing on a train when the conductor ran through shouting that Archduke Franz Ferdinand had been assassinated. The next few weeks rewrote Voska's destiny. He stayed in Austria-Hungary for the early weeks of the war, plotting with Masaryk.

Masaryk saw the war as an opportunity for Czechs. "An allied victory would mean the end of the Austro-Hungarian Empire," he told Voska. "We must make ourselves so useful that when France and Britain dictated the peace terms, they could not deny our claim to an independent republic."

Masaryk gathered military and economic intelligence about Austria-Hungary, and asked Voska to smuggle the document to London. Voska and his daughter risked death by carrying the pages of Masaryk's report, packed into hollows cut into the heels of Voska's shoes and wrapped around the wires of Villa's corset. Voska was afraid to take off his shoes on the trip and slept in them for days.

In London Voska used a letter of introduction from Masaryk to get an audience with one of the world's most important journalists, Wickham Steed, of the London *Times*. There are no US reporters working today with Steed's influence as a "statesman-journalist," who represented and shaped the interest of the British government in his columns.

Voska asked Steed for something ridiculous—he wanted a private audience with the country's secretary of state for war, Field Marshal Horatio Herbert Kitchener. At the time Kitchener was best known for orchestrating British victories in Sudan and in the Second Boer War in South Africa, though may be better known now for his ruthless military tactics.

Steed arranged the meeting in early September. Voska found Kitchener "easy, pleasant, cordial," even though at the time German troops had driven deep into France, to the Marne River, just sixty miles from Paris. Kitchener acted like the German army was someone else's problem.

What Voska needed to know was how long the war would last.

"It will be a long war," Kitchener assured him. "Three years at least, maybe four."*

A long war. That was what Voska needed to hear. If the war were to be short, his orders from Masaryk were to go home and just live his life; there would be no time to do anything else. A long war meant Voska was to organize Czechs in the United States in service of the Allies.

Voska sailed home to New York. Two days after he arrived, he gave a speech on his travels to Czech Americans at a New York beer hall. The next day, Voska answered the most important telephone call of his life. A man wanted to meet him in secret, like some sort of drug deal. And at a drug store, no less: at First Avenue and Seventy-Second Street, which was then within a Czech neighborhood.

---

* Kitchener was prescient, though he would not see the war to its end. He drowned en route to Russia in 1916, when the armored cruiser the HMS *Hampshire* hit an undersea mine north of Scotland.

As soon as Voska entered the store, a stranger called him by name. "You don't know me but I know you," the man said. The stranger had seen Voska's speech and was inspired. He said he was a clerk at the Austrian consulate in New York, and he volunteered on the spot to do anything to advance the cause of Czech freedom in Europe. Voska suspected a double cross. To prove himself, the man handed over secret consular documents showing that German and Austrian diplomats were smuggling their countrymen home through the British naval blockade with forged passports in the names of American citizens.

"For a quarter of an hour we walked the street, talking in Czech," Voska later wrote. "He informed me that he was in charge of the mail at the consulate. Further, other consular employees were Czechs. He promised to find out their attitude toward our cause and, if they passed muster, to enlist them in our service."

Voska passed the list of names from his new source to the New York correspondent for the London *Times*. The correspondent transmitted the information to the British government, so that authorities could grab the men with the forged passports, and intern them.

In New York, Voska took over a fledgling organization of Czech nationalists called the Bohemian National Alliance, and made it the base of a counterspy operation. The organization placed agents as employees in US-based German and Austrian diplomatic institutions, social clubs, and businesses, around New York and Washington, to listen for tips that could be distilled for intelligence and weaponized against the Central Powers. Voska's daughter Villa landed a job as a secretary in the office of German commercial attaché Henrich Albert.

The clerk from the Austrian consulate, still known to us only by the code name Zeno, was Voska's most valuable asset. Over the next two years, Zeno smuggled out reams of secret cables and letters. Voska rented an office in the Hudson Terminal Building, a pair of towers in Lower Manhattan, and stenciled the name of a phony medical device firm on the milky glass door: the Pneumograph Company. For authenticity, he sat a clerk out front who had studied the obscure pneumography machine, an invention to measure respiration. The real purpose of the office was in the back room, where Voska set up a photo studio for copying confidential paperwork.

And that was how a failed artist from Bohemia stumbled into becoming the head of a spy network in the United States.

❖

In the early autumn of 1914, many Americans with Austro-Hungarian roots began to ask how they could help the Allied war effort. An informal committee of foreign journalists and other influential immigrants came together in New York. Voska was among three native Czechs dispatched by the committee to Washington, to offer the group's assistance to the Allies. The Russian ambassador "seemed cool to the proposal," in Voska's opinion. The French were polite and noncommittal. The British ambassador, Cecil Spring-Rice, however, was charming and cordial, expertly stroking his guests by going on about the wonderful Czech people, so unfairly oppressed. In diplomacy, Spring-Rice was a pro. He was fifty-five years old, an aristocrat, poet, and intellectual, with a horseshoe of thinning hair, a gray-streaked Vandyke, and tiny round eyeglasses with wire rims.

Voska didn't know it at first, but he impressed Spring-Rice. Events began to click into place behind the scenes. A week after seeing the ambassador, Voska was invited to tea by the American-born wife of a Serbian diplomat. She whispered to Voska that "a man" wanted to meet him, in secret.

Yes, *another* shadowy character asking for a clandestine meeting. That sort of thing seemed to be happening a lot to Voska.

"I agreed; and she gave me somewhat mysterious instructions," Voska later wrote. "At four o'clock the next afternoon I was to report at an apartment house on the Upper West Side, take the elevator to the fourth floor and enter the first door on my right, which I would find unlocked. The apartment inside would be fully furnished—but nobody there. I was to make myself at home until 'the man' entered and identified himself."

And so Voska, half-thinking he might soon be killed, overcame his butterflies and sat down in the empty apartment and waited.

Fifteen minutes later, the apartment door opened and in walked a trim man with a youthful step, deeply tanned skin, and civilian clothes. He introduced himself by his real name, Captain Guy Gaunt. In his public life, Gaunt was the British embassy's naval attaché in the United States, a post similar to what Boy-Ed held for the Germans. In secret, though, Gaunt was part of British intelligence in the United States. His portfolio included propagating propaganda to influence the American people, and counterespionage measures against German agents.

Gaunt said Steed, the London *Times* journalist, had given Voska a sterling reference, and that the documents Voska provided on Germans traveling under forged passports had been valuable.

The men had different motivations, but the same aim: the defeat of the Central Powers in World War I.

"So we began to talk business," Voska later recalled.

At the time, Guy Reginald Archer Gaunt was forty-five years old. He had thin lips and prominent protruding ears, a nonthreatening sort of handsomeness, and easy charm. He was born in 1869, in Bellarat, Australia, a gold rush town in the province of Victoria, tucked in the southeastern corner of the continent. His brother, Ernest, was a rear admiral with a distinguished military career in the Royal Navy. His sister, Mary, was an author who wrote stories about strong, independent women.

Gaunt had trained as a merchant machine, and then at age seventeen became a midshipman in the Royal Navy Reserve. Nine years later, in 1895, he joined the Royal Navy, and climbed the ranks. He served in the Philippines and led a local troop regiment at the British consulate in Samoa during an outbreak of unrest and violence. He was promoted to commander in 1901, at age thirty-two, and served on battleships and cruisers.

He could have happily spent the rest of his life at sea, but for a gruesome disaster, which, in a few terrible seconds, swept Gaunt off the ocean and put him on the path to that Manhattan apartment to meet Emanuel Voska.

❖

What a wintry, dark, and miserable night, sailing the English Channel.

It was two weeks before Christmas, 1912. Gaunt was at the helm of a new King George V-class super-dreadnought battleship, the HMS *Centurion*. She was one of the most lethal machines of her time: six hundred feet long, some twenty-six thousand tons, bristling with armor plating and tiers of massive guns piggybacking on each other. The *Centurion* was so new, she was not quite finished. Gaunt's assignment was to take her with a skeleton crew out of Devonport, on the southern coast of England, run the steam boilers moderately hard for thirty hours to test the turbines that powered the ship, then return her to the shipyard for more work.

The overnight mission also tested the sailors. The heating system for the crew spaces was not working yet. Worse, the bridge leaked sea spray through welding gaps that had not yet been fixed. Gaunt and the bridge crew spent hours soaked and shivering, plowing through the English Channel at a swift twenty knots.

After being up-Channel during the night, the *Centurion* sliced west through dark waters on a moonless black night, shortly before daybreak. The Anvil Point lighthouse blinked its warning off to the right. Gaunt wanted a break. He left the dreadnought in the care of a lieutenant and walked a few steps to his cabin, intending to get out of his frozen boots for a while.

He barely had time to sit when the battleship trembled. Not violently, but Gaunt knew something was wrong. It was 5:38 A.M.

A fist pounded on Gaunt's door, and a crewman shouted, "Ship in collision, sir!"

Gaunt rushed out.

On the starboard side passed a fleeting glimpse of another vessel. She was an old iron steamer, peeling away into the night after being bumped by the *Centurion*. Gaunt called out to her, but the hiss of her steam escaping drowned out his voice. The other vessel blasted her siren once. Gaunt ordered the battleship's engines into reverse, to slow his ship's momentum. The old steamer vanished in coal smoke and darkness. Gaunt ordered his crew to ready for a rescue.

It took about four minutes for the *Centurion* to get its searchlights working.

The beams crisscrossed empty sea.

Nothing was there. The men scoured the area for hours. There was no sign of the other vessel. It was as if the collision had been a terrible dream, except for the *Centurion*'s crumpled bow and the gash along its side—those things were real. On deck, the crew found an oil lamp, still burning, that must have been sheared off the other ship. It was the port bow light. What had happened began to come into focus. The old steamer had been traveling in the same direction. The *Centurion* had overtaken the smaller ship and smashed her at an angle from behind. Gaunt gave up the search after daylight and brought the dreadnought home. The damage would take months to fix. The bigger worry was the other ship. What had happened to her?

Two days later, a lifeboat adrift with the body of a sailor was found off the Isle of Wight, some fifteen miles from the collision site. The sailor had died of a broken neck, probably when he dived desperately into the boat. The lifeboat had the markings of the *Derna*, an old Italian cargo steamer. The *Derna* had left Memel, now called Klaipėda, a port city in Lithuania, on December 3, heading to Wales. Nobody had seen the *Derna* for days, and now there was no doubt what ship the *Centurion* had rammed. And no doubt what had happened to her. The *Derna*'s top speed was nine knots. Slammed portside by a ship ten times as massive and traveling twice as fast, the *Derna* rolled on her beams and went under, taking the entire crew of thirty-six to their deaths.

The *Derna* remains exactly where she came to rest that night, on the sea bottom at a depth of 130 feet, according to diver Dave Wendes, who has visited and written about the many wrecks in the English Channel. Today, the degraded wreckage stands not quite two stories tall from the seabed. Ravaged by strong currents and oxygen-rich water, it is not much of a memorial to the lives lost. "We did recover a brass ship's wheel many years ago," Wendes told me, "and someone had scratched his name in the brass." It was an Italian name: Gerolimo Oliveri. Wendes was never able to confirm if the man was among those who went down with the ship. But as an epitaph for a disaster, a few letters scratched into brass will have to do.

Gaunt and his lieutenant were court-martialed in May 1913. The prosecution alleged that the *Centurion* was going too fast for conditions, and that Gaunt should have searched harder for survivors. Witnesses suggested the *Derna* did not have a light on her stern, which would have helped other ships at night determine if she were approaching or traveling in the same direction. Gaunt beseeched the court to clear him from "this position in which I find myself, through I am certain, no fault of my own."

After two days of testimony, Gaunt was acquitted. The lieutenant in charge of the watch on the *Centurion* at the time of the accident was reprimanded.

Gaunt was not legally responsible, but the verdict could not erase the horror of thirty-six dead Italian sailors, nor the disfigurement of one of the navy's newest dreadnoughts. Gaunt was briefly assigned another battleship to command, but then quickly yanked off the bridge and assigned a desk—as naval attaché in the United States. No formal explanation for the move has been found in Gaunt's writings or the archives of the British Admiralty, according to Anthony Delano, Gaunt's biographer, who concludes: "Gaunt's superiors at the Admiralty decided to park him out of sight until" the *Derna* disaster "faded from memory."

❖

Banished from the sea, Gaunt deployed to Washington, DC, in June 1914, the month Archduke Franz Ferdinand was assassinated. When Britain declared war on Germany in August, Gaunt's mission changed. He needed to quickly help stand up a spy and propaganda apparatus on a shoestring budget. In the early days of the war, Gaunt played to America's sense of right by pushing stories into the press about German atrocities in Belgium. These stories were "fairly useful cards to play in a mild way," Gaunt wrote in his memoir, but they "didn't successfully out-weigh the children's schoolbooks, wherein England is portrayed as the bully of the seas and the oppressor of downtrodden races. Bunkum, I know, but nevertheless existent."

Bunkum? The sun never set on "downtrodden races" oppressed by British colonial rule. But Gaunt was right that England was not universally revered in the United States. It can be hard to look back from the twenty-first century and imagine Americans waffling over who to support in a twentieth-century world war. But the politics of World War I were more complicated than those of World War II. Who were the bad guys in World War I? In the early days of the fighting, who could say? There were no Nazis. Hitler was an unknown army grunt painting watercolors. The 1910 US Census recorded more than eight million German immigrants and their children, a sizable base of support for Germany, when the US population was just ninety-two million. America was also home to more than four million people of Irish descent, many of whom favored Germany by default after nearly eight hundred years of discord with the English.

In the early days of the war, *Literary Digest* polled newspaper editors representing every corner of America, asking which side of the European war they and their readers favored. Of the 367 editors who responded, 105 favored Britain and the Allies, and 20 favored Germany.

New England, in general, favored the Allies, and the South leaned that way at the start of the war before heavy-handed British policies toward merchant shipping alienated southern farmers and exporters. The Midwest, thick with German immigrants, generally pulled for the Central Powers.

The majority of editors, 242, said they were neutral—as were many Americans. In big cities, such as New York and Chicago, the populations were diverse and opinions were "so mixed as to be neutral," wrote *Literary Digest*. As one California editor put it to the magazine, "We are sincerely for world peace, and we consider absolute neutrality the first international duty of every citizen and of every newspaper in the United States at the present time."

Absolute neutrality was something Gaunt could not allow to happen. He needed to push American public opinion toward the Allies. At his initial clandestine meeting with Voska in Manhattan, Gaunt offered a working partnership in counterespionage and propaganda against the Central Powers. They would collaborate and pool information uncovered by Voska's spy network with Great Britain's radio intercepts and code-breaking operations.

What the partners lacked, however, was a trusted press outlet to disseminate the German secrets they uncovered.

"Gaunt and I realized that our own best counter-propaganda would lie in the news," Voska later explained. "One provable case of a German agent plotting to blow up a ship or to arm an expedition against Canada, we felt, would outweigh a ton of pamphlets. But if the British gave out the story, it would seem tainted; while we Czech-Americans must keep ourselves invisible."

So they recruited a third member to their cabal, a certain fearless Providence newsman who knew how to sell a story.

"It was a triangle," Voska wrote, "Gaunt at one corner, I at another, and John R. Rathom at the third."

Most of the world-shaking scoops Rathom printed in the two years before the United States entered the war evolved from the triangle: Rathom, Voska, and Gaunt.

Of all the cigar-chomping editors in the world, why John Rathom? This is still mysterious. Rathom had a terrific reputation as a writer, but at that point had helmed the *Providence Journal* as its top editor for only three years. It is clear Gaunt was the one who brought Rathom into the partnership. Voska later wrote that the two Australians had met "during some war Rathom had covered in his roving years." That can't be true. Rathom's early war tales were fiction, though Voska believed them at the time.

Gaunt's story was that one day while strolling through the British embassy he spotted a "big, heavily built man chewing a cigar and impatiently trying to attract a little attention." Gaunt introduced himself and asked what he needed.

"I'm the editor of the *Providence Journal*," the big man told him. "Also, I'm an Australian, and I guess it's about time I did a bit for the old country."

"Melbourne Grammar School," Gaunt said, naming his alma mater.

"Scotch College," Rathom responded, naming a rival school.[*]

"Well, I'll be damned," Gaunt said. "It's a small world."

Gaunt claimed he took Rathom to his office and offered "then and there" to feed him secret information about German espionage operations in the United States. "A briefly told story could be worked up into two columns," Gaunt later recalled, "and I wouldn't be responsible for its complete accuracy, so long as it counter-acted the 'dope' supplied to the press" by German propagandists.

Gaunt's origin story for the triangle does not ring true, either. Gaunt and Voska were fanatical about preventing German spies from infiltrating their operations. Would Gaunt casually invite a stranger into the collaboration five minutes after meeting him? Doubtful.

The simplest explanation is likely the correct one: Gaunt read the bogus "secret rendezvous" story fed to Rathom by Gaston Means, and reached out directly or through intermediaries to dispute the story and offer facts for Rathom's more accurate follow-up.

However the trio came together, over the next two years Gaunt and Voska took Rathom into their total confidence. Gaunt spoke with Rathom or someone from his staff nearly every day. Voska leaned on Rathom for advice and shared with him the working details of his intelligence network. The thrilling spy stories Rathom told later on the lecture circuit—including his greatest hit, the "hearts on the crate" story—were largely appropriated from his private conversations with Voska.

Rathom went to extreme lengths to hide the existence of the triangle. While his stories "generally told the essential truth," Voska said, they "were usually deliberately inaccurate in detail," so German and Austrian diplomats could not reverse engineer the stories to discover their origins.

There is no evidence that Gaunt or Voska ever knew they had trusted their careers, reputations, and potentially their lives to an imposter. Rathom concealed his secrets even from the spies.

---

[*] Rathom in fact never attended Scotch College, not that Gaunt ever knew it.

CHAPTER 7

Transformation

At just thirty-one years old, Leon Thrasher had already seen more of the world than most Americans of his era ever would. As an unmarried, traveling master mechanic, his career took him to jobs around the United States, Alaska, and Europe. He had worked in Ecuador, and for a Panamanian railroad company. In early 1915 he was wrapping up a vacation in England and Scotland, and then sailing to Africa in the employ of a British mining firm.

Thrasher was a slim man, not quite 5'7". He had a high forehead and protruding ears, little round eyeglasses, and a tuft of scruff on his chin. He had not been back to his native Massachusetts since Christmas 1913, when he visited his widowed mother. Thrasher had been born in 1883 in Hardwick, Massachusetts, a farming and mill town in the geographic center of the state, which felt a long way from the cosmopolitan cobblestoned streets of Boston. His father was a farmer who dabbled in the lumber business.

Instead of following after the old man, Leon Thrasher charted his own path. In 1901, when he turned eighteen, he moved to Springfield, Massachusetts, to learn to be a machinist. Upon completing his apprenticeship, Thrasher packed his wrenches and set out to see the world.

While in England in early 1915, Thrasher wrote his mother with some news. After his vacation, he intended to return to his job with Broomassie

Mines, a London firm digging precious metals out of the Gold Coast, a British colonial region in West Africa, and what is now Ghana. Thrasher was to depart Liverpool in late March, sailing as a second-class ticketed passenger aboard the *Falaba*.

His mother would not have known the ship. The *Falaba* was an undistinguished British steamer, run by the Elder Dempster Line. At 380 feet long and 4,800 tons, she was less than half the length and one-sixth the mass of the queen of the seas, the Cunard liner the RMS *Lusitania*. The *Falaba* had a black hull painted red below the waterline, one mast forward and one aft, and a single funnel rising at midship.

The ship left England for Africa on March 27, carrying 95 crewmen and 147 passengers, all but seven of whom were men; they were largely colonial bureaucrats and businessmen.

Nearly half the souls aboard the *Falaba* would perish less than two days out of port. Their fate would forewarn of bigger tragedies to come, and test America's resolve to stay neutral in the First World War.

❖

Reports of German U-boat activity in the Irish Sea arrived by wireless when the *Lusitania* was off the southern Irish coast. For most of its transatlantic run from New York, the great liner eased along at less than full power to save hundreds of tons of coal a day. But now, with one day left in its week-long journey to Liverpool, the first week of February 1915, there was no thought to conserving coal, only burning it for speed. The *Lusitania* roared into the Irish Sea, sailing at about twenty-five knots, which on land would be twenty-nine miles per hour.

Some of the passengers refused to go to bed the last night of the trip. Better to be awake and dressed if they needed to rush to a lifeboat. It was not just the scuttlebutt about German submarines that unnerved them, but something else that seemed almost inconceivable. The ship's crew had reeled in the Union Jack flag flapping from the angled flagstick off the *Lusitania*'s stern, and unfurled the forty-eight-star American colors.

One of the greatest ships in the world had resorted to a ruse. She flew a false flag.

Captain Daniel Dow told his passengers that flying the Stars and Stripes was not intended as a disguise, exactly. You can't disguise one of the most famous liners ever built. The *Lusitania* was the largest ship in the world when she started service in 1907, at 787 feet long and 32,000 tons, like a skyscraper on its side. In fact, stood on her stern, the *Lusitania* would have been just five feet shorter than the world's tallest building in 1915, the fifty-five-story Woolworth Building in Manhattan. On each voyage, she carried enough people to populate a respectably sized town, some two thousand passengers and crew. The *Lusitania*'s hull was black, her stack of decks mostly white. The ship's four giant funnels venting black snakes of coal smoke leaned slightly backward, giving her a look of speed even at rest. Trying to camouflage the *Lusitania* with a flag would be like disguising a famous face like Einstein's with a baseball cap. But no German U-boat commander was likely to fire at a ship flying the American colors without first seeking some sort of explanation.

The trick might only work once, but Captain Dow was sure they would reach Liverpool safely. And they did, arriving on February 6.

The ruse became international news "that aroused astonishment on both sides of the ocean." Americans were uncomfortable with the misuse of their flag. Some Brits were humiliated. "The fact that our fastest liner had to change her flag has shocked our pride as much as the loss of the ship would have done," the *Manchester Guardian* reported. Follow-up stories revealed that the Cunard liner *Orduna* had flown American colors across the Irish Sea on January 31.

Germany responded to false flag tactics with an ominous escalation. German officials announced that beginning on February 18, German U-boats would treat the waters around Great Britain as a war zone, and would enforce a submarine blockade. In an effort to deny Britain supplies for fighting and for living, all enemy merchant vessels encountered in the zone would be sunk, "even if it may not always be possible to save their crews and passengers."

Neutral ships in the war zone were also in peril. "As in consequence of the misuse of neutral flags," Germany stated, "and in view of the hazards of naval warfare, it cannot always be avoided that attacks meant for enemy ships endanger neutral ships."

In other words, every ship entered the war zone at its own risk.

By issuing the statement, Germany was announcing that its U-boats would no longer be bound by the gentlemanly old rules of naval engagement, known as the "cruiser rules."

Cruiser rules were bits of international law, custom, and treaties that had evolved over centuries. The rules stated, generally, that when a warship came across an unarmed enemy merchant ship, the warship had the right to demand the merchant stop to be searched for war-related cargo, or "contraband." The warship could sink a merchant carrying contraband, after permitting the crew and passengers to abandon ship. That meant letting them get into their lifeboats if reasonably close to shore or rescue. In remote waters, the captain of the warship was obligated to take the enemy crew onto his ship until they could be dropped someplace safe.

By World War I, though, technology threatened the old ways. Many merchant ships carried wireless transmitters and could summon help if stopped by a warship. At the same time, fragile submarines, so lethal underwater, were uniquely vulnerable when surfaced.

"It was quite unrealistic to expect a submarine to stay for a prolonged period on the surface in hostile waters while a party went across to a merchant ship to search the cargo and then facilitate the evacuation of the crew," wrote the British history writer Alastair Walker. "It was also unrealistic to expect the merchant ship to sit quietly and not to use its wireless while this was going on."

As Germany's February 18 deadline arrived, Americans saw the U-boat blockade as a threat to life, world trade, the US economy, and maybe to peace. "No more momentous move in the great game of war has been taken since the conflict began than that inaugurated by Germany today to starve out Great Britain by a submarine blockade," the *Brooklyn Times-Union* recounted. "And the whole world awaits the outcome with anxiety."

❖

Officers on the *Falaba* identified the slender tower of a surfaced submarine when it was a few miles away, and closing. It was 11:40 A.M., March 28, the second day of the ship's journey to Africa. The *Falaba* was sailing in St. George's Channel between Ireland and Wales, within Germany's designated war zone around Great Britain. Captain Frederick Davies ordered his ship to flee at its top speed, about fourteen knots (a pokey sixteen miles per hour on land).

The German submarine *U-28* gave chase, making eighteen knots. When it was close enough, the *U-28* raised a signal flag ordering the *Falaba* to stop or be fired on. The submarine's commander had decided to give those aboard a chance to escape under the old cruiser rules.

Captain Davies relented and ordered all-stop. But he also directed his wireless operator to send distress calls for any British warships in the neighborhood. Most of the *Falaba*'s passengers were at lunch in the dining room when the encounter began. Leon Thrasher, probably among them, would have felt the ship slowing and heard the officers on deck running around and barking orders.

The *U-28* pulled close enough for its captain to shout by megaphone in English that the *Falaba* must be abandoned because she was to be sunk. Witnesses later disagreed on whether the commander warned that the ship would be torpedoed in five minutes, or ten, or whether he even gave a deadline. Whatever he said, the evacuation of the *Falaba* was a disaster. Passengers had no idea which lifeboats to report to. People ran around the deck, some weeping and shouting. Tangled ropes on lifeboats lowered in haste caused multiple boats to fall into the ocean or spill their passengers into the sea. Other boats swamped the instant they hit the choppy water. Survivors scrambled onto the keel of one overturned boat.

Just as the last boat was being lowered, a torpedo exploded into the side of the ship, jolting the lifeboat into the water. The *Falaba* sank in eight minutes.

Leon Thrasher was among many who ended up in the sea. Survivors later claimed that German sailors lined the submarine's deck to point and laugh at people fighting for their lives in the water. That was probably not what happened. More likely, the sailors were trying to signal to the few functioning lifeboats the locations of people struggling to stay afloat in the waves. Still, the devastating narrative stuck that the Germans had jeered at the victims.

One hundred four people died in *Falaba* debacle, including the master mechanic from Massachusetts, Leon Thrasher, who drowned.

The German U-boat war had taken its first American life.

❖

US press reaction to the *Falaba* sinking was savage, especially in New York. "The most shocking crime of the war," the *Times* pronounced; "A reversion to barbarism," the *Herald* declared; "Wickedness such as the history of war will find it difficult to match," the *Evening Post* affirmed. The *Tribune* called for the submariners to be "caught and hanged."

In Providence, Rathom wrote that the sinking illustrated "the inhuman character" of Germany's submarine blockade, which was sure to bring more tragedy. "The fact remains," he argued, "that the German submarine programme cannot be effectively carried out except at a wanton sacrifice of life."

President Woodrow Wilson believed Germany had violated international law in the *Falaba* incident, and that the United States ought to do *something*. But what? Any action might be the first step onto the slippery slope toward war. Wilson confided in Secretary of State William Jennings Bryan, "I do not like this case . . . it is filled with disturbing possibilities."

Would the United States risk a war over the death of one citizen?

Bryan, then fifty-five, was a big-boned, balding, political warhorse, a deeply faithful Christian, and probably the best orator of his generation, known for his commanding baritone. Three times he had been the Democratic Party nominee for president—in 1896, 1900, and 1908—losing twice to William McKinley and once to William Howard Taft. As secretary of state, Bryan favored staying out of the war at any cost. It was Bryan's sincere belief "that war was always avoidable and, therefore, unjustifiable," according to his underling, Robert Lansing, who would follow Bryan as secretary of state.

In the *Falaba* case, Bryan agreed with Dernburg, the German propaganda chief, who argued in the US press that Thrasher's regrettable death was as much his own fault as anyone else's. Someone who chooses to sail at personal risk into a war zone forfeits the moral gravity to pull the whole nation into a war.

In failing to forcefully confront Germany after the first American death of the U-boat blockade, the Wilson administration set the table for more. The British admiralty also took the wrong lesson from the *Falaba*, a slow, plodding ship. Fast steamers that could outrun a U-boat were perfectly safe, they believed. The admiralty insisted to the international press, "There was no ground for the belief that any of the big liners plying between New York and Liverpool would be sent to the bottom by a submarine."

❖

Over the next several weeks, war news dominated America's front pages. On April 22, German troops released liquid chlorine in the Second Battle of Ypres, in Belgium, in the first large-scale use of poison gas in the war.

Passengers continued to sail through Germany's submarine blockade. The *Lusitania* made another round trip to America. On April 17, she departed again for New York, completing her 201st Atlantic crossing. Transocean travel was never risk-free, a fact underlined by the *Titanic* disaster just three years earlier. But public concern over being torpedoed began to wear off. Part of the reason was the presumption that this new war would be fought under the genteel old rules, despite Germany's warnings and the horrific inaugural use of chemical weapons. But part also related to the psyche of the times.

The people of the age possessed "overweening confidence in the power of man-made objects to overcome obstacles like time and distance," according to Erik Larson, who wrote about the *Lusitania*'s final voyage in his book *Dead Wake*. How could they *not* feel confident? A middle-aged adult in 1915 had already witnessed breathtaking, machine-driven change in just half a lifetime. People who drove horse buggies in their youth now steered luxurious automobiles. Human flight had gone from fantasy to public fascination with airplanes and the daredevils who flew them. Nineteenth-century harbors were a jungle of ship masts and wooden vessels. By 1915 ocean travelers discussed wine pairings with the sommelier aboard floating hotels that plowed across the sea at nearly thirty miles per hour.

So when the *Lusitania* prepared to leave New York for its return to Liverpool on May 1, the ship was full. She carried 1,960 passengers and crew. Among her cargo were 4,200 cases of Remington .303 rifle ammunition and 50 tons of shrapnel shells. The ship itself was unarmed. As a Cunard official put it later with bitter hindsight, the *Lusitania* was as vulnerable to a submarine as "a Hoboken ferryboat" was to a battleship.

German embassy officials never became complacent to travel dangers in the war zone. On the morning the *Lusitania* was to depart New York, newspapers throughout the region carried an unusual warning:

NOTICE!

TRAVELLERS intending to embark on the Atlantic voyage are reminded that a state of war exists between Germany and her allies and Great Britain and her allies; that the zone of war includes the waters adjacent to the British Isles; that, in accordance with formal notice given by the Imperial German Government, vessels flying the flag of Great Britain, or any of her allies, are liable to destruction in those waters and that travelers sailing in the war zone on the ships of Great Britain or her allies do so at their own risk.

IMPERIAL GERMAN EMBASSY.

Newspapers reported at the time that the warning seemed to have no effect whatsoever. Six large liners departed New York that day, carrying in total the largest number of transatlantic passengers to leave the city in a single day all spring. The general agent of the Cunard line insisted the *Lusitania* was just too fast for submarines and her voyage "was attended by no risk."

The fact that Americans still chose to travel on a British ship was confounding to a propagandist named George Sylvester Viereck.

Viereck was an American poet and journalist. He edited the pro-German weekly magazine the *Fatherland*, published in New York. Viereck was thirty years old, clean-shaven, with full lips. His hair was carelessly swept back, and he wore little round eyeglasses. He had been born in Munich with "distinguished, if clouded, ancestry." His father, Louis, was rumored to have been the love child of Kaiser Wilhelm I, the grandfather of the current kaiser, and a German actress. George Sylvester Viereck moved with family to the United States when he was twelve.

Viereck was a writing prodigy. He published his first volume of poetry in 1904, at age nineteen. A follow-up volume in 1907 earned him a national following. Even today, his skills as a writer and interviewer stand out. His 1929 profile of Albert Einstein for the *Saturday Evening Post* is mesmerizing. The physicist gave Viereck a famous quote, still found on inspirational posters: "Imagination is more important than knowledge." The full quote continues, "Knowledge is limited. Imagination encircles the world."

As a young writer, Viereck engaged in German "social and political movements" and "gradually turned into a Germanophile" who considered it his duty to explain Germany to America, according to the author and historian Niel M. Johnson.

At the outbreak of the First World War, Viereck founded the *Fatherland* to present the German side of every issue related to the war.[*] It was a highbrow publication with a nasty side, not above doxing American businessmen profiting from the war by publishing their names and addresses. Viereck also volunteered for Dernburg's German "propaganda cabinet,"

---

[*] The *Fatherland* employed as a writer the British occultist, poet, and all-around weirdo Aleister Crowley, who would come to be known as "the wickedest man in the world." He is the subject of the 1980 Ozzy Osbourne metal ballad "Mr. Crowley."

and quietly accepted stipends from the German government to keep his magazine afloat.

While the *Lusitania* was at sea, Viereck prepared an editorial for the *Fatherland*, in which he defended an attack on another ship carrying war supplies to the Allies, and warned: "Before long, a large passenger ship like the *Lusitania*, carrying implements of murder to Great Britain, will meet a similar fate."

❖

In late April, just as the *Lusitania* was setting sail, Rathom's exposé of the fake-affidavit scheme in New York Harbor caught the notice of a very important reader: President Woodrow Wilson. The president wanted to meet this aggressive newsman from Providence. Wilson hosted Rathom at the White House on Wednesday, May 5, 1915. Their private conference was logged on Wilson's calendar.

In this meeting, Rathom laid out an incredible story. Three days ago, Rathom told the president, on May 2, while in New York, Rathom took a call at his hotel. It was from the steward of the German Club, 112 Central Park South, with an invitation. Would Rathom come to the club to speak with German naval attaché Boy-Ed? Rathom agreed, and the Germans sent a car for him.

At the club, Rathom met Boy-Ed for the first time. Boy-Ed said he was aware Rathom had an appointment with the president, and asked Rathom to facilitate some backdoor diplomacy. "We want you, when you see the president, to lay before him the suggestion that he reconsider his attitude regarding the embargo on arms," Boy-Ed said, according to Rathom's later reconstruction of their conversation.

The German offer was this: If the Wilson administration were to lean on US arms makers not to sell to the waring powers in Europe, the German Empire would signal its openness to peace negotiations, presumably brokered by Wilson. German diplomats were back-channeling this offer through Rathom, Boy-Ed explained, because Germany did not want to appear to be making the first move. He also asked Rathom to conceal his involvement—again, this is all according to Rathom.

Back in Providence two days after relaying this story to Wilson—on Friday, May 7— Rathom wrote the president for a favor.

"My dear Mr. President," Rathom's letter began,

> The *Providence Journal* and the *New York Times* are going to publish, simultaneously, the story that I outlined to you on Wednesday . . .
>
> We propose to go ahead and make public the entire incident—the statement of Boy-Ed and his request that the matter be presented to you as coming from the ambassador, etc.
>
> When I left you I, myself, suggested that we make no reference to the matter having been presented to you. It appears to me now, however, that the story will lose some of its value to us unless we can say that: "the entire matter has been laid before President Wilson," or "the statement of Captain Boy-Ed has been forwarded to President Wilson," or something of that kind.
>
> Of course I will follow your wishes exactly in the matter.

Not even in the imposter's grandest fictional biography did he partake in clandestine international diplomacy with the president of the United States during a world war. How much of Rathom's version is true? At least some. Rathom's letter is in Wilson's papers; it undoubtedly reflects the conversation the two men had just days earlier. Later, in 1918, at the height of his fame, Rathom published a long description of his May 1915 encounter with Boy-Ed. This account is larded with self-aggrandizing flourishes and what are probably made-up details, but it comports with the letter: Boy-Ed made an offer to be presented to the president.*

---

* Rathom's 1918 account also claims Boy-Ed tried to hire Rathom to overhaul Germany's public relations operation in the United States. I'd file this as dubious, but not impossible.

The article about Boy-Ed's offer apparently was scrapped. It was overtaken by world-changing news.

The very day Rathom wrote to President Wilson, perhaps the very hour, on May 7, a torpedo fired without warning by the German submarine *U-20* slammed broadside into the *Lusitania*, off the southern coast of Ireland. A massive secondary blast followed, possibly from her boilers exploding or coal dust igniting. The great liner listed hard to starboard and plunged beneath the sea in eighteen minutes.

Of the 1,959 men, women, and children aboard the *Lusitania*, 1,195 died, including 123 Americans.

❖

There was no precedent for such a sudden slaughter of so many civilians at sea. America shuddered with the palpable threat of war—"The word that no one speaks, that lies first on the tongue of all Americans," the *New York Tribune* raged.

Rathom's response was in character with most of the East Coast press. "Scores of Americans were murdered yesterday on the high seas by order of the German government," his editorial began. He printed a front-page cartoon, depicting a steely President Wilson staring out from behind his desk, with the American people, embodied by Uncle Sam, clasping one steadying hand on Wilson's shoulder and clenching the other into a fist. The caption declared: THE LAST STRAW. Rathom wrote of German "savagery," and of "the mangled bodies of hundreds of innocent non-combatants [that] lie at the bottom of the Atlantic." He foresaw a "cry for retribution" across America and the determination "which will sweep the country like a flame, that this act of frightfulness shall not go unpunished."

Rathom was never the same after the sinking of the *Lusitania*. The killing of civilians—women and babies among them—seemed to instantly transform him. It is tempting to say the massacre broke something inside him, but it may be more accurate to say something had been mended. The grifter with a penchant for exposés in the name of the greater good found his reason to be. For the next two years, Rathom committed himself to digging up the stories to turn every last American against the German Empire.

For the first time since the imposter had invented John R. Rathom, he devoted the character wholly to something bigger than himself.

Yet Wilson was determined to keep the United States out of the war. He responded to the *Lusitania* crisis with a series of diplomatic notes to Germany over the next several months. Secretary of State Bryan was so worried the strident notes would provoke a war that he resigned in June 1915. Wilson promoted Robert Lansing into Bryan's place. The diplomatic crisis was ongoing when, on August 19, three Americans died in a German U-boat attack on the liner *Arabic*, south of Ireland. America's demands that Germany change its submarine policy "now became ultimatums."

In September Germany blinked. The German ambassador, Count von Bernstorff, told Lansing that "liners will not be sunk by our submarines without warning and without safety of the lives of non-combatants," so long as the ships do not run or resist. The old cruiser rules were back. It was an uneasy peace that would be tested by additional incidents at sea, but it held into 1917, when Germany chose to unshackle the U-boat.

❖

The remains of *Lusitania* victims washed up on the coast of Ireland that summer. A corpse that came ashore on July 11 was presumed to be from the ship and assigned body number 248. But this victim was from another vessel, the *Falaba*. The body was that of Leon Thrasher, adrift at sea for more than one hundred days.

❖

It is unclear if Wilson could have taken the United States to war against Germany immediately after the sinking of the *Lusitania*, even if he had wanted to. The country may not have been with him.

New York and the rest of the East Coast were hot for reprisals against Germany. "As one went westward, however, the demands for drastic action grew less emphatic," Secretary of State Lansing later wrote. Many Americans questioned why their fellow citizens were sailing on British ships. Many thought the European conflict was not America's business and did not see the point of risking their sons for it. Those of German and Austrian backgrounds opposed war with their homelands, while a good many Irish Americans saw Great Britain as an oppressor. British sea policies had infuriated US business owners—more Americans were affected by trade restrictions than by killer submarines. And the United States in 1915, like now, was home to pacifists who opposed war on principle.

A democracy cannot be browbeaten into an all-out war; it has to demand it. Lansing, then fifty, a distinguished-looking, silver-headed diplomat, was hawkish on the German question. Yet even he accepted in the spring of 1915 that "the time was not ripe to take definitive action." The smart move was to delay, to wait for public opinion to catch up, "by a gradual process of education and enlightenment," until the American people came to see Germany as their mortal enemy.

America could be taught to want a war.

"It was a long, slow process, the process of enlightenment," Lansing wrote. "It covered a period of almost two years."

No individual did more in those two years, 1915–1917, to reeducate America than John R. Rathom. He saw America's resistance to war as much an enemy to be defeated as the Central Powers. Rathom burned out his health, sleeping six hours a night and devoting every other minute to convincing America that Germany was already at war with United States, and it was time to start fighting back. The imposter had found a purpose worthy of his heroic, made-up identity. In defending his adopted home from a foreign threat, he saw the opportunity to become the very thing he was pretending to be.

CHAPTER 8

Romancing the Dictator

On the afternoon of April 12, 1915, the liner *Antonio Lopez* chugged up the East River to its pier, after a thirteen-day transatlantic crossing from Spain. Waiting journalists charged onto the ship. They were after an interview with a famous passenger. They found him on the promenade deck gazing up at the skyscrapers of New York: Victoriano Huerta, the deposed Mexican president and former dictator, who one year earlier had fled Mexico just ahead of a firing squad.

It was widely presumed that Huerta was a murderer who had ordered the killing of his predecessor. Despite this, or perhaps because of it, the former strongman radiated grim intensity and the press could not get enough of him. He was about 5'6" and in his sixties. His eyes were small black beads, and his balding scalp was golden brown beneath a fine gray fuzz. The skin of his face appeared stretched against his sharp cheekbones, and the lines around his mouth were deeply etched, giving him "the iron-mask expression for which he was always noted."

Huerta arrived in New York dressed in a dark blue worsted suit, a white shirt with a starched collar, and a thin necktie tied in an asymmetrical four-in-hand knot. An inch below the knot, a diamond pin twinkled in the light.

Huerta bowed deeply to the horde of approaching reporters. He stood as if he had all the time in the world and let the photographers take his image.

There was one thing every reporter wanted to know: Did Huerta intend to return to Mexico to reclaim power?

"My ticket reads New York," Huerta said.

❖

The United States would have seemed like the last place Victoriano Huerta would ever visit, given recent history.

At the time of Huerta's arrival in New York, his native Mexico was halfway through a wretched decade of violence, plotting, and civil war, known as the Mexican Revolution. Regional armed factions clashed for power. The crisis had no bigger character than Huerta. He served as an army general under President Francisco Madero, until he betrayed Madero in 1913, taking power in a military coup. Madero and his vice president were shot, supposedly while trying to escape. Huerta ruled in a military dictatorship. He was a boozer, a bad administrator, and generally unpopular. The chief accomplishment of his seventeen-month reign may have been the unity he inspired—revolutionary factions united against his government in a civil war.

President Woodrow Wilson refused to recognize Huerta as a legitimate head of state. In a speech to Congress in December 1913, Wilson called Huerta a "cloud upon our horizon" and said America could not rest easily until "General Huerta has surrendered his usurped authority." Wilson stationed US warships off Mexican seaports, ostensibly to protect US property owners but also to project power.

In the spring of 1914, three months before the murder of Archduke Franz Ferdinand, a trivial incident between Huerta's government and the United States was mutually bungled and chest-thumped into a deadly military conflict. It started on the cloudy, cool day of April 9, when Huerta's forces detained at gunpoint a group of US sailors who had piloted a small whaleboat up the Pánuco River into the Mexican coastal town of Tampico, three hundred miles south of Brownsville, Texas. The sailors had come from US warships to buy gasoline from a local who had some for sale.

The sailors had done nothing wrong and were released within an hour or so. The local military governor apologized; opposition forces were in the area and his men were jumpy. The incident would have ended there, were it not for Admiral Henry T. Mayo, commander of the US Navy Atlantic Fleet's Fourth Division, stationed off Tampico in the Gulf of Mexico. Mayo was a career sailor and a hard man, with a face that looked like it was assembled from chunks of broken rock. He was outraged by the disrespect shown to personnel of the US Navy. He demanded, as a penance, that Mexican forces raise the US colors at some prominent place on shore and honor the American flag with a twenty-one-gun salute. As silly as the demand seems now, Mayo was serious. Mexican authorities kicked the demand upstairs, all the way to Huerta, who considered the terms humiliating. He offered compromises, such as saluting both nation's flags, but not the American flag alone. National pride would not allow it. "Mexico has yielded as much as her dignity will permit," the country's foreign minister said.

President Wilson backed Mayo. The president was hamstrung by what he saw as his obligation to defend national honor. Wilson set a deadline of 6:00 p.m. on April 19 for Huerta to salute the American flag or face military action. The day after the deadline, Wilson went to Congress for permission to use US armed forces to "obtain from General Huerta and his adherents the fullest recognition of the rights and dignity of the United States." It would not be a fair fight. The United States was not yet a world superpower, but Mexico was exhausted by years of internal turmoil and was no match.

US Marines came ashore into the Mexican city of Veracruz on April 21. They fought the city's defenders in the streets, captured and occupied the community of some forty thousand residents, and raised the US colors. American military losses were about 17 dead and 65 wounded. Mexico suffered at least 126 dead and 195 wounded, though accurate counts were hard to get and the true totals probably higher. The US occupation of Veracruz lasted seven months. It triggered anti-American sentiments throughout Mexico. The incursion may have hastened the fall of Huerta, who gave up power and fled to Spain that July, ahead of advancing revolutionary forces.

Karl Boy-Ed, the German naval attaché, traveled personally to Veracruz to see the US occupation. Germany took some vital lessons from the conflict. One was how easily the United States had been provoked to attack its southern neighbor. Another was how much President Wilson despised Huerta.

A year later, with Europe at war, German diplomats figured that another conflict between the United States and Mexico could benefit the Central Powers. The United States would not export munitions to Germany's enemies if it needed them at home to fight its own battles. To embroil the United States and Mexico in another conflict would require some kind of trigger. And nobody triggered Wilson like the former Mexican dictator who had just landed in New York. A plot was at hand to return Huerta to power. But Rathom's allies sniffed it out . . .

❖

By the time Huerta arrived in New York in the spring of 1915, Emanuel Voska's organization and British intelligence, through Guy Gaunt, were suppling Rathom with regular material for newspaper articles.

After the sinking of the *Lusitania*, Rathom did not bother with any pretext of impartiality. His work was anti-German. Period. He was interested only in those facts pointing toward German culpability in propaganda and sabotage plots. He did not report aggressively on the actions of British agents to influence American public opinion—he was part of them. Rathom abandoned straight journalism for advocacy. In his defense, though, the point of newswriting in his time was not *fairness* as we think of it today but *truth*. Rathom would have not understood much of today's "balanced" newswriting, the mindless presentation of all sides of an argument as equally valid.

Rathom's bias was openly threaded through everything he wrote. His readers priced his anti-German sentiments into their evaluation of his stories. In June 1915 Rathom wrote an explosive story alleging that German interests were trying to buy control of several prominent US weapons makers, including Union Metallic Cartridge Company, Remington Arms, and Bethlehem Steel. And if the Germans took over, the plants would no longer sell to the Allies.

The *Wall Street Journal* responded with a front-page story about Rathom's article, which assured nervous investors there was no chance the industrial giant Bethlehem Steel could pass into German hands.

Rathom was not above inventing details or intentionally garbling the narrative to hide his sources. But he knew credibility for his revelations depended upon some core of truth. In fact, it was true that German interests wanted to buy US weapons plants early in the First World War, to control the supply of munitions to Europe.

"In August 1914, it might perhaps have been possible to buy up the Bethlehem Steel Works, if the outlay of the necessary capital had been promptly decided on," German ambassador Count von Bernstorff wrote after the war. German agents had worked out proposals "to amalgamate the whole shrapnel industry in the United States." Officials in Berlin were unconvinced that buying stakes in the US arms industry would be worth it, and passed on the plan.

The pro-German press in the United States were among the first to recognize Rathom's rising star. George Sylvester Viereck's propaganda sheet the *Fatherland* began taking shots at Rathom months before the Providence editor became a household name. At first, Viereck needled Rathom as a rube who had fallen under the spell of the British ambassador and become England's "mouthpiece" in America.

As the year wore on and Rathom's stories grew more damaging, Viereck's attacks became proportionally more vicious. He blasted Rathom as an "intolerable nuisance." He blamed the *Providence Journal* for the ouster of Boy-Ed and Papen from America, writing that the "trail is still slimy with the repellant lies of this discredited sheet." In November 1915 Viereck called Rathom's reporting "melodramatic fiction, oozing as venom out of the fang of a serpent, from the versatile brain of its editor."

❖

Within the bustle of activity on the pier when Huerta arrived in New York, a messenger boy handed a small package to one of Huerta's associates. It was addressed "The Hon. President Victoriano Huerta, Personal." Huerta had the package under his arm when he bent into a taxicab for the ride to the Hotel Ansonia, a Beaux-Arts palace on the Upper West Side.

Later, in his suite, the old dictator noticed that the package, the size of "a two-pound candy box," looked "remarkably like a bomb."

Huerta had every reason to be suspicious. He had enemies. Ever since news had broken that he was on his way to the United States from Spain, speculation swirled that he intended to return to Mexico to lead a counterrevolution. Huerta gave perfunctory denials, claiming he had come for personal business and to see the beautiful US of A. The *New York Tribune* announced his arrival with the headline GEN. HUERTA HERE, VOWS HE'LL BE GOOD.

The situation in Mexico had remained terrible after Huerta left power. Armed factions that had worked against Huerta were fighting each other. A Huerta foe, Venustiano Carranza, was running the country. It was easy to imagine a Carranza supporter sending Huerta a Welcome to America bomb. Huerta turned the package over to authorities. An explosives expert held his breath and opened it inside the West Sixty-Eighth Street police station. Inside was the rambling manifesto of some mentally deranged person. It seemed everybody was interested in Victoriano Huerta.

The old warrior hosted twenty reporters at his Manhattan hotel a few days after he arrived, dodging their dogged attempts to divine his intentions. Huerta swore that he had nothing to do with his predecessor's death from high-impact lead poisoning. He pounded his breast for emphasis. "If I have done wrong I shall not shirk responsibility for it."

"But are you going to invade Mexico?" a reporter demanded.

One of Huerta's aides jumped in, "That's all trash."

Was it, though?

Huerta bemoaned that the situation in Mexico was almost too sad to comprehend. "Anarchy is too soft a word," he said. He suggested Mexico was desperate for a savior—someone who loved the country, grew up there, and understood its people.

"Mexico will be saved by a Mexican," Huerta said. "By a strong Mexican. Where is the man? Who is the man? When will the man appear? I do not know."

If those hints were not strong enough, Huerta spent the next several weeks meeting with former Mexican army officers and military governors, many of whom were in exile and itching to return to Mexico as the vanguard of a new revolution. Troops, they could raise. They needed guns and money. Enter the Germans.

❖

The first German spy to contact Huerta in New York appears to have been Franz Rintelen, a brash, borderline reckless navy intelligence officer, who had been dispatched to the United States to shut off the spigot of munitions to Great Britain. In his own words, Rintelen "cared nothing for America's so-called neutrality," and considered the United States the "unseen enemy" of Germany for supplying the Allies with shells.

Traveling on a forged Swiss passport, Rintelen, age thirty-six, departed in late March 1915, from Oslo, Norway, and arrived in New York on April 3, nine days before Huerta. Rintelen was clean-shaven, tall, and athletic, with "a wiry strength and easy carriage." Photos tended to capture him with a menacing look, like he was about to bark out some curse in German, though in reality he was charming and spoke perfect English. His lips were thin and "the muscles of his jaw were forever playing under the skin," the sign of tense teeth-grinding.

Rintelen was born in 1878, into a big family in Frankfurt on the Oder, a town on the Oder River on the eastern side of Germany, not the better-known city of Frankfurt. He was the son of a banker, though most other details his upbringing are a mystery. Just after the turn of the century, Rintelen went to work at a London bank. Around 1905 he apparently started a two-year stint in New York at the financial firm Ladenburg Thalmann, where he learned about America and made valuable contacts.

Early in the First World War, he was attached to the German admiralty, dealing with money transfers. How he ended up a spy in the United States is murky—after the war it seemed no one in Berlin wanted the blame for turning Rintelen loose on America. The available records show the German Ministry of War was behind his mission, according to the German historian Reinhard Doerries.

Though Rintelen was supposed to be working with Papen, they took a near-instant hate to each other. Papen later wrote that Rintelen burst into his office soon after arriving in New York and laid out grandiose plans for blowing up munition plants and orchestrating labor strikes. Papen claimed Rintelen even asked him to set up an audience with President Woodrow Wilson, so Rintelen could talk some sense into the president.

"I soon realized he was a man of limited intelligence," Papen later wrote.

Rintelen, in turn, believed Papen was a negligent boob, whose covert operations in America were run like a "lunatic asylum." Later, while serving a prison sentence in Atlanta, Rintelen passed the time fantasizing about what he would do to Papen if he got his hands on him.

Rintelen's spycraft portfolio dipped into three areas. The first was sabotage. Working with a German chemist in New Jersey, Rintelen oversaw a chemical firebomb operation. The incendiaries, known as cigar bombs or pencil bombs, were clever little devices. They were short lengths of lead pipe bisected in the middle with a thin copper or aluminum disc, to create two chambers. Sulfuric acid was drizzled into one chamber, picric acid into the other, and both ends sealed with lead or wax. When the acids dissolved the disc, they came into contact and reacted with white hot flames, igniting anything combustible nearby. The thickness of the membrane was a timer—a thicker disc could take days or weeks for the chemicals to dissolve.

German sailors manufactured the bombs on an interned German liner in New York Harbor, the *Friedrich der Grosse*. Agents bribed dockworkers to hide the bombs into the cargo holds of merchant ships carrying supplies to the Allies. Unexplained fires at sea crippled the ships or forced sailors to dump any explosive cargo. At least thirty-five ships were firebombed in 1915 and 1916.

In Rintelen's second area of espionage, he funneled money from the German Treasury to finance an antiwar political and trade group, beginning around June 1915. It started simply enough. Rintelen, using a front man, rented a hall at the St. James Hotel, a four-story white brick cube on Pennsylvania Avenue in Washington, DC, and invited antiwar activists to speak. The speakers included Congressman Frank Buchanan, a Democrat from Illinois. The next day, according to Rintelen's account, he met with German American and Irish labor leaders and hatched the idea to organize war opponents into a new trade union, called Labor's National Peace Council.

Backed secretly by German money, the group united earnest pacifists in support of a weapons boycott of the European war and strikes at American munitions plants. Congressman Buchanan was elected its president. The council attracted nationwide press for its demands that Congress nationalize the US arms industry and cut off supply to the belligerent nations. Rintelen had modest success stirring up labor unrest at docks and munition factories.

The Peace Council was low-tech Astroturf—Americans were manipulated by a foreign power pretending to be something it was not. A century later, in 2016, Russian hackers did the same thing to the United States, from the blandly named Internet Research Agency, in St. Petersburg. The hackers created hundreds of fake online profiles—digital versions of Rintelen's Peace Council—impersonating political and voter groups to organize

Americans in support of Donald Trump's presidential campaign and to sow chaos.[*]

Rintelen's final area of espionage concerned returning Huerta to power in Mexico, to rattle the United States into another military action. "If Mexico attacked her, [the United States] would need all the munitions she could manufacture, and would be unable to export any to Europe," Rintelen wrote in his 1933 memoir, *The Dark Invader*.

Was Huerta likely to invade the United States from Mexico? No. But the Germans realized that injecting Huerta back into the ongoing Mexican chaos would further destabilize the region, demanding intense focus from the United States. The United States may respond by stockpiling munitions that otherwise would be sold to Britain. President Woodrow Wilson had proven he would use any flimsy excuse to intervene militarily in Mexico. Another Veracruz could tie up US supplies and attention for months.

Some sources suggest Rintelen first met Huerta in Spain in February 1915, and persuaded the old dictator to sail to America to begin his march back to power. There does not seem to be any evidence of this meeting. Rintelen's account says he met Huerta for the first time in New York that spring, and Rintelen was not shy about boasting about his spycraft.

Germany offered to support a new, Huerta-led Mexican revolution. Many details needed to be worked out. An agent attached to the German embassy traveled to New York to choose a quiet space for a conference between Huerta and Germany's representatives. That man was a plant, working for Emanuel Voska's organization.

The meeting was set for the Hotel Manhattan, a vaguely French-looking tower at Madison Avenue and Forty-Second Street. The day before Huerta arrived, an electrician showed up with a doctor's bag stuffed with

---

[*] For instance, in May 2016 the Russian-made Facebook page Heart of Texas, posing as a conservative Texas political organization, called for an armed protest at an Islamic center in Houston. Another Russian-created group, United Muslims of America, called for a counterprotest at the same time and place. Americans on both sides showed up. Police managed to keep the peace, but the day easily could have ended in violence. As the *New York Times* put it, foreign agents had acted as "puppet masters for unsuspecting Americans."

cables and equipment. Hotel staff co-opted by Voska sneaked the man into Huerta's suite and stood guard while he wired a microphone into the folds of the drapes and ran the wire into the adjoining room, where Allied agents would be listening.

Franz Rintelen largely represented Germany in the meeting with Huerta and his aides, though Boy-Ed "dropped into the party now and then," Voska later wrote.

Germany's opening offer was weapons for Huerta's revolution. The old dictator countered with demands for heavy financial support and personal guarantees that Germany would bail him out of trouble if things went sideways. Negotiations dragged for several weeks at other locations in the city. The outlines of an alliance came into focus. Some $900,000 was deposited in accounts accessible by Huerta, with promises of more cash once Huerta's revolution was launched and proved its viability. Talks wrapped up by the end of May, and military planning began. Weapons would be "accumulated along the border and envoys would be sent to incite desertions" among the other armed factions.

Huerta prepared to ride back into Mexico at the head of a revolution.

Meanwhile, John Rathom conferred with Voska, with whom he was always in steady contact, on Germany's Huerta plot, and got to work on a blockbuster news story almost too outrageous to believe.

CHAPTER 9

The Creation of John Revelstoke Rathom, Part 2: Love, Sex, and Poison

The young woman, still new to San Francisco, descended onto Market Street with a dangerous shopping list.

She was slim and very pretty, with a long neck, wide cheekbones, and a sharp chin. She likely would have been dressed in a frilled blouse with a high neckline, a meticulously tailored coat, and a long flowing skirt that just cleared the ground, like most of the women shopping along the busiest commercial street in the city. Her hair would have been pinned up and tucked under a brimmed hat trimmed with flowers or bows.

She came from a distinguished family, was educated at pricy schools, and carried herself with an easy grace, though on the inside she was heartsick, anxious, and desperate.

It was 1899. At this time John Rathom was still an ace reporter at the *San Francisco Chronicle*. San Francisco was thriving, still seven years from the great earthquake. Market Street slashed across the city through a wide canyon of distinguished granite and marble buildings, packed with stores and restaurants on the street level and offices above. At the far end of the canyon the tall outline of the clock tower on the Union Ferry Depot marked the edge of San Francisco Bay. It could seem everyone in the city had crowded into Market Street at the same time, in a loud, smoky, barely controlled chaos. Men in dark suits and bowler hats jumped out of the way of streetcars. Horse buggies, motorcars, and delivery trucks weaved around each other like they were making braids. People pedaled in every direction on bicycles, swerving around those on foot.

At a Japanese shop on Market Street, the woman bought a small, oblong wicker basket; a dainty craft item, suitable for giving as a part of a gift.

She also stopped at the Emporium, at Fifth Street and Market, maybe the most magnificent department store on the West Coast. It had opened three years earlier, in a massive seven-story building with a façade full of columns and arches. Inside were a tiered restaurant under a glass dome and fifteen acres of retail space.

At the Emporium, the woman bought a bag of candy-glazed cherries.

Two blocks away, at the fifteen-story Baroque tower that was home to the *Call* newspaper, she left the Market Street bustle behind, turned onto Third Street, and went into Blake's Drug Store for the poison.

Arsenic, please, she told the clerk—half an ounce. For killing vermin, she explained, and then asked if the powder would mix up well with turpentine.

That should mix up fine, the clerk said.

The woman gave the clerk a fake name, and an address that did not exist, then paid a dime for the poison. Now she had all the ingredients for a sinister plot that would become the biggest threat yet to Rathom's career.

❖

The genesis of the plot that came together on Market Street dated back two years to late 1897.

Rathom, an ace *Chronicle* reporter, took a week's vacation to Santa Cruz, a beach town about seventy-five miles south of San Francisco on Monterey Bay. Traveling without his wife, Mary, he checked in around November 13 to the finest hotel in the city, the Pacific Ocean House.

The Ocean House was a leisure spot for the upper classes of California society. It packed about a hundred rooms in a thick, redbrick building, with a long veranda above the first floor, like an elevated walkway. Guests reclined along the veranda in armchairs, listening to the thump of women's heels on the wooden sidewalk below. The hotel made up for a lack of water view with a backyard that opened into aromatic gardens of roses and orange trees. Guests dined in the hotel restaurant on fresh trout pulled from local streams and fresh duck blasted out of local lagoons. Men puffed cigars to the clack of ivory in the billiard room and pounded drinks at the hotel's mahogany bar, watching themselves in a wall of mirrors. Framed oil paintings hung on the opposite wall of the barroom, including one of a naked woman painted by A. D. M. Cooper, a California artist with a drinking problem who sometimes settled bar tabs with art. He would be known as the Rembrandt of the saloon nude.

At some point during his stay, Rathom met another Ocean House guest, a young West Virginian named Florence Mildred Campbell. Florence was twenty-four, unmarried, strikingly good-looking, ambitious, a feminist ahead of her time—educated at Hiram College in Ohio. She was politically active, too, having organized West Virginians behind Republican William McKinley in the presidential election of 1896.

Rathom did not know it then, but he was destined to be with Florence for the rest of his life. The love story they would write together would be entangled with lies, betrayal, and a sensational attempted murder plot.

Florence was the daughter of a Civil War veteran from back east, Milton B. Campbell, a Union Army lieutenant in the war. He died when Florence was sixteen. Her uncle, John A. Campbell, a well-wired lawyer, professor, banker, Republican politician, and judge in New Cumberland, West Virginia, took a role in raising her.

Three months before she met Rathom, Florence received an invitation to join a star-studded, fifty-four-member West Virginia delegation that crossed the country by train to witness the commissioning of a new gunboat, the USS *Wheeling*, in San Francisco. The ship had been named for what was then West Virginia's capital city. The mayor of Wheeling was part of the cross-country mission. So were the sheriff, county commissioners, local businessmen, and several journalists—it seemed everyone who could plausibly defend joining the junket was on the train. Six sitting congressmen headlined the delegation, including an ex-Confederate general, James A. Walker, who represented neighboring Virginia's 9th District.[*]

When the delegation swept through Santa Cruz on a California tour in September, Florence Campbell stayed at the Pacific Ocean House, where she struck up a quick friendship with the proprietor, E. B. Pixley, who ran the hotel with his wife. A few weeks later, Florence wrote to Pixley for advice. The rest of the West Virginians were going home, but Florence wanted to spend the winter in California. She intended to support herself as a paid public speaker, presenting a talk she had originally delivered in West Virginia on the "new woman," a hot-button term for the women's liberation movement of the 1890s.

Pixley was a respected local businessman and show promoter, and he pulled strings for Florence. As it happened, the Santa Cruz Fourth of July and Encampment Committee had partied too hard in celebration of Independence Day 1897, America's 121st birthday, and overspent itself into a $400 deficit. With Pixley's coaxing, the committee agreed to host Florence's lecture as a fundraiser at the Santa Cruz Opera House on November 12.

Florence's talk was advertised in the *Santa Cruz Sentinel*. Tickets cost fifty cents for good seats, about $16 today. It was a provocative topic, the new woman, more than two decades before the passage of the Nineteenth Amendment. It took some courage for Florence to lecture a packed house of strangers, some three thousand miles from home, on a pointed political and social controversy. The Irish writer Sarah Grand is credited with coining the term *new woman*, originally referring to women who objected to the power imbalance of marriage, though the term had evolved to include women who wanted equality in work and civic life. Traditionalists of the late nineteenth century despised the new woman the way social

---

[*] Already famous for his war exploits, Walker would become an even bigger name, when, after losing reelection in 1898, he contested the vote and was wounded when a gunfight broke out during a deposition.

conservatives loathed the feminists of the 1960s, or, for that matter, the feminists of today.

Reporters covering Florence's speech figured on being harangued for a miserable hour. They were happily surprised. "It was imagined that she would appear in bloomers or mannish costume," the *Sentinel* reported the next day. "Instead an attractive young lady gowned in white, which was relieved by a bunch of carnations, stood before the audience. There was not a trace of the new woman as she is generally represented about her. She looked more like a sweet girl graduate at commencement exercises." Florence spoke nervously, a little too softly for the big room, and in her gentle southern accent. There is no known transcript of her remarks, and only the barest summary in the paper: "Miss Campbell contended that women have the right to engage in any of the professions or in business if they were capable of doing so."

Reviews of her speech were polite, though some attendees came away thinking they had just heard "a schoolgirl's essay," and the show marked the beginning and end of Florence's California tour.

She went back to her room at the Ocean House, and at some point over the next several days made the acquaintance of a certain big-boned Australian.

Florence cultivated a friendship with Rathom. She moved to San Francisco. Rathom helped Florence get some light newspaper work, possibly at the *Oakland Enquirer*. He encouraged her in journalism, coached her, and for a short time Florence stayed with John and Mary Rathom, outside San Francisco in Mill Valley. The women became close, confiding in each other and often exchanging letters.

Rathom and Florence became even closer. They began having an affair.

❖

Around the time Rathom and Florence were first getting together, another San Francisco journalist was already eyebrows-deep into an extramarital affair that would have deadly effects. It would blow up his career and reputation, put his liberty at risk, titillate newspaper readers across the nation, and unintentionally inspire a copycat that would push John Rathom's life to the edge of a precipice.

Journalists, even competitors, are tight-knit, and it is likely that Rathom, a reporter for the *Chronicle*, would have known John Dunning, the San Francisco bureau chief for the Associated Press. Dunning was a plain-faced guy with a half-hearted mustache. He was a drunk, a problem gambler, and an insatiable womanizer. In 1897 Dunning was thirty-three and married to Mary Elizabeth Pennington, the daughter of a former Delaware congressman. Dunning was also two years into a raucous affair with a married woman.

Dunning had met his paramour, Cordelia Botkin, in Golden Gate Park, while fixing his bicycle after it had broken down during a ride. Botkin was stout, frumpy, and ten years older than Dunning, but fun and flirty. She lived a largely separate life from her estranged husband, a grain broker. Dunning asked Botkin out on a date, and soon they were shacking up among empty whiskey bottles at her apartment on Geary Street in San Francisco, laying bets together at the racetrack, and hosting booze and card parties like a frat house. Dunning's life quickly ran off the rails. He gambled himself into debt and was fired for embezzling money from the Associated Press. His wife left him, took their child, and moved home to Dover, Delaware.

The outbreak of the Spanish-American War in April 1898 revived Dunning's career. The Associated Press gave him another chance, rehiring Dunning to cover the war in the Caribbean. He bid good-bye to Botkin at a train station in Oakland, where he dropped some bad news. He missed his wife and wanted to save his marriage. When his war assignment was done, he was moving to Delaware to reconcile with his family. Botkin wept and begged him to reconsider. Dunning was firm—it was over.

It was not over for Botkin.

Soon, Dunning's wife in Delaware began receiving bitter, anonymous letters in the mail, handwritten in messy swirls, as if by someone who was drunk, describing wild affairs her husband had enjoyed in California. The letters warned Mary not to take John Dunning back.

Then, on August 9, a package from California arrived by mail in Dover, addressed to Mrs. John P. Dunning. Inside was a lady's handkerchief, a box of chocolates, and a note:

With love to yourself and baby—Mrs. C.

Mary had a couple of friends in California with names beginning with *C*, and she did not know which one had sent the package. All of Mary's friends knew she was a chocaholic. Relaxing on the veranda at her parent's home, Mary ate some candy and passed the box to her sister, her sister's children, and a couple of family friends.

Everyone who ate the candy fell violently ill.

The children and friends recovered, but Mary's sister died after two days.

A doctor visiting on the morning of August 12 found Mary deathly ill, "in a state of collapse," drenched in a cold sweat, her eyes and face swollen. Her lips were blue, and the membrane in her mouth and nose was inflamed and slimy. Her pulse was too weak to read at the wrist and she struggled to breathe. She told the doctor of a tingling throughout her legs and feet and "a burning and boiling sensation" in her stomach. The symptoms intensified throughout the day, until Mary died in agony around 8:45 that evening.

In the midst of the tragedy, Mary's father realized the handwriting on the note that had come with the candies was similar to that of the angry anonymous letters Mary had received. He began to investigate. A chemist who examined the leftover candies concluded they had been laced with arsenic, a deadly poison both tasteless and odorless.

Mary Dunning and her sister had been murdered.

John Dunning received the news of his wife's death while in Puerto Rico. He immediately left for Dover. Botkin had written Dunning hundreds of letters over the course of their affair. The moment he saw the anonymous notes sent to his wife, he knew who was responsible.

Cordelia Botkin was indicted in San Francisco on two counts of murder. The newspapers, not overly concerned with the presumption of innocence, dubbed her "the Dover Assassin."

Botkin's trial in December 1898 was a massive spectacle. No one had ever seen a case like it. Murder by mail. A steamy story of sex, booze, and adultery. Newspapers blew out their entire front pages chronicling the testimony. Wire services reported the happenings nationwide. Spectators jammed the court gallery every day and overflow crowds by the hundreds lingered around the courthouse waiting for morsels of news to leak out.

On December 30, 1898, Botkin was found guilty. She was spared the noose and sentenced to life in prison.

❖

In late 1898, when Rathom had recovered from the case of the yellow fever he contracted covering the war in Cuba, he moved out on his wife and joined his mistress, Florence, at an apartment at 610 Ellis Street, a two-story clapboard boarding house about five blocks from what was then San Francisco City Hall. John and Florence falsely told their landlady, a dressmaker named Elsie Scheib who also lived in the building, that they were husband and wife. Florence presumed, or maybe just hoped, that her married lover would get a divorce.

Mary Rathom lived just two blocks away, on Polk Street. Mary did not blame Florence for the affair, not at first, and remained courteous to her, believing the younger woman was a lost soul, far from home, and that Rathom was the one at fault. The women continued exchanging civil letters.

Around February 1899, Scheib, the landlady, learned that Rathom and Florence were not married and confronted them.

"We have been deceiving you," Rathom admitted. "I'm very glad this has all come out. I feel more relieved tonight than I have in many months. There has been some trouble between me and my wife, and there were many reasons why I could not get separated from her. But now I am able to put Miss Campbell in the position to which she is entitled and make her my wife. She deserves it."

Florence, who was there, seemed delighted, but time passed and nothing came of it. Scheib, who was friendly with Florence, urged her to leave Rathom. Florence stuck by him.

The next month, Mary showed up several times at the apartment house on Ellis Street to speak with Florence, usually making appointments for when Rathom would not be there. Mary wanted her husband back and asked Florence to break off the affair. Florence, though, was too deeply in love. On one Sunday evening, Rathom and the two women had a hot argument at the Ellis Street apartment, which left Florence angry and feeling sick for days.

"Rathom had told each woman he was trying to get rid of the other," Scheib later told the *San Francisco Examiner.*

Rathom and Florence moved out of Ellis Street in the spring. It is unclear where they went, but it was not far. Florence continued to receive her mail at Elsie Scheib's place and would swing by every week to pick it up.

In early June, Florence and Mary met for a private talk. They walked together to a park on Turk Street, probably Jefferson Square Park, which at the time was a sprawling forest of trees and shrubs over rolling hills. They argued. Mary was out of patience. She threatened to file for divorce and to name Florence as a co-respondent, outing her publicly for adultery with a married man and calling witnesses to prove it.

A couple of weeks later, on June 30, 1899, six months to the day after Cordelia Botkin met justice in a San Francisco courtroom, a package arrived for Florence in the care of Elsie Scheib. Florence came to pick it up the next day.

The beautiful little package was carefully wrapped in glossy baby-blue paper and tied up with white twine. There was no return sender, but the handwriting on the address was definitely Mary Rathom's. Oddly, the handwritten address seemed to have been clipped from an old envelope and pasted on the package. Scheib encouraged Florence to open it. Inside was an oblong willow basket, six by three inches, with a hinged lid. It was filled with three-quarters of a pound of candy-glazed cherries. Somebody in the room joked about whether it had been sent by Cordelia Botkin. Florence ate several of the candies. Elsie Scheib ate three pieces.

Scheib's husband playfully warned that they ought to know not to eat candy that comes through the mail. "But we paid no attention to him," Florence said later.

That night, both women fell ill.

Scheib woke at two o'clock in the morning and began to vomit. She was restless and had a bad headache.

Florence, feeling ill, panicked. She was convinced she had been poisoned with arsenic. She tried to think back to the news stories about the Botkin trial. Was arsenic a fast poison or a slow one? What she mostly remembered about the case was that two women had died. She took dry mustard in water to induce vomiting. Florence told Rathom the cherries had made her sick and that Mary Rathom had sent them. Well, the handwriting on the package was definitely Mary's, Rathom agreed.

Both women got better in a couple of days.

While Florence recovered, Rathom took the leftover cherries to a chemist who had been quoted in the press in the Botkin affair. When the cherries tested positive for a tremendous amount of arsenic, Rathom saw no choice but to bring the matter to the San Francisco police. The case fell to the same officer who had investigated Botkin, police chief Isaiah Lees. He was a grizzled Colonel Sanders lookalike, sixty-eight years old, with a dangling triangle of wispy white beard.

The story broke in the papers one week into July. The press was flabbergasted. *Another* sensational attempt of murder by mail? This copycat crime was a made-for-tabloid-TV story, but the print reporters of the late nineteenth century did their best with it.

The *San Francisco Examiner* splashed the story under a banner headline across the top of page 1: CANDIED CHERRIES WERE FULL OF ARSENIC; MYSTERY VEILS THE NAME OF THE SENDER.

Accompanying the *Examiner* article was a front-page illustration of Rathom, looking slimmer in the face and more hangdog, maybe due to circumstances, than in his later Providence days. In addition to an article of several thousand words, a front-page text box in large typeface summarized the scandal:

Last Thursday afternoon a package was delivered at 610 Ellis St. addressed to Miss Florence M. Campbell. The address was in the handwriting of Mrs. John R. Rathom, whose husband left her several months ago because of his affection for Miss Campbell. The address was cut from an old envelope which had been sent with a letter in ordinary correspondence between the women. The police believe Mrs. Rathom did not send the package and are investigating to locate the person responsible. An arrest may be made soon. Miss Campbell denies any responsibility in the matter, and Rathom says he believes neither of the women sent the stuff through the mail. The candy was examined by Chemist Thomas Price, and he reported that "it contained enough arsenic to kill a herd of cows."

Mary acknowledged it was her handwriting on the address label, but denied sending the cherries. Florence huffed at the suggestion she might have had something to do with it. "I have been informed that I am suspected of having prepared the poisonous package myself," Florence told the *Examiner*, "and my answer to this suspicion is this: Would I, knowing the candy contained poison, offer it to the best friend I have on earth?"

Rathom defended both women in press interviews, but much more strenuously defended his wife, which suggests he had some idea who was behind the scheme:

> I'm absolutely certain that my wife knew nothing whatever about it. She knew she had not sent it, and I knew she had not done so. I have been married about nine years and I think I know something about my wife's character.

Rathom's own paper, the *San Francisco Chronicle*, did him the favor of burying its initial article on the scandal on page 5. The wire services blasted out a version of the story by telegraph on July 8, where it was reprinted for readers in every corner of the country, with local editors coming up with their own headlines:

JEALOUS WIFE OF A NEWSPAPER MAN UNDER SUSPICION
—Indianapolis Journal

ARSENIC IN THE CHERRIES
—Brooklyn Citizen

RATHOM MAKES A CONFESSION
—St. Louis Globe-Democrat

That last headline refers to a quote from Rathom in the wire story, in which he admits that at some level he was responsible for the imbroglio. "I have made both these women suffer," Rathom said. "It is my fault. Say what you want of me. There is no excuse for my conduct. But spare the women, who are innocent. My wife has never upbraided me for my attention to Miss Campbell and has never said an unkind word to Miss Campbell."

The *San Francisco Call* concluded that the guilty party had to be among the three main suspects: Florence, Mary, and Rathom. The *Call* story reported:

> A box of poisoned candy through the mail, two women who claim to have been made ill by eating it, and a strange reticence on the part of all concerned in the matter made a case which puzzled the police for a short while yesterday, and then dwindled into the uncovering of another story of a man's duplicity and a wrecked home.

Over the next three weeks, Chief Lees and his detectives traced the arsenic and the basket back to their sellers, Blake's Drug Store and a Japanese retailer on Market Street. The chief invited Florence to his office for another chat, and secretly arranged for the druggist and the clerk from the

Japanese store to be there. They identified Florence as the perp. Confronted with the facts, Florence cracked. The whole thing was a frame-up inspired by the Botkin affair, she admitted. Florence *sent the basket to herself* to get leverage over Mary.

"My only object in mailing this poisoned candy was because she threatened to use my name [in a divorce filing] and make it public," Florence confessed. "I intended holding the poisoned candy matter over her head and thought possibly I could frighten her from using my name publicly and that was my whole object in doing it."

She had poisoned only the candies on the bottom of the basket, slicing them with a knife and inserting the arsenic.

"I had no intention of ever touching the poisoned candy myself, and certainly did not intend that Mrs. Scheib or anyone else should partake of it, and thought it was perfectly safe to partake of the candied cherries from the top."

The candies on the top were not poisoned. But after eating some Florence began to think *what if the cherries were stirred up in transit?* She began to perspire and feel sick. When Elsie Scheib mentioned that she, too, was feeling unwell, Florence unraveled. It is possible Florence consumed a small amount of poison that night, or was made ill by the power of suggestion, multiple doses of vomit-inducing mustard, and the terrifying thought that an entirely innocent woman could be hanged if anyone died from the plot.

Chief Lees referred the case to the district attorney, who concluded that the lawmakers of California never anticipated someone like Florence Campbell. Arsenic was not a controlled substance—you could buy it at the drugstore. And it was not against the law to mail it to yourself. So what was the crime? Florence was not prosecuted.

Newspapers that had published the details of the sensational mystery followed up with stories on the deflating conclusion. The *New York Times* headlined its story MISS CAMPBELL CONFESSES. A headline in the *Topeka State Journal* sounded disappointed: A NICE PLOT SPOILED.

After Florence was unmasked as the culprit, Mary Rathom left San Francisco—alone—to return to British Columbia. It is unknown if

Mary walked out, or if Rathom sent her away. She arrived in Victoria on August 4, and moved back in with her mother. Mary told her local paper that she would not file any legal action against Florence. The whole mess had been embarrassing enough. She did file for divorce and named Florence as a co-respondent.

With Mary out of the way, Rathom and Florence were free to be together. In Florence Campbell, Rathom found a soulmate for his roguish side, someone who loved him enough to frame another woman—his wife!—for attempted murder. And far from being deterred, Rathom was more committed to Florence than ever. After their humiliation in San Francisco, it was time to start over, as Rathom had done before. They would keep the good parts of their story, paper over the bad with inventions and lies, and head east, toward new fame and danger.

CHAPTER 10
Minister without Portfolio

O n the hot afternoon of Saturday, July 24, 1915, George Sylvester Viereck, editor of the *Fatherland*, arrived at about two o'clock at the offices of the German-owned Hamburg-American steamship line, at 45 Broadway in Lower Manhattan. The nine-story brick and masonry building, jutting several floors taller than its lower neighbors, had a wide, arching entryway, and its name, HAMBURG-AMERICAN BUILDING, painted in giant capital letters high on its side. Around the rear, the building backed up to the Sixth Avenue El, an elevated train line.

Viereck stayed about an hour, and then left at three o'clock with a key figure in Germany's covert operations in the United States, Heinrich Albert, who kept an office in the shipping building. Albert was the most important character in German espionage and propaganda efforts in America—because Albert controlled the money.

"He spent thirty million at least—and only Germany knows how much more—in secret agency work, also known by the uglier names of bribery, sedition and conspiracy," wrote author John Price Jones, in *The German Secret Service in America, 1914–1918*. "He admitted that he wasted a half-million or more."

Albert's jobs involved floating German loans in the United States, supervising "all financial deals involving German business interests," financing clandestine copper and cotton shipments to Germany, seeking to buy US factories for the German war effort, and advising the German embassy "on all commercial matters," Viereck later wrote. Albert also supplied the money to pay for Dernburg's German propaganda office.

Albert, then forty-one, the son of a bank owner, was from an affluent German family. He spoke excellent English and knew the United States well; he had helped organize Germany's exhibit in the 1904 World's Fair in St. Louis. He was commonly called Dr. Albert, though he probably never held a doctorate. He had studied law. Albert was about 6'1", 190 pounds, "and wore the somber frock coat of the European business man with real grace," Jones wrote. His eyes were "blue and clear," his face clean-shaven but for a small moustache, like two tiny diagonal slashes over his upper lip. His chin had a deep cleft in its center, and one side of his face was "faintly saber-scarred."

"His greeting to visitors, of whom he had few, was punctilious, his bow low, and his manner altogether polite," Jones wrote. "He had none of the 'hard snap' of the energetic, outspoken, brusque American businessman. Dr. Albert was a smooth-running, well-turned cog in the great machine of Prussian militarism."

Leaving the Hamburg-American Building together that Saturday afternoon, Albert and Viereck walked around the block and climbed the stairs to the Rector Street station to wait for the next El train heading uptown.

At Albert's side, and never far from his touch, was his bulging tan leather briefcase.

Albert's briefcase was fat with records and letters relating to Germany's covert activities in the United States. There were so many secret documents in the briefcase that Albert had lost mental track of some of the paperwork he had amassed.

As Viereck would later ruefully recall, "It was a veritable mare's-nest of intrigue, conspiracy and propaganda that reposed placidly in Doctor Albert's briefcase."

In a few minutes, a train from South Ferry pulled up. Passengers alighted, others stepped in, and the train continued its run. Albert and Viereck sat together in the middle of the train car and chatted quietly in

German. The Gothic revival spire of Trinity Church passed just off to the right. The train rattled north along Trinity Place, and then Church Street and West Broadway, before turning west to Sixth Avenue.

From the street level, the Sixth Avenue El was a hideous, sunshine-blocking monstrosity; a railroad on cumbersome stilts. It roared unpleasantly overhead, shook windows, and dripped oil on pedestrians. From the train car, though, the visual sensation was like riding a floating carpet among the buildings of Manhattan, at the altitude of their third-floor windows.

After about ten stops, Viereck got off at Twenty-Third Street. A young woman took the open seat beside Albert and opened a book to pass the time. Albert's stop was still ahead. He was living at the German Club on Fifty-Ninth Street and needed to get off at Fiftieth Street and then take a short shuttle.

Albert also took out something to read. His briefcase sat beside him on the seat, resting against the wall of the car.

About five stops later, the train pulled into the Fiftieth Street station. Riders bustled off and on. Not Albert, though, who was engrossed in his reading, zoned out like a typical rail commuter. Just as the train was ready to move again, Albert looked up and realized he was about to miss his stop. He leaped from his seat and hurried to the door, shouting to the railmen for wait.

The moment he hopped off the train, he realized in cold terror that he had left behind his briefcase.

Instantly, he tried to run back onto the car, but a very large woman was in the doorway, asking a question of one of the rail employees. Albert needed a moment or two to squeeze past her and run back to his seat.

The briefcase was gone.

How was it possible? It was there *seconds* ago. The woman who had been sitting next to Albert told him some man had grabbed the bag and disappeared out the other end of the car.

Some man? Albert ran off the train after him, whoever he was. The big German's footsteps landed heavily on the wooden planks of the loading platform. A loose crowd that had just departed the train flowed toward the stairs. Nobody had the briefcase, not that Albert could see. How was that possible? This was like an evil magic trick. The train pulled away. With rising panic, Albert rushed down the stairs. No one had his bag. He ran into the street to get a better view of the crowd.

And there!

A stranger descended from the El platform with Albert's precious briefcase, walking like he owned it. He was a smallish man, this briefcase thief, half a foot shorter than Albert, and slightly built. How Albert had overlooked him on the platform was a mystery, but a mystery to sort out later.

For now, he barreled straight at the thief in a rage.

The thief was quick. Extremely quick. He dashed away on fleet feet and caught up to a fast-moving surface streetcar heading uptown. The athletic little bandit leaped with the briefcase onto the car's running board.

Albert chased after the streetcar, shouting for it to stop. His heart banged hard against his ribcage.

The thief said something to the conductor, who eyed Albert warily. The conductor spoke an order to the motorman and the car took off. It turned west on Fifty-Third and left Albert behind—sweaty, winded, and aching with dread.

Two days after the robbery, a sad little classified ad appeared in the *New York Evening Telegram*:

> Lost—On Saturday, on the 3:30 Harlem elevated train, at 50th St. station, a brown leather bag containing documents. Deliver G. H. Hoffman [Albert's secretary] 5 East 47th St., against $20 reward.

Albert tried to tell himself it would be okay. Imagine the disappointment of some common thief when he ransacked the briefcase to find no money and only paperwork, most of it in German. He would probably just pitch the whole thing in the trash.

Wouldn't he?

The Germans had other problems to take their minds off the missing portfolio—problems in the large, hulking shape of John R. Rathom.

❖

By the summer of 1915, Rathom's primary sources—British spies and Emanuel Voska's Bohemian National Alliance—were supplying all the tips, documents, and rumors Rathom could handle. Rathom also sought to develop additional sources inside the US government, and maintained a confidential relationship with Gaston Means, the mercurial German agent. No matter how unreliable Agent E-13's information could often be, Rathom could not bring himself to quit Means.

The month of July began a run of sensational stories for Rathom:

First, on July 1—

Rathom alleged in a widely reprinted story that a German-owned wireless station at Sayville, Long Island, had been violating American neutrality rules. With its Atlantic cables cut, Germany depended heavily on radio messages between the United States and Berlin. Under US government rules, the station was not allowed to send messages in secret code unless US censors were provided the code ahead of time. Rathom alleged the station's operators were giving the censors fake codes to disguise the true nature of the messages the station was sending. He wrote:

> The *Providence Journal* has been collecting these messages for many months and last month handed to Federal authorities at Washington copies of every line of wireless that had been sent from and received by Sayville. These documents prove conclusively that the Government has been persistently fooled by the German Embassy at Washington and that under the very eyes of the censors the German ambassador have violated every obligation of neutrality.

Rathom's language was intentionally imprecise. *The* Providence Journal *has been collecting these messages. . . .* Collecting how? Rathom did not say. He planted the false impression that the newspaper had intercepted German wireless transmissions. It was a feint to disguise the true source of the material: the British government. Later, Rathom's feints became bolder, until he began to claim outright that *Journal* wireless stations on Block Island, a tiny, teardrop-shaped vacation isle about twenty miles off Long Island, intercepted and catalogued all German radio transmissions from Sayville. The lie was reprinted so many times in newspapers across the country that it came to be accepted as an uncontested fact.

Other newspapers quickly followed up the *Journal's* Sayville story, confirming that Navy Secretary Josephus Daniels and other federal officials had met with Rathom in Washington, DC, to see his proof. "The Navy Department is convinced that much of the editor's evidence is well-founded," the *New York Tribune* reported.

National readers finally had a name to connect to the *Providence Journal's* newspaper's scoops: John Revelstoke Rathom.

On July 2—

Rathom published a blistering attack on former Secretary of State Bryan, whom he accused of engaging in unsanctioned negotiations over ship and submarine policy with the Austrian ambassador. Rathom alleged that Bryan made promises he did not relay to President Wilson. The story was reprinted by the *New York Times*, and a number of other papers. The *Washington Times* reported that the story "attracted wide notice." The *Rutland Daily Herald* (Vermont) editorialized on the story, describing its source as, "The Providence Journal, an irrepressible New England newspaper which makes a specialty of giving departments and foreign delegations cold chills."

On July 21—

Rathom printed a story alleging that German spies were trying to bribe labor leader Samuel Gompers to persuade his union brothers to strike at US weapons plants. Gompers had already been president of the American Federation of Labor for nearly thirty years. He was famous in his time and is among the most important people in the history of organized labor in the United States. Later that summer, Gompers confirmed publicly that foreign interests had tried to bribe labor leaders to instigate strikes. It was more validation for Rathom, even if Gompers stopped short of substantiating

Rathom's charge that Gompers was personally offered enough money to retire in luxury if he called for strikes at munition plants.

On July 29—

Rathom printed allegations that German agents intended to squeeze off the Triple Entente's access to loans from US banks, by threatening the banks with a boycott by German American clients and financial firms.

"The movement means, in brief, that the banks under German-American control will be used as a medium to make impossible American participation in future loans to the Allies," the story charged.

As usual, Rathom fuzzed the sourcing for the story. "The *Providence Journal* has secured the facts of this movement," he wrote, "from one who has worked among German agents since the inception of this scheme." That language clearly describes Gaston Means, who played both sides of the propaganda war, depending on how it benefited himself.

The *New York Times* reprinted the story beneath the headline SAYS GERMAN AGENTS SEEK TO AWE BANKS, and the now famous opening line: "The *Providence Journal* will say tomorrow . . . "

Rathom's impressive run of stories in July was only the prelude. Next, he pulled together threads of information passed along by Voska, and published startling allegations beyond what most Americans at that time could have imagined.

❖

From the moment deposed Mexican dictator Victoriano Huerta arrived in the United States in early 1915, everyone figured he would try to retake power in Mexico.

In late June, Huerta made his move.

The former strongman left New York by train. At a stop in Chicago, he told curious reporters that he was on his way to see the Panama–Pacific International Exposition, a world's fair in San Francisco celebrating the opening of the Panama Canal.

Instead, he took a hard left turn, taking a train south toward Mexico. The train stopped at "a little desert station" in Newman, New Mexico, about twenty miles from the border town of El Paso, Texas. Huerta, wearing dark round glasses, stepped off the train as a big morning sun cleared the horizon.

Huerta's plan, contemporary news articles reported, was to cross the border at El Paso, where he would take command of a garrison of soldiers that would mutiny against their leadership. Those troops would link up with thousands of Mexican fighters loyal to Huerta on both sides of the border. Huerta would declare himself the rightful leader of Mexico, set up a provisional national capital, and then fight to the sea to capture a harbor for the import of more arms and supplies. From there, the revolution would compete for the hearts and minds of the people, and, where necessary, shoot people in their hearts and minds.

The plan's big weakness, however, was how obvious it was that Huerta intended to do this exact thing. He was being watched, and US officials were a step ahead of him. A deputy US marshal and a compliment of American troops were waiting to arrest Huerta when he got off the train in New Mexico. Huerta gave up peacefully, claiming he had come to the border only to visit relatives in El Paso. There was a bridge for sale in Brooklyn for anyone who believed that. The old dictator was taken to Fort Bliss and charged with the crime of planning an attack on another nation from the United States.

Huerta's arrest was a sensational news event throughout the country. The story monopolized front pages for days, in part because Huerta welcomed newspaper interviews while out on bail. He was funnier and more charming than your average blood-stained strongman, and he made great copy. The cyclone of attention around Huerta's arrest set the scene for Rathom's most outrageous story.

On July 23, 1915, Rathom again met with President Wilson. The event is logged on Wilson's calendar, scheduled for 11:00 A.M. I've been unable to find a record of their conversation. It is likely Rathom offered the president a preview of the crazy story he was reporting.

On August 4, 1915, Rathom published his *Mona Lisa*.

He accused German embassy officials of conspiring with Huerta to destabilize Mexico to such a degree that the United States would be forced to intervene militarily. In essence, Rathom accused German diplomats of trying to goad the United States and Mexico into a shooting war.

The *New York Times* published Rathom's story the same day it ran in Providence:

SAYS GERMANY USED HUERTA AGAINST US, PROVIDENCE JOURNAL TELLS OF A JOINT PLOT TO EMBROIL THIS NATION WITH MEXICO

PROVIDENCE, R.I. Aug. 3—The *Providence Journal* will say tomorrow:

The arrest of General Huerta at El Paso on June 27 closed the first chapter of a plot to embroil the United States with Mexico and put a stop to the exportation of munitions of war to the Allies, a plot directed and almost brought to a conclusion by the German ambassador, Count von Bernstorff, and Captain Boy-Ed.

. . .

The German Embassy, using Huerta's ambitions for its own purposes, simply made him a cat's paw (a dupe) and attempted by vague promises of the support of many thousands of German reservists in this country to bring about a condition in Mexico that would compel the United States to intervene.

Rathom hid his sources, as usual. The bones of the story came from Voska and his group's espionage on the conference between Huerta and Rintelen in New York.

The story alleged that Boy-Ed and other unnamed German officials met "many times" with Huerta in New York. Rathom did not mention Franz Rintelen, who would later admit he organized the conference with Huerta. Instead, Rathom blamed Bernstorff and Boy-Ed, probably because at the time Rintelen was a nobody and the other two diplomats were famous.

"The purpose of this plot," Rathom's report continued, "was five-fold":

- To distract an American public still enraged about the sinking of the *Lusitania*.
- To give the United States a reason to stop munition exports to the Allies. If the United States went to war with Mexico, it would need those munitions at home.
- To compel the United States to lease for its war against Mexico the German-owned ships languishing in interment in New York Harbor.
- To frustrate Mexican oil exports to the Allies.
- To compel President Woodrow Wilson to impose an arms embargo on Mexico, which would showcase the administration's hypocrisy over permitting arms sales to Britain.

"Germany had everything to gain and nothing to lose by a war between the United States and Mexico or by American intervention in Mexico," Rathom wrote, in analysis that Boy-Ed and Papen would have agreed with, if they were being honest.

The American press reacted to the story with shock and in some cases disbelief:

CAPTAIN BOY-ED DESCRIBED BY NEWSPAPER AS INSTIGATOR OF
HUERTA'S PLANS—*Washington Times*

PLOT TO EMBROIL THE UNITED STATES TRACED TO GERMAN
EMBASSY
—*Daily Globe*, Fall River, Massachusetts

IS GERMANY BACKING HUERTA?
—*El Paso Times*

BERNSTORFF LED HUERTA IN PLOT, PAPER DECLARES
—*Evening Public Ledger*, Philadelphia

PROVIDENCE JOURNAL INSISTS HUERTA IS A GERMAN TOOL
—*Daily Capital*, Topeka, Kansas

OFFICIAL WASHINGTON WAS STARTLED BY RECENT STORY IN NEWSPAPER
—*Greenville News*, Greenville, South Carolina

The story got traction from Maine . . .

PROVIDENCE JOURNAL VS. VON BERNSTORFF
—*Bangor Daily News*

all the way to Alaska . . .

SAYS GERMANY WAS BEHIND HUERTA ACTIVITY
—*Alaska Daily Empire*

Count von Bernstorff denied Rathom's story in a letter hand-delivered to Secretary of State Lansing, which the secretary accepted. "As the department [of state] has no information on the subject, it regards this expression of the ambassador as satisfactory," Lansing's office said.

A Boy-Ed spokesman called the Huerta story "too absurd to discuss. It's funny, ridiculous, crazy." Boy-Ed laughed it off, "I have nothing to say except that in Providence, apparently, the heat has been even worse than here."

In truth, the allegations did seem ridiculous.

"The story in the Providence Journal that the German embassy at Washington planned the present trouble between the United States and Mexico looks startling in print," the skeptical *Wilkes-Barre Record* reported, "but it is hardly likely that the embassy would leave so many clues uncovered."

Some of the more blistering criticism came from Herman Ridder, publisher of *Staats-Zeitung*, an influential German-language paper in New York. In a column published on August 9, Ridder snarked that he had followed the dispatches from the *Journal*—"an unheard-of-paper in an insignificant New England town"—that were reprinted in the *New York Times*.

"We need not delve deeply into these matters when we are informed that the shining editorial and proprietor light of the Providence Journal is not an American but an Australian," Ridder wrote. "I should like to see some of the allegations of the Providence Journal proven or retracted."

Rathom's responded with a journalistic middle finger: On August 15, he ran a long story—again, simultaneously published on the front page of the *Times*—alleging that the US government was preparing prosecutions against the perpetrators of German spy schemes. The story is notable for two things.

The first is that Rathom reported that Werner Horn, the German army reservist who bombed the Vanceboro railroad bridge, had signed a confession in which he admitted the attack had been ordered by a superior officer inside the United States. Rathom correctly exposed Horn's unnamed superior as the German military attaché Franz von Papen, while vaguely suggesting US government sourcing.

Nearly all of this reporting on Horn was dead-on. Horn did sign a confession, and Papen was the officer who gave the order. If the government had not quite yet confirmed Papen's involvement, it was true that Bielaski, chief of the Bureau of Investigation, strongly suspected Papen.

Horn was desperate to protect his superior. He responded with a sharp denial issued through the Boston law firm representing Horn in his criminal case for transporting explosives. "My client authorizes me to say that the accusation against Captain von Papen is unqualifiedly false and the alleged 'confession' is a sensational fake," Horn's lawyer said in widely published statement.

Rathom slashed back with a decisive follow-up story, reporting specifically that Horn's confession was not only in the hands of the Department of Justice, it was "in typewritten form and was voluntarily signed by him with the following words above his signature: 'I declare the above to be true on the honor of a German officer."

That was exactly right.

And the most plausible source for that level of confidential detail was the special agent who took Horn's confession and typed the document for him—Bielaski.

The Horn stories demonstrate that by mid-August 1915, Rathom and Bielaski had formed a confidential relationship, and that Bielaski was feeding Rathom information. The relationship is well-documented in the later months of the year. The lawman and the imposter kept up regular contact at least into 1918. Their secret affiliation would become valuable to both parties, until the relationship would go disastrously awry for one of them.

The second thing that made Rathom's August 15 story notable is this passage:

> The Government has been placed in possession of a bag of documents which was found in the hands of a secret service agent of the German Government, and among these documents has been found positive proof of German official activities against the peace of the United States.

After three weeks of uneasy silence, Dr. Albert's stolen briefcase was about to explode into an international scandal. It is unclear where Rathom got the tip. Maybe from Means, who remained in the orbit of the German embassy, perhaps close enough to smell the panic.

❖

In early August, German diplomats learned that the *New York World* was making inquiries into Dr. Albert's business affairs. Soon they deduced that the newspaper somehow possessed documents from Albert's briefcase. Albert was incredulous. He blew up in a meeting of Dernburg's propaganda cabinet, unable to comprehend how an American newspaper could publish his property. "They are private papers!" he shouted.

"This is a world war!" responded Hale, the group's American advisor.

The cabinet strategized about how to block publication of Albert's materials. They considered filing in court for an injunction, but decided that would only bring more attention to the documents. Viereck and Albert made "a hectic automobile trip" to see an influential lawyer. The lawyer called everybody he knew with a scintilla of political power. He talked to President Wilson's secretary. He talked to a member of Wilson's cabinet. No luck. There was no way to keep Albert's papers secret.

Beginning August 15, Albert's documents and their English translations were splattered across the front page of the *New York World*, reprinted across America, over three long days. As the author Heribert von Feilitzsch summarized:

> Albert's papers revealed the German ownership of the Bridgeport Projectile Company, the investments in American munitions, market-cornering efforts, investments in newspapers, bribes to American politicians, links of the Deutsche Bank . . . to the German operation, and payments of the German government to George Sylvester Viereck and the Fatherland. Every day new headlines seemed to top the ones of the day before.

The damage to German espionage was incalculable. "The inner workings of the propaganda machine were laid bare," Viereck later wrote. "The exposure of Albert's activities destroyed the element of camouflage, essential to propaganda success."

The *World*'s exposé, backed up by documented proof, enhanced Rathom's sensational reports, which came from anonymous sources. The *Sacramento Bee*, for instance, collected all the allegations from the *New York World* and the *Providence Journal* in a massive round-up story. The *Bee* reported that federal officials in Washington were "highly aroused over these charges." Many newspapers speculated that certain German diplomats would be thrown out of the United States.

German diplomats blamed British spies for stealing Albert's briefcase, but they were guessing. They had no idea who took it.

With the truth a mystery, the imposter saw an opportunity to leverage the situation. He would play the protagonist for an American public eager for a good story. In June 1917, two months after the United States entered

World War I, Rathom would spin a caper tale right out of a spy novel, starring himself and the reporters he commanded. He debuted the story in his first major wartime speech, before the Canadian Press Club in Toronto.

In Rathom's version, a *Providence Journal* reporter directed by Rathom to shadow Albert, followed the German official into a New York leather goods store. After watching Albert buy a briefcase, the *Journal* man bought an identical case. A day or so later, undercover *Journal* reporters staged a fistfight on Albert's train, and when Albert was distracted a third man swapped Albert's briefcase for the identical portfolio, which was stuffed with old newsprint.

"This happened on a Saturday morning," Rathom said, with his flair for irrelevant details that make a lie *feel* like the truth. "Albert, in a statement later, said that he discovered the trick the same day, but we know for a fact that he did not discover until Monday morning."

Rathom's version of the story was picked up by newspapers across the country, reprinted countless times, and celebrated by reporters and editorial writers.

Seventeen years after Rathom's death, Voska retold Rathom's version of the briefcase caper as the gospel truth in a 1940 article in the *Saturday Evening Post*. In his memoir, released the same year, Voska reported that just as his book was going to print, he learned what really happened to the briefcase, and that Rathom's story was not true. "When he gave me a very different account of this operation, I believed him," Voska wrote of his friend.

Voska was among John Rathom's closest confidants. The two men were entangled in each other's secrets, collaborating in a spy venture in which one slip could ruin everything, or even get somebody killed. There was no one on whom Rathom relied more. And yet, the imposter never broke character, not even to Voska.

Souls need other souls; it is a necessity of humanity. But Rathom's soul had to keep a distance from even his closest friends. How lonely it must have been.

The question that remains: If Rathom did not steal Albert's briefcase, who did?

The culprit was the US government.

A week after the torpedoing of the *Lusitania*, President Woodrow Wilson ordered US Treasury secretary William McAdoo to deploy the Secret Service to spy on figures connected to the German and Austrian diplomatic corps in the United States. Secret Service chief William Flynn assigned a crew to follow key individuals. Franz von Papen, to his credit, became good at identifying and shaking his shadow. He would duck into a Macy's or Gimbel's, switch elevators at every floor, and eventually slip out the back door.

Not everyone was so skilled.

On July 24, 1915, the day Viereck arrived at the Hamburg-American Building, an undercover Secret Service agent named W. H. Houghton was on his tail. At 2:30 P.M., Houghton found a telephone and called his office in the Custom House building, two blocks away on the other side of Bowling Green Park. Houghton wanted help staking out the shipping building. He spoke to Secret Service agent Frank Burke.

Burke, in his mid-forties, was 5'7", 135 pounds. He was one of those undersized tough guys who would not be fun to mess with—and he was fast, too. It was said Burke could run the hundred-yard dash in ten seconds. The world record was 9.375. Burke had hoped to take the afternoon off to see a baseball game, but duty called. He joined Houghton's stakeout.

Viereck emerged around three o'clock, in the company of a tall stranger. The two Secret Service agents could tell by the deference Viereck showed the man that he was a VIP. Burke noticed faint scars on the man's cheek, and recalled a description he had heard from a customs lawyer about Heinrich Albert, the "most important representative of the German government in the United States." Burke was sure of it—this was Dr. Albert.

Another thing Burke noticed: Albert carried a well-stuffed brown briefcase.

The agents followed the men to the Rector Street El station and then onto an uptown train. Agent Houghton sat directly across from the

Germans. Burke sat right behind them. He could hear the men chatting softly, but Burke did not know German and could not understand what they were saying.

Viereck got off the train at Twenty-Third Street. Houghton slipped out to follow him.

Burke stayed with Albert.

At the Fiftieth Street station, when Albert bounced up and ran to not miss his stop, the briefcase was *right there*, alone and unguarded, tempting like the ripe fruit of the Tree of Knowledge. Burke was an agent of the US government, and he did not have a warrant for Albert's property. Taking the bag would be a crime. Getting caught would probably cause a diplomatic confrontation between the United States and Germany.

"I decided in a fraction of a second to get it," Burke later recalled.

The woman who had sat beside Albert noticed the briefcase and called out to him, but he was already out on the platform. Burke told the woman the case belonged to him, grabbed it, and fled out the other door.

Out of the corner of his eye, Burke saw Albert trying to get back onto the train, squeezing around a woman in his way. Seconds later, Albert barreled out of the train again, onto the platform, looking for the thief.

"He seemed," Burke would recall, "greatly disturbed." The Secret Service agent blended in with the light crowd. Albert was between Burke and the stairs, and the agent did not dare run for the street. Instead, Burke pressed the briefcase against a wall and then turned around and leaned against it, pinning it to the wall with his back. With his hands free, he coolly pretended to have trouble lighting a cigar, striking several matches. Albert was fooled. He ran down the stairs.

Now what? Burke thought. The train had left. If Albert came back up, Burke would be trapped on the platform. He decided his chances to get away were better on terra firma. He went down the stairs.

Albert was in the street, his eyes dissecting the crowd, "panic written on his face." He immediately recognized the briefcase and charged at Burke.

Even lugging the heavy bag, Frank Burke was fast. He ran, jumped on a moving streetcar, and told the conductor that the fellow chasing him was crazy; the guy had just made a scene at the El station and if he got on board the streetcar he would "cause trouble."

The conductor considered the howling, red-faced, bug-eyed man chasing his streetcar and agreed: That guy looked like trouble. He told the motorman to skip the next stop, and the car left Albert in the dust.

Burke switched to another streetcar at Eighth Avenue, heading south. He got off after a few blocks and ducked into a drug store to call his boss for a ride. Upon receiving the portfolio later that night, Treasury Secretary McAdoo understood the volatile nature of the stolen documents. But though many of the German plans were underhanded, they were not prosecutable, especially against diplomats with immunity. Complicating matters, Burke had taken the briefcase illegally, so the government could not just hand out the contents. Instead, McAdoo and Chief Flynn struck a deal with Frank I. Cobb, the trusted editor of the *New York World*. Cobb could have some of the documents if he swore to keep the source secret.

Albert issued a prolonged statement defending himself after the *World* published his dirty laundry. It read like a brief written by an angry lawyer, which is what it was.

Viereck thought highly of Albert's response on a technical level. "But the propagandist who is compelled to explain himself is already lost," he conceded. "He can no longer fire from ambush. His guns are no longer concealed. The loss of the Albert portfolio was like the loss of the Marne"—the key defeat early in the war that blunted the German advance toward Paris.

Viereck decided to go on offense, to crush Germany's enemies in the press. It was time to fight back with ruthlessness. He made it his mission to unearth some damaging skeletons in the mysterious past of John R. Rathom.

CHAPTER 11

"Idiotic Yankees"

The first American wounded in the 1898 Spanish-American War was a newspaper reporter: James Francis Jewell Archibald, who was writing for *Scribner's* magazine. It is very likely that Archibald and Rathom met while banging around the military encampment in Tampa for many dull weeks, looking for news.

Archibald was a New York native, twenty-six at the time, small and slim, and prematurely balding. His enthusiasm for war reporting had already taken him to the First Sino-Japanese War and the US Army's campaign against American Indian tribes.

A month before the main US invasion of Cuba, Archibald and several other scribes joined American troops on an ill-fated mission to deliver Springfield rifles to insurgents on the island. The mission was a comic failure. The operation was supposed to be secret, yet sixty or so news-famished reporters in Tampa splashed the mission's relevant details on front pages across half the world. Rathom wrote that the operation's commander promised to "get every rifle safely ashore and in the hands of the insurgents as fast as steam can take him south."

A droll reporter for the *San Francisco Call* later wrote, "The Spaniards may not be able to shoot very well, but some of them can read."

The operation sailed from Florida to its planned landing site at Mariel, a port west of Havana. Several hundred Spanish soldiers were waiting there "as though by special appointment." The ship bypassed that site and put ashore its troops and embedded reporters further west, unknowingly near a Spanish fort that garrisoned two thousand soldiers. The mission devolved into a fighting retreat, back to the beach, into the landing boats, and back to Tampa. No weapons made it to the rebels. "That the failure was unattended by any loss of life on our part seems due more to good luck than to good judgement," a *New York Herald* correspondent wrote.

In the retreat, Archibald was shot through the arm. Becoming the first American wounded in the fight with Spain earned him some celebrity.

In the years that followed, Archibald sought out warfare wherever he could find it. He marched alongside British forces in the Sudan campaign in 1899, and then with the Boer in South Africa during the Second Boer War; he embedded with Russian forces during their disastrous conflict with Japan in 1904–1905; and in 1910 Archibald visited the French military pacification of Morocco. He chronicled numerous lesser conflicts, revolts, and skirmishes in between the larger battles. If men in different-colored laundry were shooting each other somewhere in the world, Archibald was there.

Archibald wrote vividly, bringing faraway soldiers alive on the page, and then either made them heroes or snuffed them out. He became the most famous war correspondent in the country, though he would soon learn how short was the step to infamy.

The outbreak of World War I seemed like Archibald's moment, as if his entire life had been a training program for this unprecedented conflict. Archibald, by then forty-three, rushed to Europe in the fall of 1914. He embedded for five months with the German army, living among the troops, touring both fronts of the war, enjoying access to German and Austrian trenches, bases, airfields, and commanders. He took photographs and shot film.

He sailed home to America in February 1915, and turned his experience into a paid speaking tour called "5 Months with the German Army." It was advertised as "an uncensored lecture with his own marvelous motion pictures." Archibald was a halting speaker with a meandering style, but his material was compelling. His talk provided a glimpse of a new kind of warfare, combining brutal trench fighting, airplanes, and modern artillery—all presented with an intimacy most Americans had yet to see.

The German soldiers in Archibald's colorized photographs wore big grins as they marched, drilled, dug, built fortifications, and moved big guns. "The German army," the *Leavenworth Times* (Kansas) recounted in its review of the talk, "is made up of a cheerful, apparently contented lot of men." In Archibald's telling, the German army moved with clocklike precision. The troops were expertly led. And they conducted themselves with honor. Stories of German "atrocities" in Belgium were exaggerated, he said.

The lecture's political slant could not be missed. "Mr. Archibald's talk was enlightening," reported the *Asbury* (New Jersey) *Park Press*, "from a pro-German point of view."

It happens sometimes in the journalism business—reporters who immerse themselves into a subject can become emotionally captured by what they cover. In newsroom lingo, Archibald had "gone native."

Emanuel Voska had long thought Archibald was a cosplaying wannabe. "He enjoyed war," Voska wrote, "between wars, he loved to pose as a mysterious figure of great international importance." But once Archibald showed German sympathies, Voska's group began to pay attention to him.

In late August 1915 Archibald booked a trip to Europe from New York on the Dutch liner *Rotterdam*. On the eve of his departure, he dined with German ambassador Count von Bernstorff and his counterpart, Austro-Hungarian ambassador Constantin Dumba, a mild-looking fifty-nine-year-old with a droopy cookie duster mustache. Lots of people saw them together at the Ritz-Carlton roof-garden café.

Archibald made a generous offer to the diplomats: He would be happy to carry any private dispatches they wanted delivered overseas.

Count von Bernstorff declined. Dumba, however, embraced the offer. He figured Archibald would never let sensitive documents fall into enemy hands. Archibald was an amateur magician "who readily produced eggs and coins from the noses and ears of his friends," Dumba later wrote. If Archibald were ever cornered by the British, the reporter would make the documents disappear.*

Meanwhile, Voska's agent in the Austrian embassy noticed a pile of documents being wrapped for transit. Based on whispers and deduction, Voska understood the cache was for Archibald to carry to Europe. In a twist maybe too charming to be true—this part of Voska's account was emphatically disputed—Voska learned that a German spy also intended to present Archibald with a gentleman's walking stick. This simple cane had been hollowed and stuffed with more secret dispatches written on tissue paper. Voska passed the description of the package and the cane to British intelligence through Guy Gaunt. British agents would know what to look for when the *Rotterdam* lumbered into Falmouth to be searched for contraband.

"Twenty-five hundred miles overseas lay the perfect trap," Voska wrote, "and Archibald was heading right into it."

The first news flashes on the British search of the *Rotterdam* were short and vague, reporting only that the American correspondent James F. J. Archibald had been detained on a charge of "performing an unneutral service" by carrying documents from the German and Austrian embassies in the United States.

Archibald spent a night in jail, and then was sent home on the *Rotterdam*'s return voyage. The British promptly leaked the documents. The most damaging was a letter from Ambassador Dumba to the Austrian foreign minister, asking for money to provoke strikes at US factories.

"We can disorganize and hold up for months, if not entirely prevent, the manufacture of munitions in Bethlehem and the Middle West, which, in the opinion of the German military attaché [Franz von Papen], is of great importance and amply outweighs the expenditure of the money involved," Dumba wrote.

---

* Seems like a good time to mention that Voska thought Dumba was a stone-cold moron.

The letter was ruinous. The Wilson administration declared Dumba unsuitable to be a diplomat in America, and sent him home in humiliation.

Papen had also trusted Archibald. In a letter to his wife sent with the reporter, Papen described the fallout over the publication of papers from Dr. Albert's stolen briefcase. "You can imagine the sensation among the Americans," he wrote. "Unfortunately, some very important things from my report were among them, such as the buying of liquid chlorine and about the Bridgeport Projectile Company, as well as documents regarding the buying up of phenol, from which explosives are made."

In a throwaway line, Papen's letter paid tribute to the German soldiers fighting Russia. "How splendid on the eastern front. I always say to these idiotic Yankees that they had better hold their tongues. It is better to look at all this heroism with full admiration."

That offhanded slam echoed across the United States. A headline in the *New York Times* read: CAPT. VON PAPEN CALLS US "THESE IDIOTIC YANKEES."

One thing the British did not find on the *Rotterdam* was a cane stuffed with secret documents. "The cane is still a mystery," Voska later wrote. "When we saw it was beyond recall, Rathom published in the *Journal* a guarded and purposely garbled account of its adventures."

Inspired by Rathom's story, the national press became obsessed with Archibald's phantom walking stick. Dispatches about the cane were published coast to coast, from the *Washington Post* to the *Oregon Daily Journal*. The US Secret Service interrogated Archibald about the missing cane. *What cane?* Archibald insisted. He swore he never had one.[*]

The Archibald imbroglio brought immediate consequence. Said Voska:

> These stories made a sensation, of course. The indignation aroused by the *Lusitania* affair, four months before, had died down. The Albert papers had only warmed it up a little. But

---

[*] The document scandal shattered Archibald's reputation. He died by suicide in 1934, in Hollywood, California, at the age of sixty-two. His suicide note read: "Don't blame this one on Hollywood."

now the pro-Ally element buzzed again like a swarm of hornets. Americans who had been trying to preserve their personal neutrality "in thought and deed" swung by the hundreds of thousands to the side of the British and the French.

❖

By the autumn of 1915, Rathom enjoyed regular benefits from his secret friend, Bureau of Investigation chief Bielaski. On October 16, Rathom published an alarming story about an Austrian spy. The backstory to the article is a web of covert relationships, manipulations, and intrigue, with Rathom sitting as the spider at its center.

The story reported that an Austro-Hungarian army officer in the United States, Eugene von Tomory, had acquired military defense plans for New York City and smuggled them home to Austria. Rathom clearly got the story from Voska.

The *New York Times* reprinted Rathom's piece under the headline PROVIDENCE JOURNAL SAYS AUSTRIAN CAPTAIN CARRIED OUR DEFENSE PLANS.

The story held frightening possibilities. If true, foreign nations would know the defensive weaknesses of the most important city in America.

The genesis of the story was Voska's undercover man in the Austrian embassy. He noticed another cache of documents being prepared for transport, and learned the documents were to be delivered to Tomory's New York apartment just before Tomory was to sail. Voska gave a description of the package and of Tomory—middle-aged, smooth face, bulldog expression—to British authorities to intercept at Falmouth.

Somehow, though, the British missed the courier when they searched the ship. Maybe he slipped away. Maybe he had a disguise and fake identification. They never found him.

The day Rathom's story was published, a Bureau of Investigation agent in New York was dispatched by his boss to interview British naval attaché Guy Gaunt for more information about Tomory—information that Voska and the British government wanted US authorities to have. Who connected the bureau to Gaunt? Most likely Rathom, the one person secretly linked to everyone involved: Voska, Gaunt, and Chief Bielaski.

In a private interview, Gaunt told the bureau agent about Tomory and the documents he smuggled to Europe, provided Tomory's former New York address and the name of his landlady, and offered intelligence on an alleged spy ring that had fed Tomory the information.

"Capt. Gaunt insists that his statements regarding Tomoroy [sic] are absolutely true," the special agent wrote in his report. "He declined to give me the source of his information, stating that he was unable to do so on account of the highly confidential nature thereof."

Bielaski's agents investigated. Once the bureau had done its legwork, in walked Rathom, who persuaded the Bureau of Investigation to leak what it had found. We know this is the case because Bielaski gently rebuked the special agent in charge of his New York bureau, William M. Offley, for giving Rathom documents related to the Tomory inquiry: "I desired to get specific authority from the department before letting [Rathom] have the data he desired," Bielaski wrote. "Please do not give him any further information but refer him to me in all cases."

Voska's spy had identified the Austrian courier. British intelligence passed the tip to the Department of Justice. Bielaski's special agents dug out additional facts, and gave them to Rathom. All the backstage intrigue was invisible to the reader, who knew only that Rathom had published another sensation.

❖

By the latter months of 1915, Rathom and Bielaski were in near constant contact by confidential telegrams, letters, and telephone calls. Rathom's burgeoning national reputation as a German spy hunter attracted "tips" from all over the country. Suspicious Americans felt duty-bound to report the unneutral activities of their neighbors to *somebody* who would take the matter seriously. That somebody was Rathom. Often these tips were unpublishable—half-baked rumor or quarter-baked speculation, yet Rathom passed many of the tips to the Department of Justice.

Rathom became a government informant, though it is more precise to consider him an information broker with government clients. He traded knowledge as a commodity with federal agents, sometimes getting little in return but occasionally landing a windfall.

In one instance, Rathom sent Bielaski a list of employees working for the Austro-Hungarian consulate in New York—a list compiled by Voska's inside man. The object was to help Bielaski identify witnesses for the Archibald document investigation. Rathom flagged one employee who was "easily rattled," and suggested the Bureau of Investigation could pressure him to crack.

In return for all the information he provided, Rathom boldly and frequently asked Bielaski to leak him sensitive information about federal investigations. Late in 1915, in one spectacular example, Rathom sent Bielaski a list of five typewritten names of German and Austrian diplomats in the United States. In an accompanying letter, Rathom wrote:

> I enclose with this, a slip of paper containing the names of five persons whom I have every reason to believe are about to be jolted off the box.[*] It is vital to me to know whether my judgement is good in this respect. I want you to send this slip back to me in the enclosed envelope, with a check mark or even an infinitesimal pin prick alongside of the names I have guessed right about. I will find the mark no matter how small it is, and you will be doing me a great favor.

Did Bielaski mark the paper? Impossible to know. The Bureau of Investigation chief's answer for the record was that he could not help Rathom in this case. Rathom went ahead and published a damning story about one of the men on his list, a German consul general in San

---

[*] This is some mystifying slang. Near as I can tell, it means "knocked off one's high perch."

Francisco, Franz Bopp, suggesting he masterminded plots to destroy Canadian railroad bridges to interrupt munitions shipments. Eight weeks later, a federal grand jury indicted Bopp. Stories about the indictment credited the *Providence Journal* for its prescient coverage, and the Rathom legend grew a little larger.

❖

On Friday, November 12, 1915, Rathom rattled the underpinnings of US neutrality.

And for once, he named his source.

This blockbuster story was essentially a long statement from a former Austro-Hungarian diplomat, Joseph Goricar. Practically no one in the United States knew Goricar before the story, and history has since forgotten him. But for a brief time in 1915, no informed American could miss Goricar's name in the papers, and what he had to say.

Goricar was in his early forties. He had light, drowsy eyes, and wavy hair swept off his forehead. His eye-catching feature was a bushy mustache that had a distinct part down the middle, as if two ink-black woolly bear caterpillars had been placed head-to-head, but not quite touching, at sloping angles beneath his nose. Goricar had served about fifteen years in the Austrian diplomatic corps, stationed in the United States since 1909. He was a "South Slav by birth," Voska later explained, who underwent "a sharp inner struggle" when the war began. Goricar felt greater loyalty to his South Slavic roots than to the political amalgamation called Austria-Hungary. He resigned his West Coast diplomatic posting in December 1914, and traveled to New York. There, he offered his services to his fellow South Slavs, the Serbians, who were at war with Austria. "Knowing about our work, they passed him over to us," Voska wrote. Goricar became a key member of Voska's network.

Goricar claimed to have deep-rooted knowledge of Austrian espionage in the United States. Rathom printed his revelations under the headline FORMER AUSTRIAN CONSUL EXPOSES SPY WORK HERE. The lede reads:

Dr. Joseph Goricar, who has been in the Austro-Hungarian Consular Service for fifteen years, and who resigned his office on Dec. 20 of last year, made a statement yesterday to the Providence Journal in which he declared that the United States is honeycombed with German and Austrian spies, and that every Austro-Hungarian consulate in the country is the centre of a hotbed of propaganda for the destruction of munitions factories, for the creation of strikes among labor men working in such factories, and for every act of violence that is being committed here today having these objects in view.

Goricar charged that his consulate bosses pressured him to acquire schematics for fortifications in San Francisco Bay. He alleged that the office of the Austrian consul general "is the centre of the entire plot for securing fraudulent passports" for German and Austrian military officers in the United States. He said the consulate strong-armed laborers of Austrian ancestry to strike or quit their jobs at US munitions factories. He said German spies had already spent more than $30 million on propaganda in the United States.

Austro-Hungarian officials dismissed the allegations as "false and absolutely base," and called Goricar a traitor. Boy-Ed laughed off the charges: "I have nothing to say—nothing, only that the Providence Journal is the best comical paper of the United States." Yet the Goricar story went national over the wires. The *New York Times* reprinted Rathom's report at the top of page 1. The International News Service reported that President Wilson discussed the Goricar allegations with his cabinet.

Several news outlets reported that Chief Bielaski was eager to interview Goricar for more details. In fact, Bielaski telegrammed Rathom after the story appeared:

Please wire immediately government rate collect where Joseph Goricar may be interviewed by agents of this Department. Will appreciate you forwarding any additional info you may have in addition to that published.

And then telegrammed his agents in Providence:

> See Rathom Providence Journal and procure from him as full
> information as possible present whereabouts Goricar.

Rathom responded:

> Cannot reach Goricar for several days. Am printing in morning
> however conclusive proof by facsimile documents of guilt of
> Austro-Hungarian Consulate in New York in connection with
> passport frauds.

Rathom's follow-up story included reproductions of original letters and
their translations, appearing to show that an Austrian military officer had
departed the United States with a false passport, and that top Austrian
diplomats knew all about it.

Bielaski, Rathom, and Goricar arranged a conference for November
16–17 at the Hotel Astor, a magnificent Beaux-Arts building the size of
a city block in Times Square. News of the conference was plastered in
newspapers across the United States. The government's top investigator was
beseeching a *newsman* for information on foreign espionage. Nobody had
ever seen anything like it. After the meeting, Bielaski and Goricar declined
to comment to reporters. Rathom was unusually guarded, saying only that
Goricar "went into details" about the charges he had made.

The tantalizing secrecy created a kinetic air of mystery, and drove fever-
pitched speculation about which Central Powers diplomat would be the
next kicked out of the United States.

Bielaski's notes from the conference show that Rathom and Goricar
presented a great deal of innuendo, a bit of rumor, and many legitimate
letters that Voska's inside man at the Austrian consulate had steamed open
and copied, or just stole. Rathom and Goricar named low-level consulate
employees who helped with the fraudulent passport operation. They alleged
that the head of the German Secret Service spent the month of June on a

boat at the New York Yacht Club, holding conferences with secret agents from across the United States.

Rathom named a New York socialite and novelist, Charlotte Teller Hirsch, as the person who allegedly tried to bribe labor leader Samuel Gompers. Goricar described German and Austrian pressure campaigns through ethnic clubs to threaten workers into quitting jobs in the munitions industry. Rathom gave names he said appeared on forged passports over the past few days. Goricar alleged that certain foreign-language newspapers were on the take from Austria-Hungary.

None of the proof was ironclad. But Bielaski took many of the allegations seriously. He ordered his New York office to pursue more than a dozen lines of inquiry raised by Rathom and Goricar. In the case of Charlotte Hirsch, accused of trying to bribe Gompers, the bureau scrutinized her phone records. Bielaski asked his New York bureau chief, "Is there anyone who was employed in the Hirsch's home or who lived there who might be able to throw light on their activities during the period referred to by Mr. Rathom?"

Another important group that took Rathom's charges seriously: the Germans.

The Goricar stories had drawn blood. So much so that the *Buffalo Commercial* joked that the *Providence Journal* should "publish in a bomb-proof shelter."

Count von Bernstorff sensed the political damage, following so soon after the Archibald revelations. On November 16, the day of the Bielaski/Rathom/Goricar conference in New York, the German ambassador complained bitterly to Secretary of State Lansing:

> The continuation of the baseless attacks on myself and the colleagues of my embassy in the columns of the Providence Journal impels me to ask whether your excellency cannot see your way to make it clear that these attacks are not countenanced by the American government. Such slanders against the representatives of a friendly power who have the right to claim the protection

and hospitality of the United States authorities would be incom-
prehensive, were it not a matter of common knowledge that the
Providence Journal is a "hyphenated" Anglo-American paper.

Lansing never replied. Instead, two weeks later, he informed the ambassador that Boy-Ed and Papen were no longer welcome in the United States.
They would have to leave.

The Wilson administration did not detail why the diplomats were being
recalled. The press consensus was that the decision was based on a cumula-
tion of scandals. Rathom published an explanation, reprinted on the front
page of the *New York Times*, that Boy-Ed was sent home for his link to the
passport fraud operation, his connection to the phony affidavit/tugboat
scheme, and his alleged association with the Huerta plot in Mexico—all
related to stories Rathom had broken or advanced.

Boy-Ed's seething farewell attack on Rathom, handed out to reporters
at that chaotic scene on the Hoboken pier, inspired a sense of pride among
Rathom's former colleagues. The *San Francisco Chronicle* reminded its
readers that the famous spy hunter was a *Chronicle* alum: "Some sleuth he
was, too, in those days."

Rathom wrote that Papen was ordered home because the Archibald
documents linked him to labor schemes at US munitions plants, and the
fact that Papen had sent with Archibald two coded letters, for which
the US government had not been given the key. Rathom acquired from
his British sources a copy of one of Papen's ciphers, a menacing cluster
of letters and numbers. Rathom shared the letter with the *New York
Times*, where it appeared "By Courtesy of The Providence Journal," on
December 4, the day the decision to recall Boy-Ed and Papen became
public.

Papen departed New York for Germany on December 22. "Certain
newspapers have made reckless charges which could not be supported by
evidence," he said in his good-bye message, "but the United States government never intimated that it believed these charges to be true. To this I have
nothing to add," he said, and then added, "After all this war will not be won

by the *Providence Journal* and the *Evening Telegram* with their hyphenated supporters. It will be decided by the success of invincible German arms."

The British government guaranteed safe passage to Germany for Boy-Ed and Papen—but not for their stuff. When Papen's ship docked at Falmouth for inspection, the British confiscated the documents he carried. Papen, for some reason, had entered the war zone with self-incriminating paperwork.*

The paperwork included checks written to saboteurs, such as $700 to Werner Horn on January 18, two weeks before Horn bombed the Vanceboro railroad bridge. Other checks linked Papen to the bombing attempts against the Welland Canal. Some letters discussed the effectiveness of bombs against trains. One was a long screed by a supporter blasting the *Providence Journal*. "This lying sheet has made charge after charge since the inception of the war," complained the writer, N. Lindheim (probably Norvin Lindheim, a lawyer for the German embassy).

Papen also had a letter from George Sylvester Viereck raging over Papen's ejection from the United States. Viereck promised to forgo any further "restraint" and to increase the volume of his crusade for "justice and fair play" for Germany.

High on Viereck's to-do list: destroy Germany's chief tormentor in the American press, John R. Rathom.

❖

On December 29, 1915, the front cover of Viereck's *Fatherland* carried a banner headline: THE MYSTERY OF JOHN REVELSTOKE RATHOM, PRESIDENT WILSON'S CONFIDANT.

The story began:

Why does President Wilson countenance the reprehensible acts of John Revelstoke Rathom? How comes it that this man, who

---

* Hard not to think of the television series *The Wire*: "You taking notes on a criminal fucking conspiracy?"

holds no position of recognized consequence, enjoys the confidence of the Administration and the members of the Cabinet?

Who is Rathom? A man of British birth, sprung from obscurity, who obtained a fleeting notoriety years ago in San Francisco in an unpleasant "poisoned cherry" scandal.

Rathom is the editor of a newspaper in a small New England city, the Providence *Journal*. But he is rarely in Providence. He makes his headquarters in New York City, at the Hotel Astor and the Hotel Manhattan. And we see this man hiring spies, investigators, secret agents, who dog the diplomatic representatives of the countries with whom the United States is at peace, *but England is at war.* We see him handing out for publication private correspondence admittedly stolen from diplomats. We see him trying to inflame public opinion against the enemies of his native land.

The *Fatherland* called for Congress to investigate Rathom. The story also drilled down into the man. It flung more sordid details from the sixteen-year-old poisoned cherry fiasco in Rathom's face, and reported that "many of Rathom's statements about his biography are under dispute by various persons." Viereck came as close to the imposter's secrets as anyone had ever done, though he could not land a knockout blow.

❖

Around midday on November 7, 1915, in the Mediterranean Sea off the coast of Tunisia, passengers on the Italian liner *Ancona* were just getting to lunch. The *Ancona* was two days into a voyage from Naples to New York, carrying about five hundred people.

Suddenly, a submarine broke through the dour sea. The sub flew the red-white-red standard of the Austro-Hungarian navy. It blasted a cannon shot ahead of the liner to warn it to stop. Instead, the captain ordered the *Ancona* to flee. In the chase, the sub hit the ship three times with shells, before the liner stopped. The sub raised a flag commanding everyone to leave the ship before she was sunk.

Like on the *Falaba* back in March, the evacuation was hasty and chaotic. Lifeboats put into the sea while the liner was still moving immediately capsized. One group of passengers was simply too scared to move and refused to leave. The submarine encouraged them with another shell into the *Ancona*'s prow, but that only made the panic worse.

The submarine captain sensed he had spent too much time sitting vulnerable on the water's surface. He had given the passengers a chance to live, and they had refused. He submerged his boat and torpedoed the liner. The *Ancona* disappeared beneath the waves, taking those who failed to evacuate. The exact death toll is unknown; one estimate says about two hundred people died, including at least nine Americans.

The sinking plunged the United States and Austria-Hungry into a diplomatic crisis, similar to the crises with Germany after the sinkings of the *Lusitania* and the *Arabic*. In this case, though, the United States treated the incident as a first strike against Austria, despite press speculation that the incident was a German "false flag" attack. President Wilson demanded Austria-Hungry denounce the sinking and pay compensation for Americans killed and wounded.

In December 1915, Rathom published a story about the *Ancona* that risked bringing the United States directly into the war. Again quoting Goricar, a former Austrian diplomat, Rathom reported "it is common knowledge" at German and Austrian consulates in the United States that the submarine that sank the *Ancona* was in fact a German U-boat, falsely flying an Austrian flag "as a cloak for Germany's crimes."

It was an outrageous accusation, yet it passed with hardly a national ripple. Goricar was Austrian, so he might be biased. And the Austro-Hungarian government had taken responsibility and denounced the attack.

Except that Rathom was right—it *was* a false flag attack. The sub that sank the Italian liner was the German *U-38*, flying Austria's flag because in late 1915, Germany was technically not at war with Italy, while

Austria-Hungary was. Austria took the rap for the sinking to prevent a cratering of US-German relations that likely would have led to war.*

"That piece of deception is the critical act of the *Ancona* incident," wrote the historian Gerald Davis in the *Journal of Modern History*. "It prevented one of the most explosive issues of the period of American neutrality from taking form and postponed a showdown on the submarine issue."

Had more Americans believed Rathom's report, the United States might have entered the war more than a year sooner, and changed history in ways we might not even imagine.

---

* The United States confirmed the sub was German in 1925.

CHAPTER 12
Good Friends/High Places

The winter sun had been down for hours. It was a cold night in Ottawa, Ontario. Hard snow lingered on the grounds of the grandiose Parliament Building, seat of the Canadian government, perched on a bluff above the Ottawa River.

The people's business on the legislative calendar that evening was light and a bit dull. Samuel Francis Glass, MP, a member of the House of Commons, let himself into the Parliament reading room around quarter to nine. Glass was fifty-five, clean-shaven, and wore his hair parted straight up the middle. He perused the shelves of newspapers for fresh editions from London. Finding none, he grabbed that afternoon's copy of the *Ottawa Evening Journal*, February 3, 1916, a Thursday, and settled down at a long table to catch up with the news.

There were six long tables in the reading room, laid out in a row. Horizontal shelves installed under the tables held all sorts of newspapers. Around the room, books and more periodicals were organized—in some cases simply piled—on even more shelving. Just about all the fittings in the room were made from soft white pine; dry old wood oiled and varnished to a sheen.

The top headline in the *Evening Journal* reported speculation that President Woodrow Wilson had sent an envoy to Germany to try to broker peace in Europe. Glass devoured the gossipy political notes column on the front page, perhaps looking for his own name—no luck there—and then became engrossed in a story about the *Appam*, a British steamship captured at sea by the Germans, when suddenly he felt a whoosh of heat passing alongside of him, as if somebody had flicked the switch of a hot air blower.

Glass turned and caught a whiff of burning paper. Flames flickered from a file of newsprint beneath the next table. Glass threw up his hands and called out, but the caretaker was not in the room. The MP ran to the door and shouted for the constable in the hall to get a fire extinguisher. In those precious seconds, the fire became too big for one person to put out. Flames spread with startling speed out of the reading room and into corridors ornamented with polished, highly flammable wood paneling.

In the chamber of the House of Commons, a couple dozen members wearily debated a proposal related to retail fish prices when the chief doorkeeper burst in and shouted, "There is a big fire in the reading room! Everybody get out quickly!"

A big fire? None of the members smelled fire. They calmly gathered their things and locked their desks. When they opened the door to leave, choking black smoke poured into the chamber. The members of Parliament and the spectators in the gallery had to run for their lives, hands over their faces, through a hot death fog. A newsman crawled from the gallery on his hands and knees. A worker cut a portrait of Queen Victoria from its frame and sprinted it to safety just ahead of the conflagration. The Canadian prime minister, overwhelmed by smoke, was helped from the building by a page boy.

The automatic fire alarm struck at 8:57 P.M. Two minutes later, firefighters in an engine truck pulled onto Parliament Hill. The center block of the Parliament Building loomed over them in Italian Gothic splendor, like "an old-world cathedral city rising free from its bastioned hill," the *Star-Phoenix* newspaper of Saskatchewan reported. The building was 470 feet long, three stories high, and ornamented with towers and turrets, like a cross between a palace and a fortress, built from cream-colored sandstone accented with red stone over the doors and windows. Above the main entrance rose the two-hundred-foot Victoria Tower, "surmounted by a great iron crown over which the Union Jack floated when Parliament was in session."

Fire broke through the roof. It was beyond control.

Survivors clambered down rescue ladders. Others repelled from windows on ropes made from knotted towels. People threw themselves from the building into nets held by firemen.

The flames lit the night sky like a slice of the sun. Thousands of citizens from the neighborhoods of Ottawa were drawn like moths. They stood hypnotized, in the bitter cold, watching the fire destroy the jewel of their city and a symbol of their nation.

The Victoria Tower put up a hard fight against the irresistible fire. As a reporter from the *Ottawa Citizen* witnessed:

> First the flames could be seen steadily creeping up foot by foot, each successive row of tiny windows changing from darkness into yellow blaze. Then the flames struck the winding stairs above the tower room and the fire shot up the superstructure bursting out of every opening in the edifices. With flames all around it, the old clock kept up "Business as Usual," and struck out the midnight hour.

The tower clock stopped at twenty past twelve, and then at 1:21 A.M. the guts of the tower gave way and the clock's cast-metal bell plunged to the earth.

By morning light, the breathtaking scope of the destruction was clear, and all of Canada was in anguish. Only the attached Library of Parliament building was saved; protected by a steel door that had sealed out the flames.

Two women visiting Parliament as guests of the speaker and his wife suffocated in the smoke. A police officer and two men holding a water hose were crushed when a stone tower collapsed in the inferno. The remains of a law clerk would be discovered in the ruins. The seventh and final body recovered from the rubble would be that of Bowman Brown Law, MP, a Massachusetts native who grew up in Nova Scotia.

The ruins were still smoldering when newspapers across Canada delivered another jolt to their shell-shocked readers.

A rabble-rousing editor in distant Providence, Rhode Island, was claiming he had notified the Department of Justice three weeks before the fire that German spies were plotting to destroy the Canadian Parliament.

Yet no warning ever made it to Ottawa.

❖

John Rathom's claim resounded in hundreds of headlines across the United States and Canada, though his story was frustratingly vague. It came in a short preface to an article on the destruction of the Parliament Building:

> The Providence Journal three weeks ago notified the Department of Justice that it had received information directly through employees of the German embassy that the Parliament Houses of Ottawa, Rideau Hall, the home of the Governor-General of Canada at Ottawa, and large munitions plants in Ontario were to be the next objects of German attack on this continent, in the order named.

The Canadian press was incredulous. Who had received this warning? How had they acted on it? Rathom had not specified which nation's Department of Justice he had notified; Canada had one, too. Canadian officials were emphatic: *Nobody told us anything*.

Reporters interrogated US attorney general Thomas Watt Gregory, who had no clue what Rathom was talking about. Gregory informed the press he had not heard from Rathom in two months. Unnamed justice officials leaked to reporters that the department had no affidavits or other paperwork to substantiate Rathom's claim.

It soon began to look like Rathom made it up.

The editor's entire identity was a lie, but he would not stand to be accused of telling one. On February 5, Rathom sent a furious telegram to Attorney General Gregory: "We are greatly concerned and humiliated by your statement yesterday to several newspaper men in Washington, practically charging the Providence Journal with falsehoods."

Gregory answered Rathom privately, saying he had only told the truth—he had heard nothing from Rathom or anybody else about a planned attack on the Canadian Parliament.

To protect himself, Rathom publicly outed H. Snowden Marshall, the US attorney for the Southern District of New York, as the official he had warned about an attack on Parliament.

Reporters tracked down Marshall, who acknowledged Rathom had mentioned something or other about German sabotage in Canada about three weeks earlier, but that Marshall had been under the impression that Rathom had *already* notified the Department of Justice, and since the matter had nothing to do with the Southern District of New York, Marshall "paid no further attention to it."

By exposing Marshall, Rathom shed the bad light off himself and cast it onto the Department of Justice. A high-level US official had been forewarned of an alleged terror plot that killed seven and came within a frantic minute of wiping out the government of a friendly nation, and yet by some stupid misunderstanding nobody had warned Canada.

It is a measure of how high Rathom's public star had risen and how valuable the government believed he could be that after Rathom gave the Department of Justice such a black eye, the department's response was not to back away from the editor but to tighten its clandestine relationship with him.

Before the week was out, Bureau of Investigation chief Bruce Bielaski and John Rathom would agree to cooperate on an unusual joint venture. Together, the lawman and the imposter planned a secret intelligence-gathering operation. They would collaborate on an undercover sting to flush out more clues about pending attacks by German saboteurs.

The target of the sting was the secret source who had warned Rathom that the Canadian Parliament would be attacked.

On the evening of Saturday, February 5, barely forty-eight hours after the Parliament fire, two Bureau of Investigation special agents sent by Bielaski arrived at offices of the *Providence Journal*. With Rathom's guidance, the agents planted a Dictaphone microphone in his office, and then threaded the cables to a hidden listening post in another part of the building, where the agents could eavesdrop on a conversation between Rathom and his secret source.

Rathom's role in the sting would be to coax his source into revealing operational details about upcoming plots, and if the source happened to incriminate some German spies while the Bureau of Investigation special agents listened on the line, that was gravy.

Everyone took their places the next morning, Sunday, February 6.

At 10:30 A.M., the target of the sting strolled into the *Journal* office, blasting people with his thousand-watt smile. It was Rathom's old frenemy, the North Carolina confidence man, Agent E-13—Gaston Means.

❖

After winning the confidence of the Department of Justice over the second half of 1915, Rathom entered the new year with an unrestricted secret backchannel to Chief Bielaski. Information and rumor flowed both ways between the men.

On January 3, 1916, for instance, Bielaski sent Rathom information about an individual the editor was investigating, a US representative for a German electric device company.

"Harry Perissi, in whom you are interested, arrived in New York on the Steamer Rotterdam December 23rd," Bielaski wrote to Rathom, disclosing the businessman's business to the bureau's press ally. The Bureau of Investigation also had interest in Perissi as a potential spy; Bielaski had just received a field report from a special agent who watched the customs inspection of Perissi's bags at the docks in Hoboken,

New Jersey. Bielaski informed Rathom: "He apparently had nothing with him of interest."[*]

The very next day, January 4, Rathom appealed to Bielaski for a gigantic favor, though not for a news story this time. This request was personal . . .

Rathom's paranoia about the infiltration of German spies in America was sincere. He saw spies everywhere, including in his own offices. Rathom believed Germany had an agent inside the *Providence Journal*. He had convinced himself that the head of the *Journal*'s photo engraving department, a Massachusetts-born tradesman named Arthur L. Artesani, was a covert German agent.

"As you know, I have been worried for some months over the belief that we were so unfortunate as to have in our employ a hired agent of the German Secret Service," Rathom wrote to Bielaski. "I have now reached the point where I must ask you to do all in your power to help me in connection with this man."

Rathom believed that Artesani was moonlighting as the editor of a new "bitterly pro-German" weekly newspaper in Rhode Island called the *Cranston Citizen*. He alleged that Artesani had been mailing copies of the *Citizen* to the German embassy in Washington, and that every Friday he sent a registered letter from Providence to Count von Bernstorff, the German ambassador, in an envelope sealed with red wax.

Rathom presumed that *he* was the subject of those secret letters.

"What I want to ask you is whether you can possibly let me know in a general way the contents of the next of these letters to be sent?" Rathom asked Bielaski.

Bielaski's direct response is not recorded, but we know he took a hard pass at intercepting the mail of a US citizen based on no actual evidence, because Rathom was "bitterly disappointed" by Bielaski's answer. "I have felt that, under the circumstances, the government puts itself in a rather

---

[*] Federal authorities would arrest Perissi with two other men in June 1917, accusing them of espionage in a plot to smuggle information out of the United States, through Mexico, to Berlin.

helpless position with regard to espionage of this character if it does not fight fire with fire," Rathom complained to Bielaski on January 8.

Rathom pleaded: Was there nothing Bielaski could do?

Sure, there was—these were the benefits of good friends in high places.

The Bureau of Investigation chief ordered a covert federal investigation into a possible "neutrality violation" by the head of the *Providence Journal*'s photo engraving department. On January 10, 1916, Bielaski sent a coded telegram to his special agents in Boston:

> Confer Rathom Providence Journal concerning his letter [January] eighth to me. Arrange any practical way secure access documents possession alleged German Agent.

Thirty-five-year-old Art Artesani of Cranston, Rhode Island, did not know it, but on his boss's suspicions alone, the chief of the Bureau of Investigation, US Department of Justice, was now referring to him as "alleged German Agent."

In an interview with one of Bielaski's investigators, Rathom claimed his desk had been broken into and his mailed tampered with. No, he didn't have any proof it was Artesani, but who else would it be? He insisted the federal agents search the offices of the *Cranston Citizen*, because no doubt Artesani would have kept copies of whatever letters he had sent to Count von Bernstorff.

The puzzled agent asked the obvious question: If you believe your employee is a German spy, why haven't you fired him?

"When I get ready to discharge Artesani," Rathom raged, "I will have one of the greatest newspaper stories that was ever published in this county. I will charge the German embassy at Washington with being directly responsible for Artesani's employment at the Providence Journal."

Bielaski next directed his agents to interview postal officers in Providence and Washington, including the carrier who delivered the mail to the German embassy, to determine if Rathom's employee had indeed been sending mail to the ambassador. "Please give this matter special attention and let me hear a report as early as practicable," Bielaski ordered his men.

On January 25, a post office official in Washington, DC, called a bureau agent to view a suspicious package. It was twelve inches long by two inches wide, an inch deep, and quite heavy, as it if contained rolled newspapers or other documents. It was tied with twine and sealed with red wax. The package was addressed to Count von Bernstorff at the Imperial German Embassy. The return address was from A. L. Artesani, Cranston, Rhode Island.

"I was advised by the Chief of the Bureau that no further action be taken in this matter," the agent said in his report, which did not say whether the bureau opened the package.

On February 4, a month after Rathom had first asked for help, Bielaski reported to the editor—yes, you might have a spy. "The matter seems to be about as you suspected in this particular case," Bielaski wrote to Rathom. "Please do not make any reference in your paper to the fact that this matter has been taken up with the Department."

Bureau of Investigation archives record no further action in the case. There was no law against writing columns favorable to Germany—not yet. If Rathom was waiting for Artesani to slip up so he could fire him, he did not live to see the day. Artesani's career at the *Providence Journal* continued into the 1940s, two decades after Rathom's death. He got his kid on the newspaper's payroll, too.

❖

By early 1916 Rathom's reputation as a spy hunter had grown so big, the Department of Justice found itself swimming in his wake.

Three weeks after the Canadian Parliament fire, on February 27, Rathom splashed on his front page what purported to be documentation of an Austrian government bribe to a Czech-language newspaper in the United States. It came in the form of a letter, signed by an Austrian diplomat in Washington, Baron Erich Freiherr Zwiedinek von Südenhorst, a typo waiting to happen, known in the US press for brevity's sake as Baron Zwiedinek.

Rathom charged that the letter "conclusively proves that Baron Zwiedinek is continuing in greater measure than ever before his gifts of money to various alleged 'neutral' newspapers printed in the Bohemian language, for the purpose of promoting German and Austrian propaganda in every possible way."

That was certainly how it looked. The note from Baron Zwiedinek directed Austrian consulate officials in Chicago to pay bribes to subvert an influential Bohemian newspaper in that city, the weekly *Vesmir*. The letter was titled: "Concerning the Subvention for the Weekly Vesmir." *Subvention* is an old-fashioned word for a government payment. It was an oddly descriptive title for a memo about paying bribes. Suspiciously so.

The letter stated that the Austrian government "decided to continue to pay a monthly subvention of $200 to the above-mentioned paper." The letter instructed the consulate general to "hand the enclosed check for $800 to Dr. Frank Iska," *Vesmir*'s publisher, "as a further subvention for the months of January, February, March and April, 1916." That would be about $20,000 in today's money.

Other papers picked up Rathom's story and a national scandal rained down over Baron Zwiedinek. The diplomat claimed the letter was "a fabrication of whole cloth." But who would believe that?

Frank Iska, publisher of the *Vesmir*, denied ever receiving one dime in bribes from anyone. But who would believe that? For Iska, Rathom's story was more than bad press, it was a health hazard. Iska was besieged with death threats from local Czechs who thought he was an Austrian collaborator. How mad were these people? One threat warned: "Burning up is a death too sweet for thee; into four pieces thou shouldst be torn and to swine thou pieces shouldst be left fed."

Iska, age fifty-two, was a native of Bohemia, like Rathom's trusted source, Emanuel Voska. Iska was a former Catholic priest who had studied law in Vienna and became a political agitator. He visited the United States in the early 1900s on a lecture tour about the historic struggles of the Bohemian people. A sketch of him from 1903 showed a thick-necked man with heavy dark eyebrows and a black Vandyke. He moved to the

United States around 1904, and founded his Bohemia newspaper about five years later.

The US government answered Rathom's story by immediately launching an urgent investigation into the Baron Zwiedinek letter and the alleged bribe. Rathom had the Department of Justice on a string. He tugged and the country's most powerful law enforcement organization came running.

Iska told the Bureau of Investigation he suspected the letter was a setup by a zealous faction of the Bohemian community. This faction wanted Iska to use his influence to persuade Bohemians in Austria-Hungary to rebel against their government. Iska urged a more moderate course; he thought open defiance of the Austrian government would bring only harassment and violence.

A second prong of the BOI investigation focused on whether the letter was authentic. Bielaski personally borrowed Rathom's copy, which was in fact only a photograph of a typewritten letter. Federal agents acquired writing samples from every typewriter in the Austro-Hungarian embassy in Washington. The samples were analyzed by a typeface expert, to determine if any of the embassy machines could have produced the alleged Baron Zwiedinek letter. After two months of meticulous study, the expert concluded that the letter had been typed on an L. C. Smith & Bros. typewriter with an imperfection in the lowercase *a* that caused the letter to smear. None of the machines in the embassy were a match. A second analysis concluded that the embassy letterhead on the bribe letter was of an older style no longer in use.

Ultimately, the Bureau of Investigation concluded the letter was a forgery.

Iska's enemies had used John Rathom, the preeminent source of news about German and Austrian plots, to destroy an innocent man's reputation and embarrass the Austrian government. Rathom's obsession with German and Austrian intrigue made it impossible for him to question whether the information could have been faked.

The Bureau of Investigation publicly announced that the letter was forged but kept the evidence secret. Nobody could get the details—not even Rathom, who tried to get them through Bielaski. Without these details, Iska could not shake the stink of suspicion. He begged for a public exoneration in plaintive open letters to President Wilson. He never got one. Even worse, the postmaster general suppressed the *Vesmir* in early 1918 under the Trading with the Enemy Act, according to Bureau of Investigation files.

Iska had to sell his printing office "at considerable loss."

Meanwhile, the people who had cast Iska into the grinding gears of history simply moved on and never looked back. No one was ever held responsible for the forgery. But we can guess about who did it. Iska's more conservative approach to challenging Austria-Hungary put him at odds with Emanuel Voska's Bohemian National Alliance. Bureau of Investigation files speculate that the group was behind the forgery. Voska may have use the "spy hunter" he helped create to take down a political adversary.

❖

Rathom and Gaston Means remained in touch even after Means conned Rathom in the spring of 1915 into publishing the false exposé about British ships being coaled out of New York Harbor. The Department of Justice was aware of their ongoing relationship. Bielaski told the attorney general that Means's duties as a paid German agent included "keeping watch on Rathom of the Providence Journal and giving him misinformation."

So that's why Means stayed in touch with Rathom. But why would Rathom take his calls? By November 1915, at the latest, Rathom understood that Means was working for the Germans and was therefore unreliable. Rathom told Bielaski that he had to divide everything Means told him into two piles: "that which is of value and that which is deliberately given . . . to mislead."

Rathom put up with Means because Agent E-13 was dimples-deep into the German propaganda machine and had access to information Rathom would do anything to get. Means was like a slot machine. He strung Rathom along with the occasional nugget, while maintaining the aura of a potential jackpot to keep Rathom from walking away.

In the days after the Canadian Parliament fire, Rathom finally saw a way to beat the house. He arranged the sting with Bielaski to trick Means into revealing details of pending sabotage plots the Department of Justice could investigate.

It was an odd spot for Rathom. He and Means were clearly friendly. They had traits in common, such as innate aptitude for lies and grifting. Game recognizes game. The war, however, had driven John Rathom and Gaston Means down different paths. Rathom saw the First World War as his call to be something bigger. It was his opportunity to attain the made-up greatness of his own fake identity. Means, on the other hand, saw the war in terms of what it was worth to his bank account.

By joining the feds in a sting against Means, Rathom was selling out a confidential source in the worst way possible. There are almost no words to describe the magnitude of the sin against journalism. Here again, Rathom is acting more like a spy than a newsman. Rathom knew that Means could go to prison if he happened to incriminate himself during the sting. If the thought troubled Rathom, he managed to put it aside. Means's liberty was a price Rathom was willing to pay.

When Means arrived at the *Providence Journal* on February 6, Rathom sat him down in his bugged office. Two Bureau of Investigation special agents, along with Rathom's secretary, taking notes for a transcript, listened in as Rathom went hard at Agent E-13:

> RATHOM: Well, you people have pulled it off again according to schedule. If you know any of the exact facts as to how the Ottawa fire started, I mean what mechanical means were used, I want you to tell me.
>
> MEANS: Well, I told you over the telephone about the firebomb in the library and if you want to know anything about the way

in which some of the flames were spread through the corridors, get your friends in Ottawa to see if they can save out some of the fire extinguishers and see what is in them.

RATHOM: What do you mean by that?

MEANS: I mean that with the aid of one man in the office of the superintendent of the building, a lot of these extinguishers were substituted for others with the outside cases exactly the same, and filled with benzine or gasoline.

Means invented that amazing detail. There had been nothing wrong with the fire extinguishers in the Parliament Building. But what a diabolical lie. So specific and outrageous. With the facts unknown at the time, it sparkled with *potential truth* that reinforced Rathom's belief that German agents were homicidal thugs. The best lies merely tickle our own inner biases.

Rathom argued that a reckoning was coming for German saboteurs, and that Means should get on the right side of it.

Means scoffed:

MEANS: Germany is a thousand times right. She has a perfect right to burn and destroy everything in Canada she can lay her hands on. This is war, not a tea party.

RATHOM: I am simply saying that your German friends cannot go to Canada from the United States and make whatever war they want to on the public buildings there.

Both men spoke as if there was no question that the Germans were responsible for burning down the Parliament Building. But it is unclear to this day whether sabotage had anything to do with it. The cause of the disaster was never identified. A royal commission investigated the blaze for months, exploring every theory. The commission asked Rathom to give testimony in Ottawa, but he refused. Instead, he sent the commission a statement that essentially repeated what he had published in the newspaper.

The investigation found "many circumstances connected with this fire that lead to a strong suspicion of incendiarism," according to the commission's report, but no definitive proof the fire was set.

A paid German agent had told Rathom ahead of time the building would be attacked—that is pretty good circumstantial evidence of arson. A cigar bomb tucked under a pile of newspapers would have done it. On the other hand, Means was a one-man disinformation factory. He could easily have invented the Parliament plot, like so many of the fantastic stories he spun to Rathom, only to be shockingly proven right by a carelessly discarded cigar. Means may have been the rooster taking credit for the sunrise.

Their discussion continued:

> MEANS: What do you mean in your editorial this morning by using the word *vandalism* in connection with the destruction of the Ottawa Parliament Building? It is not vandalism. This is war and it is the duty of every German in this country to make war on Canada . . . I deny the scruples of nations, and if a few people have to die by the destruction of a public building, that is the fortune of war.

> RATHOM: Well, there is just one thing, Means. Just as sure as you are born, you ought to be square in this matter and act like a decent American citizen and go tell authorities all you know.

> MEANS: Isn't everything I told you up to date absolutely true?

> RATHOM: No, it isn't. You have tried deliberately two or three times to throw me off the scent.

The two men then fell into an argument about the tall tales Means had woven for Rathom in the past, such as the whopper that German diplomats paid a bribe to have William Jennings Bryan removed as secretary of state.

Finally, Means got to pending plots against Canada:

MEANS: You ask me why Germany didn't start earlier [with sabotage] in Canada? It took them a long time to perfect the system there and now it is perfected. Now listen and I will tell you what's going to happen.

[Means consults his notebook]

Montreal and Toronto will be the first to go by fire. After that, explosions are planned for Vancouver and Winnipeg, in that order.

RATHOM: What about the new government buildings in Montreal?

MEANS: They are not out to destroy a few buildings. They will destroy the whole city.

At this point, Means swerved the conversation into a pointless round-about of lies and grievance. Out of nowhere he accused Secretary of State Lansing of passing sensitive information to the Germans.

Rathom was unmoved by the bullshit. He sheepdogged Means back on track:

RATHOM: Now let's get down to tacks about this present Canadian situation. Do you know today of any public buildings in Canada that are still to be destroyed?

MEANS: All right. Put this down. The city of Toronto and the city of Montreal will be destroyed by fire on the same day as soon as the high winds late in this month or early March begin

in Canada. You don't realize the way these people go about
their business. They have even taken the meteorological observations of the past twenty years to show them about what dates
they can expect the beginning of the high winds, and I tell
you they have copped out all the plans necessary to give them
full information about the reservoir system and water mains,
especially in Montreal, which is three times more vulnerable in
this way as Toronto.

Water mains in Montreal *three times more vulnerable?* Means was making
up these details as he went along. None of the things he predicted came to
pass. It is an open question, though, whether the whole story was nonsense,
or these were real aspirational plots that were later abandoned.

Means's information was maddeningly vague, leaving the Bureau of
Investigation no solid leads to investigate. Yet the federal government
treated the information gravely. The Department of Justice dispatched
Bielaski to hand deliver the transcript of the Rathom/Means conversation
to the counselor for the Department of State, "in order that you might, if
you deem it desirable, communicate such portions of this statement as seem
proper to the officials of the countries concerned."

After the sting, Rathom warned Bielaski that Means might try to
leave the country. He asked if Means had applied for a passport. Bielaski
answered on February 8, writing to Rathom as he would to a colleague.

"No application has been made by any one in the name of Gaston B.
Means for a passport," the bureau chief said. "Have you a good photograph
of this gentleman or can you obtain one on some pretext. If you have one or
could get one, would you send us a copy, as possession of this photograph
will make it more difficult for him to get a passport under some name
other than is own."

Rathom wrote back, "Will see what I can do."

They were a team, after all.

With friends in such high places, it was tempting to think one could
get away with anything.

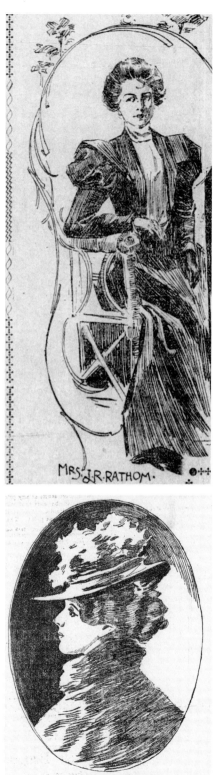

TOP LEFT: The Imposter—writer and editor John Revelstoke Rathom, photographed around 1918. Courtesy of *The Providence Journal-USA TODAY* Network. TOP RIGHT: The Imposter's wife, Mary Rathom. After she was betrayed by Rathom, she became a prolific poet in Western Canada. Courtesy of San Francisco Call, July 8, 1899. BOTTOM RIGHT: A newspaper sketch of the West Virginian who stole Rathom's heart, Florence M. Campbell, who became Rathom's wife in name, though not under the law. Sketch dates from the poisoned cherries fiasco. Courtesy of *Saint Paul Globe*, St. Paul, Minnesota, August 20, 1899.

The key characters of the poisoned cherries fiasco: Mary Rathom, a hangdog-looking John Rathom, Florence Campbell, and landlady Elsie Scheib. Courtesy of *The Call*, July 8, 1899.

ABOVE: Vanceboro bridge bomber Werner Horn, who risked capture so that he would not endanger innocent life. Courtesy of the Library of Congress. BELOW: The crew of the German submarine U-53 are on deck to greet the locals during the sub's surprise visit to Newport in 1916. Courtesy of the Library of Congress.

ABOVE: Archduke Franz Ferdinand, whose murder triggered the First World War. Courtesy of the Library of Congress. BELOW: The passenger liner *Lusitania*, thought to be too fast for any German submarine, shown docked in New York in 1907. Courtesy of the Library of Congress.

ABOVE LEFT: Karl Boy-Ed, the German Empire's naval attaché to the United States, and one of Rathom's favorite targets. Courtesy of the Library of Congress. ABOVE RIGHT: Count Johann Heinrich von Bernstorff, the German Empire's ambassador to the United States in the critical years before the U.S. entered the First World War. Courtesy of the Library of Congress. BELOW LEFT: Rathom's enemy in the pro-German press, journalist and poet George Sylvester Viereck. Photo from 1922. Courtesy of the Library of Congress. BELOW RIGHT: Franz von Papen, Germany's military attaché in the United States, who was as much spy and saboteur as a diplomat. Courtesy of the Library of Congress.

ABOVE: One of the most notorious criminals of his generation, Gaston B. Means, also known as German agent "E-13." Courtesy of the Library of Congress.

LEFT: *World's Work* Magazine launched a nationwide advertising campaign to promote Rathom's articles about his investigations into German spies. Courtesy of the *Chicago Tribune*, December 7, 1917.

ABOVE LEFT: US Attorney General Thomas Watt Gregory at first welcomed Rathom's help, and then ordered Rathom to be blackmailed into silence. Courtesy of the Library of Congress. ABOVE RIGHT: A. Bruce Bielaski, the head of the Bureau of Investigation, an inside source for Rathom, and then his tormentor. Courtesy of the Library of Congress. BELOW: The ticket to Rathom's 1917 speech in Boston, where the federal government began its blackmail campaign to shut Rathom's big mouth. Courtesy of FBI files, the National Archives.

On the trail of the Kaiser -

Pilgrim Publicity Association Dinner in Honor of

JOHN R. RATHOM

EDITOR AND GENERAL MANAGER PROVIDENCE JOURNAL

Speaker's Subject: Three Years of Germany's
War against the United States

Boston City Club, Wednesday, Nov. 21, 6:30 P. M.

Admission and Dinner, $2.50   Table No. C8

Rathom offended the Wilson administration with his attacks on the 1920 Democratic presidential ticket, Ohio Gov. James Cox, left, and Franklin Delano Roosevelt. Shown here in Washington after meeting with Wilson. Courtesy of the Library of Congress.

Was the rumor true that Rathom tried to take his own life after his firing in Astoria? He contributed a suicide poem for this drawing in the San Francisco *Call*. Courtesy of *The Call*, January 21, 1900.

CHAPTER 13

The Creation of John Revelstoke Rathom, Part 3: Tried by Fire

Years before Rathom could prove himself as a clandestine counterspy partner for the nation's top cop, he had to prove himself once again as a journalist, under some of the hardest circumstances imaginable.

On the brisk afternoon of December 30, 1903, on Randolph Street, in the heart of Chicago's commercial district, the Iroquois Theater drew another capacity crowd, mostly mothers and their young children, still on Christmas break. It was a magnificent theater, just five weeks old, looking from the street like the edifice of an exclusive bank for millionaires. Patrons filed in between towering stone pillars and beneath a high archway faced with glass.

The show onstage was *Mr. Blue Beard*, a silly musical and romantic comedy. It had charmed critics with lavish sets and costumes, a huge cast of singers and dancers, and the spectacular special effect of a flying ballerina—a dancer suspended on a wire who soared over the audience. It was the first major show staged at the new theater, and nearing the end of a successful run. After *Mr. Blue Beard* packed up in January, *Ben-Hur* was due to begin production.

During the second act, around 3:15 P.M., the house lights were down. Eight chorus girls and eight male dancers held attention to the stage. The orchestra blasted through a waltz called "Let Us Swear By the Pale Moonlight," and a lighting specialist bathed the stage in a dreamy moonlight effect.

The first sign of danger was a small tongue of flame on a stage curtain.

Close to two thousand people were inside the theater. They tapped their toes to the music and sang along with the cast, and then, in a matter of a maybe a minute, as the fire spread as fast as the eye could follow, panic drove them into a monstrous stampede.

The scope of the Iroquois Theater disaster is hard to comprehend—602 people were killed. It was then—and still is—the deadliest single building fire ever in the United States.

Every available reporter in Chicago jumped on the story. Journalists at the *Record-Herald* on Washington Street, three blocks from the theater, were close enough to hear the sirens. This was not just a news story; this tragedy would be etched forever into history. *Record-Herald* editors needed a writer for a nearly impossible deadline task—to take the dictated news feeds phoned in by reporters at the fire scene and the hospitals and weave these disjointed snapshots into an unbroken narrative that conveyed both the facts of the disaster and the overwhelming emotional power of the moment.

They assigned the job to a feature writer on the staff, still new to the *Record-Herald* after coming from San Francisco in the wake of scandal—John R. Rathom.

❖

There is a unique pressure in writing on deadline about a news event that will be in the history books. Time speeds up for the writer. The clock on the newsroom wall gobbles up the hours before publication. Editors hover about, their worried eyes silently screaming for progress. *Give us something to read!* The blank page (or the blank screen) waiting for words becomes an abyss, ready to swallow any sentence not profound enough to do justice to a news event bigger than the writer, bigger than anyone.[*]

Rathom dipped his pen and scratched out a deadline news lede for the ages:

> More than six hundred men, women and children met a fearful death at the new Iroquois Theater yesterday afternoon—tortured and incinerated by fire, suffocated by smoke and gasses, and crushed into nothingness by one another while struggling to escape the impending doom.

Rathom then led the reader through the disaster, moment by moment. First, a pop from a hot calcium light on stage, which ignited a curtain or a ribbon of tinsel. The star of the show, comedian Eddie Foy, a big name at the time, broke character to urge the audience to be calm. A fireproof asbestos curtain snagged when stagehands tried to lower it. Actors fleeing out the stage door fed fresh air into the auditorium, which the fire inhaled in an explosion that splashed flame across the ceiling. In seconds, Rathom wrote, "black, choking fumes beat down in a cloud of death from every wall."

"That was all," he wrote on. "Fear, uncontrollable and terrible, reigned. Men and women fought like wild beasts, filled only with the desire for self-preservation."

Babies slipped from their mothers' clutch and were crushed underfoot. Girls threw themselves off balconies and lay broken and wailing until suffocated by smoke. The lights went out. People thumped into walls. Bodies toppled into piles.

The story described rescue attempts, successful and not. And then Rathom brought the reader outside the theater, pulling back like a movie

---

[*] I stared into the abyss of the blank screen, juggling too many news feeds to count, on deadline as a reporter in the *Boston Globe* newsroom, on April 15, 2013, when domestic terrorists bombed the Boston Marathon.

camera, in passages that when I first read them clotted my chest with grief for strangers who lived far away and long ago:

> From every business street of the city, men, whose wives and families had gone to the matinee, streamed, with white faces and eyes blinded with half-frozen tears, over to the theater, and screamed like madmen the names of those they were seeking.
>
> Many of them found their loved ones safe, but still half-crazed, in surrounding stores and hotels; others discovered them among the dead, identified by some particle of dress, a half-charred hair ribbon, a shoe, or a locket. Others are still searching and will continue to search before they can finally assure themselves that the happiness of their lives has gone forever.

This is writing history on deadline: It is more than reporting what happened. It is to take the pain and sorrow of Chicago on that day in 1903, and put it into the hearts of readers in the next century. Rathom's Iroquois Theater story was a deadline masterpiece, crafted in a few hours under unthinkable pressure. This is why Rathom got so many second chances in journalism. He could flat-out *write*.

New doors would soon open for someone of his talent, offering new opportunities—and new troubles.

❖

Rathom was thirty-five at the time of the fire. He had moved to Chicago within months of the poisoned cherries debacle in San Francisco, probably in late 1899 or early 1900. With his wife, Mary, back in Canada, Rathom's lover, Florence Campbell, was on his arm when he arrived in the Midwest. John and Florence lived together in Chicago, pretending to be husband and wife. They could not legally marry, as Rathom was still wed to Mary. Their divorce was not finalized until 1909.

Rathom and Florence lived an austere life on a reporter's salary. In a letter to Florence in 1901, while she was visiting relatives back east, Rathom complained their apartment was cold and lacked hot water for three days. He asked Florence in another note how he should address letters to her while she was staying with her sister in Ohio. He wanted to know if Florence had told the sister she was going by the name Florence Rathom. There is no record that John and Florence ever married, but clearly Rathom loved her. "Oh, Florence," he wrote as her trip was ending, "I am more glad than I can tell you to know that on Monday night you will be in my arms again."

Exactly when Rathom joined the *Record-Herald* staff is hard to pinpoint. He published a Thanksgiving poem in the newspaper in 1899, when the paper was called the *Times-Herald*. The poem, about turkey hunting in Cuba, was not very good, but may have been his entry to a job. He started as a copyreader, but his talent was too big for a desk. By 1901 Rathom was a roving feature writer tackling an array of interesting assignments. He wrote a long explainer on the workings of the New York subway system. He profiled the sportswriter/gunfighter Bat Masterson, whom Rathom likely met while covering the Corbett-Fitzsimmons fight in Nevada in 1897. He interviewed Booker T. Washington, the educator and civil rights leader, about whom Rathom wrote, "Nobody who talks with him can ever fail to become impressed."

Rathom was fascinated by Chicago's ethnic groups and created a lecture on what he saw as the characteristics of each. He presented his talk with colored lantern slides, like a primitive film strip, to civic groups around the city in 1904 and early 1905, most likely for paid stipends. Little record of his presentation survives; most of what does is cringeworthy: The Greeks are good students. Scandinavians are wholesome. Italians "live on olive oil and macaroni."

But for all the denigrating racial stereotypes Rathom promulgated, there was one critical bias he argued against. Immigrants, contrary to conventional thinking, are generally *not* "of the criminal class," he insisted. The newest Americans were mostly peasants, he said, industrious and eager to work, sometimes driven to crime by desperation or bad environment.

Rathom still spent more money than he earned. Florence and he fled apartments in Chicago whenever they fell behind in their rent. They first lived a few miles south of downtown on Calumet Avenue, and then hopped among three flats on Superior Street. They ghosted one landlord, suddenly moving out while owing a month's rent and $5 borrowed. Their next landlord obtained a $10 week lien on Rathom's salary to get what he was due. The couple skipped out of yet another rental while the landlord was on vacation. Then they sold their furniture and "flitted from one boarding house to another."

Rathom left the *Record-Herald* sometime in early 1905. For the first time since he began playing the character of journalist John R. Rathom, the imposter left the newspapers business. He was lured by a fat salary to the advertising firm of Michaelis & Ellsworth, headquartered in the new Orchestra Hall on Michigan Avenue in downtown Chicago.

His new job was to produce black propaganda as fast as he could write it.

❖

In the summer of 1905, editors of rural newspapers around the Midwest began receiving regular correspondence from the mysterious firm of "Rathom & Crawford," which purported to be based in Omaha, Nebraska. In these packages were prewritten articles opposing bills in Congress that would regulate how railroad companies set prices for transporting freight. The editors were told they may publish the material for free.

Around the same time, a gifted public speaker by the name of John R. Rathom began appearing at county fairs and farm gatherings in Iowa, such as the Interstate Live Stock Fair and the Poweshiek County Agricultural Society. Rathom delivered beautifully crafted speeches to sun-scorched planters and ranch hands about the "farmer's best friend"—the railroads. He suggested that the *last thing* such a good friend needed was more government regulation.

It wasn't long before Midwest editors began asking in their pages: "Who is John R. Rathom?"

What the editors eventually learned was that Rathom was an agent for the most powerful corporations in America, the railroad companies—the Apple, Google, and Facebook of the early twentieth century. In an era before commercial flight and interstate highways, railroads were the one fast and secure way to ship goods around America's vast landscape. Railroad companies were routinely accused of colluding to keep freight rates high. President Theodore Roosevelt believed railroads had too much power, and at his urging Congress was considering bills to strengthen the government's hand to influence shipping rates.

Eager to beat back these bills, a number of major railroad companies quietly agreed to cooperate on a stealth campaign to shape public opinion against rate legislation. In May 1905 the companies established a black propaganda operation, which came to be known as the Railway Press Bureau. Based in Chicago and New York, and run by the Boston advertising firm Michaelis & Ellsworth, the press bureau offered big bucks to lure "scores" of energetic journalists out of America's newsrooms and into an organization that churned out reams of exquisitely written articles and opinion pieces opposing railroad regulation.

Beyond just writing propaganda, the Railway Press Bureau dispatched its agents to meet with small-town newspaper editors, offering in some cases to pay, secretly, to have bureau-written material printed as an unsigned editorial—the column normally reserved for the official position of the newspaper. Running as an editorial not only camouflaged the source of the piece, but bestowed upon the propaganda the accumulated credibility of the publication.

The railroad effort was aggressive and expensive. In Nebraska the *Central City Republican-Nonpareil* complained in the summer of 1905 that the shadowy firm of "Rathom and Crawford" delivered by mail "a dose of anti-railway regulation argument every twenty-four hours."

The muckraking journalist Ray Stannard Baker investigated the propaganda campaign. Baker was friendly with President Theodore Roosevelt. While Roosevelt was researching a speech to Congress on the railroad issue, he asked Baker if he knew a guy named Rathom and what he was doing in the Midwest.

"Rathom appears as the farmer's friend," Baker told the president, "not the hired railroad agent which he really is. His letterheads declare him a lecturer. Thus by deceit these publicity agents not only seek to influence public opinion, but they employ all the great leverage of the power of the railroads, their advertising, their passes, their political influence."

By midsummer, rural news editors came to suspect railroad money was behind the news blitz. Some mocked the campaign. Wisconsin's *La Crosse Tribune* recalled that the mysterious John Rathom had called railroad rate legislation "the most vicious measure" to ever come before Congress. "That's what John R. Rathom said to the farmers of Iowa," the paper asserted. "Of course John did not want it understood that he was doing his talking for the benefit of the railroads. Just for the farmers, of course."

Other newsmen undercut the campaign by writing openly that the railroads were trying to bribe them. "The editorial page of a newspaper is its soul," reported the Marshalltown, Iowa, *Times-Republican*, in October 1905. "The editor who sells it puts himself on the market as certainly as any hog or steer sold at the stockyards."

The paper predicted: "The trick will fail. It's hope of success lay in secrecy. Now that it has been uncovered popular opinion will take care of it."

Barely a month later, the prediction proved true. Once the facts of the scheme were widely known, no editor could publish the bureau's propaganda without appearing to be on the take. The press bureau laid off its pricy staff and shut down in November 1905, after six months in operation. The railroads reportedly poured $2 million into the campaign, about $60 million in today's money.

Rathom had gambled on a new venture with a big salary and was now out of a job. Of all the lessons he might have taken from the experience, the one that appeared to stick is that black propaganda is a magician's trick that depends on deception: the audience must never learn the true source of the material they are being fed.

He would carry this lesson into the last job he would ever have.

❖

The unemployed imposter stepped off the train in downtown Providence, Rhode Island, in March 1906, about four months after the Railway Press Bureau shuttered. Rathom had been job hunting, probably in New York, when he heard that a newspaper in Rhode Island lost a good chunk of its staff to a crosstown rival and was looking for experienced hands.

Rathom was thirty-seven. No longer the trim athlete from his twenties, he had ballooned to 260 pounds, give or take a British stone. His hairline had crept high up his forehead, and he parted his thin black hair far on the left side, practically above his ear.

There is no known record of what happened at Rathom's job interview at the *Providence Journal*.

The *Journal* was then a well-established paper, dating to 1829, respectable and staid, with ho-hum design aesthetics and a conservative personality left over from its service as a house organ of the Republican Party before the paper became politically independent in the late nineteenth century. Its direct audience was small, with a circulation of 17,466 daily and 20,146 on Sundays. The evening edition, the *Evening Bulletin*, had a daily circulation of 37,653.

Rathom left his interview with an offer to become managing editor, and a $200 advance on salary. He went home to the Midwest to gather his stuff and his pretend wife, and tend to one final task in Chicago: on March 25, Rathom raised his right hand and swore the oath to become a US citizen—notwithstanding the lies in his citizenship application about his name and when and where he arrived in the United States. Once John and Florence moved permanently to Providence, neither lived anywhere else full-time for the rest of their lives.

Providence today is about the 150th largest city in the United States by population, largely overlooked nationally, though underrated in the eyes of those who know it well. In Rathom's time, Greater Providence was much more influential, as a manufacturing power of cotton and wool goods, machine tools, base metals, jewelry, refined sugar and molasses, as well as an important eastern port. In 1900 Providence was the twentieth largest city in the country, roughly equivalent to Boston or Washington, DC, today. The capital of Rhode Island was a bustling, crowded hodgepodge of brick factories and foundries breathing through tall smokestacks. A field of railroad tracks splayed out downtown beneath a gleaming new state house made from white Georgia marble. Rathom settled on the city's East Side, where bankers and mill owners had built grand homes.

The tangled strands of Providence's DNA made it the ideal habitat for a morally flexible character such as John Revelstoke Rathom. Tiny Rhode Island has long produced an abundant share of both political corruption and oddball news stories, known in the business as "news of the weird." The place has been called Rogues' Island since the 1700s. To this day, its citizens take perverse pride in the comically inept exploits of the state's deep strategic reserve of hucksters, boneheads, and crooked pols.

It all goes back to the founding. Providence was established in 1636 by religious dissenter Roger Williams, after Williams was kicked out of Massachusetts Bay Colony for being annoying and disagreeable, and spouting radical ideas, such as treating Native Americans fairly.* Rhode Island evolved as a safe haven for religious heretics, which fostered a reverence for independence and a mistrust of outside meddling. On top of the Rhode Island State House dome stands an eleven-foot figure of bronze and gold, known as the Independent Man. He holds a spear and wears only a loincloth. Dress codes are tyranny.

In Rathom's time in the early twentieth century, Rhode Island quaked with stormy, ethnic-driven politics, in an era when different kinds of white people battled for power, largely Irish Catholic Democrats and Republican WASPs. Immigrants came in waves in the nineteenth century: French Canadians by train, Germans and Swedes by boat. Refugees from southern and eastern Europe followed near the end of the Gilded Age, bringing Portuguese, Armenians, Poles, Jews, and Italians. These groups settled in enclaves and clung to their old traditions, making Rhode Island more of

---

* In an abundance of caution, Massachusetts waited three hundred years before overturning its ban on Roger Williams.

a "mosaic" than a melting pot, wrote Rhode Island historian and author Patrick T. Conley.

"At century's end the streets of Rhode Island's major cities sounded with the babel of new tongues," Conley wrote. "Inner city neighborhoods and blocks took on old-world characteristics; parishes, ethnic congregations, and synagogues sprang up; factories flourished with the cheap and abundant labor these newcomers provided."

Newspaper competition was fierce in Rathom's era. Rhode Island was home to fifty-five regular news publications, including fourteen daily papers and twenty-five weeklies. Newsstands were all-you-can-read buffets. Among the Providence-based publications: the *Advance* was the newspaper for Black readers. The *Alba* and *Eco Del Rhode Island* were for Italians. The *Anzeiger* was for Germans. The *Bahag* was one of two papers for Armenians. The *Visitor* was for Roman Catholics. The *Issue* and the *Outlook* were for "drys" who wanted to outlaw booze. The *Journal* competed daily with the *Providence News* and the *Providence Tribune*, weekly with the *Rhode Island Examiner*, and monthly with *Corbett's Herald*.

Boston was an hour by train. At the time, nearly 700 newspapers were being published in Massachusetts, with the large ones on sale throughout Providence. Papers across the United States were linked by the national newswires. Newspapers were the medium that knitted the enormous country into a single whole. In 1915 about 23,000 publications delivered news to American readers, including 2,502 daily papers—twice the numbers of dailies today.

Into this cacophony of voices strode one talented, shameless imposter. To this job he brought a great gift for writing, a love of screaming black headlines and scorching editorials packed with rage and wit, and an inclination to throw bombs and make trouble. In 1912 the *Providence Journal* promoted Rathom to editor and general manager. There would be no meddlesome bosses looking over his shoulder. The guardrails were down. A notice of Rathom's promotion appeared in the industry journal *The Editor and Publisher*. With it was a picture of the imposter, perhaps the earliest surviving photograph of him. His hair is a bit unkempt and his youthful face is plumped in middle age. The notice read, "Mr. Rathom is one of the best known newspaper men in the country and enjoys the warm friendship of hundreds of members of his profession."

Less than two years later, in June 1914, Rathom plastered his front page with a story from the international wires. An obscure archduke and his wife had been assassinated in Sarajevo. War drums beat across the Atlantic. The actor playing the part of John R. Rathom threw himself into the role of a lifetime.

CHAPTER 14

Shock & Awe

On September 17, 1916, at the German naval station at Heligoland, an archipelago about forty miles off the coast of Germany, the attack submarine *U-53* glided from a berth into the North Sea, beginning a long, audacious, and top-secret journey ordered personally by Kaiser Wilhelm. The sub handled lethargically in the waves; she was so overloaded with supplies. It seemed every inch of free space had been stuffed with water, rations, extra fuel, and extra weapons. She carried six torpedoes, two more than normal; one of them was stored under the captain's bunk. For this special voyage, the *U-53* added two extra machinist's mates to keep the sub running, in addition to the standard crew of thirty-four men. Engineers who designed the U-boat had pegged its maximum range at five thousand miles, but on this mission the *U-53* may have to go twice that far.

The submarine traveled underwater for about ninety miles in the North Sea, to evade British warships, and then surfaced for much of the trip west, avoiding normal sea lanes toward the open ocean. Ventilation was bad on U-boats and everything was damp, including the bedding. The sailors passed a flu virus around. It seemed like something mechanical broke every day on the 213-foot sub—either the short-range radio antenna had to be fixed, or some oil leak repaired. The crew came within a couple minutes of drowning when an exhaust vent locked open during a dive and seawater poured into the starboard engine room.

The *U-53*'s mission was so secret its sailors had not been told where they were going.

Their commander, Lieutenant Hans Rose, was thirty-one years old. He was fit, leading-man handsome, and wore a vaguely sinister vertical goatee down the middle of his chin. He had originally hoped to command a destroyer, but switched to the submarine force in 1915 because the kaiser was reluctant to risk the German surface fleet in battle. "The underseas boats were the only ones getting into the fracas, and that's where I wanted to be," he later recalled.

Three days into the voyage, as the *U-53* entered the Atlantic, Rose called the crew together for an announcement. They met in the control room, "which was about as big as a suburban dining room and full of equipment," wrote Wellington Long, a United Press International chief correspondent in Germany, in 1966. Control wheels, dials, and valves stuck out from everywhere. "In the middle of the packed room was the gyroscopic compass, as big as a barrel, and the elevator for raising and lowering the periscope."

Rose finally told his men what they were doing: "We have been ordered to travel to the United States."

Kaiser Wilhelm had dispatched the *U-53* to introduce the U-boat to the American people, to prove that Germany's lethal submarines could appear anywhere, anytime, even under the nose of the US Navy.

"Convinced the Americans were essentially spineless, [Kaiser Wilhelm] reasoned that a German U-boat sally into a US naval harbor would be so intimidating as to keep the United States out of the war," Long wrote.

The commander of Germany's U-boat fleet, Commodore Hermann Bauer, chose Rose for the mission because the sub commander was both bold and methodical. Bauer personally assured Rose that after his show of German might in America, "the submarine weapon would be freed of its shackles." Germany would defy the United States and declare "unrestricted submarine warfare," the only way, Rose believed, to choke off supplies to Britain and end the war.

"My heart really beat faster at this news," Rose later recalled. "All we German submarine commanders had been praying for this order for more than a year," ever since Germany capitulated to US demands after the sinking of the *Lusitania* and agreed to protect neutral lives at sea.

But first, Rose had to make a dramatic splash in the United States. And where best to do that?

Berlin chose to send the *U-53* to Naval Station Newport, in Rhode Island, home to the US Atlantic destroyer fleet, and the backyard of Germany's most influential critic in the American press, John R. Rathom.

❖

The *U-53* was not the first German sub to embark for the United States during the war.

On July 9, 1916, two months before the *U-53* began its US voyage, a very special German submarine, the *Deutschland*, motored into Chesapeake Bay and nestled against a pier near historic Fort McHenry, in Baltimore Harbor. The *Deutschland* was not a warship and she carried no weapons. She was a commercially built merchant vessel, essentially an unarmed light cargo hauler that could travel underwater to defeat the British blockade.

Baltimore reacted to the *Deutschland* like the Martians had landed. The *Evening Sun* blew out its front page with a photograph of the submarine under a double-deck banner:

FIRST OF FLEET OF GERMAN UNDERSEA

MERCHANTMEN DOCKS AT LOCUST POINT

The newspaper marveled at the "daredevil journey" of the *Deutschland*, which had departed from the German port of Bremerhaven, and slipped beneath British warships on a sixteen-day trip to the United States, taking the scenic route up and around Scotland.

The *Deutschland*'s captain, Paul Koenig, announced that he had brought a cargo of dyestuffs to trade, a commodity the United States had been unable to import due to British sea policy. "While England will not allow anybody the same right on the ocean because she rules the waves, we have by means of the submarine commenced to break this rule," Koenig bragged. His vessel was only the first German merchant sub. He said the United States should expect a visit soon from the *Deutschland*'s sister ship, *Bremen*.

Captain Koenig and his crew became overnight celebrities. The *Baltimore Sun* saluted them:

> Without regard to party, creed or class, everybody who admires daring, skill and indomitable determination will take off his hat and give three cheers and a tiger for the Deutschland and her brave sailor men. True Americans draw no international lines when it comes to admiration for genius and courage.

Members of the *Deutschland*'s crew went sightseeing in Washington, DC. They visited the Navy Department and met its assistant secretary, Franklin Delano Roosevelt. German ambassador Count von Bernstorff came from Washington to tour the submarine with the mayor of Baltimore.

It seemed the Germans had finally discovered how to capitalize on US anger over the hardships imposed by the unpopular British embargo. The sub earned Germany its best press since before the *Lusitania*. Count von Bernstorff later wrote, "The days after the arrival of the Deutschland were the pleasantest I experienced in America during the war."

The *Deutschland* departed on August 2, with a cargo of bulk rubber, nickel, and tin. A US destroyer escorted the sub to the three-mile limit, where American waters ended and international waters began. The *Deutschland* arrived safely home in three weeks.

Years later, after Germany had lost the war, Count von Bernstorff pondered a painful what-if. What if Germany had sent ten merchant subs to build upon the *Deutschland*'s charm offensive in America, while maintaining the U-boats' deference to passenger ships? A sea policy of all carrot, no stick may have kept the United States out of the war, and shaped a vastly different century.

❖

A cloudless blue sky hung over Narragansett Bay on October 7, 1916, a perfect autumn Saturday in Newport, Rhode Island. Warm sun beat down. A breeze flicked white caps into the waves. One writer noticed how the "slender black ships" of the US destroyer fleet "rode easily at anchor."

It was the opening day of the World Series—the Boston Red Sox vs. the Brooklyn Robins.[*] Just as game 1 was scheduled to begin, at about two o'clock, something extraordinary happened. American sailors spotted a surfaced submarine powering through the East Passage, a channel of water between Newport and Conanicut Island, the narrow band of land that splits the mouth of Narragansett Bay. The submarine was so thin for her length that she looked like a knife blade slicing through sparkling blue sea.

This was no merchant sub. She flew the German man-o'-war ensign at her bow, a black-white striped flag with the Iron Cross in the center. The sub's two eighty-eight-millimeter deck guns were clearly visible, as were her torpedo tubes. "Incredulous crewmen rushed to the railing of the American destroyers to watch the audacious stranger, as the *U-53* swept steadily into harbor and finally dropped anchor," Long wrote.

The sub's crew stood at attention on her deck. The sailors were in smart blue uniforms. The officers were practically in tuxedoes: white dress shirts with high starched collars, dark ties, and double-breasted black coats.

A small motorboat approached the submarine. An Associated Press reporter in the boat shouted up to the men on the sub. "Have you come here to be interned?"

Lieutenant Rose answered, "No. But I've brought a letter for the German ambassador. Will you mail it for me?" He passed down an envelope. Rose didn't really care if the letter got mailed. It was a just gag, a short note to Count von Bernstorff saying hello.

---

[*] The Red Sox would win the series in five games. Babe Ruth pitched thirteen shutout innings in game 2. The Red Sox won the World Series again in 1918, and then began a bit of a drought.

Rose went ashore and exchanged strained pleasantries with Admiral Austin Knight. The U-boat captain insisted he wanted no supplies or repairs—"I just wanted to visit you, Admiral," Rose said. Next, Rose called on Admiral Albert Gleaves, commander of the US destroyer flotilla. Gleaves apologized that on the "dry" base he could not offer Rose a drink.

Rose got grim confirmation from the Americans that the merchant sub *Bremen*, sister ship to the *Deutschland*, had not arrived in the United States. The *Bremen* was overdue, and Rose presumed, correctly, that the sub had sunk.* Admiral Gleaves brought his wife and daughter for a tour of the *U-53*. Rose offered cake and champagne, and allowed Gleaves's daughter to peer through the periscope at her father's ship, the view a sub commander would have before he attacked.

And then just as suddenly as it had arrived, the *U-53* was on its way.

Game 1 of the World Series was wrapping up in a 6–5 Boston win, when Rose ordered his deck cleared of the Rhode Island tourists who had come out in boats and clambered aboard the warship. The U-boat's stay in Newport was barely two and a half hours, but its effect was everything Germany had hoped.

The next day, every major newspaper in America was plastered with photos and shrieking black headlines about the peculiar port call of the *U-53*. Newswriting about the event carried the bewildered tone of *what the hell was that about?*

"Just what mission brought the grey undersea fighting machine to Newport, its commander declined to tell," Rathom's *Providence Journal* reported.

The *U-53* anchored overnight near *Nantucket Lightship*, a floating lighthouse that marked the dangerous Nantucket Shoals, some forty miles south of Nantucket Island.

Rose's mission in America was to *shock and awe*. His cameo in Newport was only the shock.

The next morning, at 6:53 A.M., a few miles south of the lightship and outside the three-mile limit of US territorial waters, the *U-53* stopped the

---

* The fate of the *Bremen* remains a mystery.

British steamer *Strathdene* by firing a warning shot across her bow. Rose followed cruiser rules to the letter. He ordered the steamer's crew into lifeboats, and then torpedoed the empty ship and sank it.

At 8:03 A.M. the sub stopped the Norwegian tanker *Christian Knudsen*, loaded with diesel oil bound for London, forced the crew off, and torpedoed and shelled the ship to the bottom.

Less than three hours later, the *U-53* halted the British freighter *West Point* and raised the signal flag to "abandon ship." The crew left in lifeboats. Rose sent his men to the empty ship in an inflatable boat; they attached explosives to the ship and destroyed it.

Responding to urgent wireless reports from *Nantucket Lightship*, seventeen American destroyers steamed to the attack zone. The US warships crowded so close to the *U-53* that Rose had to reverse engines at one point to avoid colliding with one.

Yet the German commander proceeded with icy efficiency.

He stopped the Dutch steamer *Blommersdyk* and the British freighter *Stephano*. The ships were evacuated. American warships picked up the passengers. Rose sent a wireless message urging one US destroyer to withdraw to a safe distance so the *Blommersdyk* could be sunk. The warship backed off. So long as the U-boat was in international waters, the US Navy could do nothing to stop it. That was what it meant to be neutral in the war. The *U-53* sank the last two ships with explosives, shell fire, and torpedoes.

At 10:30 P.M., after firing its last torpedo, the *U-53* turned toward home.

Though there was no loss of life in the attacks, five ships destroyed in one day by one submarine practically on America's shores stunned the US public. Newspapers across America furiously typeset bulletins about the sinkings for the next morning's front pages.

In downtown Providence, people crowded around the *Journal* building all day and late into the night to read news dispatches on the sinkings, which the newspaper posted in the ground-floor windows as they arrived. Most in the crowd were shocked at the brazenness of the German submarine captain. Some wondered if the sinkings violated the law. And many commented aloud that the rapid-fire attacks "shows what the Germans could do if they went to war with us."

For Lieutenant Rose, it was mission accomplished.

❖

One hundred days after the *U-53* flexed its power for America, on January 17, 1917, two civilian cryptographers employed in London by British Naval Intelligence started work on decoding a German dispatch plucked from the air by wireless listening posts. The message looked like a typical German cypher; it was a long list of numbers, most of them four- or five-digits.

The Germans believed their codes to be unbreakable. But the secret British codebreaking operation, itself code-named Room 40, was painstakingly unraveling the complicated German encryption.

Working from fat books containing all of Britain's accumulated knowledge on German cyphers, the cryptographers first decoded who had sent the message: *Zimmermann*. That would be Arthur Zimmermann, the German Empire's secretary for foreign affairs.

In a scene described by the historian Barbara Tuchman, "The code book pages flipped back and forth with an agitated rustle while sheets of paper filled up with words tested and discarded, with more words fitted together, until, after two hours and in spite of many gaps in the sequence, an intelligible version had come clear."

The cipher was in fact two messages.

The first, addressed to Count von Bernstorff, notified the ambassador that Germany was about to make a risky wager. On February 1, Germany would declare a policy of unrestricted submarine warfare. That meant any ship, including neutral ships—American ships—would be torpedoed without warning. The new policy rescinded Germany's pledge to safeguard the lives of neutrals after the sinking of the *Lusitania*. The United States would be outraged. It could mean war. But Germany was running out of time. Its people were starving from the food blockade. The German high command was betting that even if the United States responded by declaring war, a ruthless submarine campaign would cripple Britain before the United States could do much to affect the conflict. Bernstorff was ordered not to tell the Wilson administration of the new policy until the very last minute.

The rest of the cipher fell somewhere between astonishing and bloody unbelievable. This part of the message was meant for Count von Bernstorff to forward to Germany's foreign minister in Mexico, Heinrich von Eckardt. It was a hedge in case the new submarine policy drove the United States to war. Zimmermann's message offered Mexico an alliance: If the United States declared war on Germany, Germany and Mexico should make war together on the United States, and invite Japan to join them. Then Mexico could recover territory lost to the United States in the 1840s through annexation and the Mexican-American War.

What Rathom had outrageously alleged nearly two years earlier was now happening: Germany was orchestrating a war between the United States and Mexico to keep America too busy at home to interfere in Europe.

British officials knew this explosive revelation was precisely the sort of evidence that could bring the United States into the war on the side of the Allies. There was one problem: How could they get the telegram in front of the American people without tipping off the Germans that their codes had been broken?

❖

On January 31, 1917, Count von Bernstorff arrived at about four o'clock for a meeting at the Washington office of Secretary of State Lansing, in the massive State, War, and Navy Building, now called the Eisenhower Executive Office Building, next to the White House.

Lansing sensed something was wrong as soon as Count von Bernstorff walked in. The German diplomat normally radiated cheer. Now he was unable to even fake a smile. He eased into a plush chair beside Lansing's desk and handed Lansing some papers, in German with English translations.

"I've been instructed to give this to you," Count von Bernstorff said, as if distancing himself from the documents.

Lansing read the notice slowly to himself:

> Germany will meet the illegal measure of her enemies by forcibly preventing after February 1, 1917, in a zone around Great Britain, France, Italy and in the Eastern Mediterranean all navigation, that of neutrals included, from and to England and from and to France . . .
>
> All ships met within that zone will be sunk.
>
> The Imperial Government is confident that this measure will result in a speedy termination of the war and in the restoration of peace which the Government of the United States has so much at heart.

Lansing had presumed Germany might eventually come to this grave decision. But so soon? Unrestricted submarine warfare was to begin *the next day*.

"I am sorry to have to bring about this situation," Count von Bernstorff said, "but my government could do nothing else."

"You must know that it cannot be accepted," Lansing told him.

"Of course, of course. I understand that—I know it is very serious, very, and I deeply regret that it is necessary."

The ambassador rose to leave, and the men shook hands. There were tears in Bernstorff's eyes.

The American response was as negative as Count von Bernstorff had anticipated. The *Brooklyn Daily Eagle* ran a front-page cartoon snarking, "The Freedom of the Seas will now be enjoyed by icebergs and fish." On the same page, the paper solemnly reported that a diplomatic break with Germany was likely, and that such a break would be "equivalent to war, or as certain to result in war within a very short time."

"The President is shaping his course with full realization of the fact that upon his decision may rest the whole future of humanity."

Three days later, Wilson made his choice. The United States severed diplomatic relations with Germany and ordered Count von Bernstorff out of the country. Not just the ambassador, but his entire diplomatic operation, nearly two hundred people. Count von Bernstorff's parting message was simple: "I hope that war may be averted and the old friendly relations between the United States and Germany may soon be restored."

President Wilson, too, clung to slim hope that the United States could stay out of the conflict. He offered to mediate among the waring nations in Europe, to craft a "peace without victory," before German submarines caused some new outrage that forced his hand.

Tense days followed. With the United States teetering on the precipice of war, Great Britain pushed.

❖

A week after America's diplomatic break with Germany, on February 9, Rathom published one of the most prophetic and mysterious stories of his career. The headline read: GERMANS ORGANIZED FOR ATTACK ON AMERICA ACROSS BORDER LINE.

"If Germany succeeds in dragging the United States into war," the story said, "her first blow against this country will be struck through Mexico." The story and a related editorial alleged that Germany had sent to Mexico hundreds of its military officers, along with money, arms, and rabid anti-American propaganda. "In what way it is proposed [that Germany] strike a blow at the United States through Mexico is not fully understood."

The story gave no hint of its sourcing. Perhaps a combination of things overheard by Voska's spies and Rathom's Department of Justice contacts, mashed together with educated speculation. A number of newspapers reprinted the story, but it was overshadowed by the avalanche of news about the break with Germany and the anticipation of war.

By the end of the month, Rathom would again look like a soothsayer.

❖

On February 10, a British spy in Mexico acquired a copy of the coded Zimmermann message from a telegraph office. This was the version of the message *after* it had been relayed by Count von Bernstorff. As the British had hoped, the relayed version contained "small but significant differences in dateline, address, and signature" from the original sent from Berlin. If *this* version were made public, the Germans would presume the telegram somehow leaked after it was decoded in North America, and they may not suspect that the British had broken their code.

From this point, the British plan picked up speed.

On February 19, British codebreakers finally filled in all the missing gaps in the Zimmermann telegram, and the decoding was complete. Four days later, a British high official presented the telegram to Walter Hines Page, the US ambassador to Great Britain.[*] Page passed it to the US State Department. President Wilson ultimately decided the American people should see it.

Lansing suggested leaking the telegram—with no fingerprints—to the press. He chose to give the story to Edwin Hood, a straight-shooting Associated Press reporter, then about sixty years old, and no bomb-thrower like Rathom. In 1881 Hood broke the news of the shooting of President Garfield. Now E. M. Hood, as he was known, would break the biggest story of the young new century.

Americans read the text of Zimmerman's telegram in their newspapers on March 1:

> On the first of February we intend to begin submarine warfare unrestricted. In spite of this it is our intention to endeavor to keep neutral the United States of America.
>
> If this attempt is not successful, we propose an alliance on the following basis with Mexico: That we shall make war together and together make peace. We shall give general financial support and it

---

[*] Page was the former editor of *World's Work* magazine in New York, which he turned over to his son, Arthur, in 1913. The younger Page would soon become instrumental in the public fall of John R. Rathom.

*is understood that Mexico is to reconquer the lost territory in New
Mexico, Texas and Arizona. The details are left to you* [Heinrich
von Eckardt, Germany's representative in Mexico] *for settlement.*

*You will inform the president of Mexico of the above most secretly
as soon as the outbreak of war with the United States is certain and
add the suggestion that he should, on his own initiative, invite
Japan to immediate adherence and at the same time mediate
between Japan and ourselves.*

*Please call the president's attention to the fact that the unrestricted
employment of our submarines now offers the prospect of compelling
England to make peace within a few months. Acknowledge receipt.*

After a relentless two-year diet of news about German intrigues, the
telegram was the final outrage. President Wilson scheduled an address
before a joint session of Congress to make the case for war.

On the evening of April 2, the president's car arrived at the US Capital
at 8:20 P.M., flanked by two cars of policemen. The Capital dome was lit.
Searchlights panned over it. In the dim, shadowy plaza below, US caval-
rymen in formation raised their sabers and created a lane for the president
through a mass of people who had gathered. The crowd gave Wilson a
generous ovation.

Inside the House chamber, the Supreme Court took seats directly in
front of the rostrum. Members of the Senate entered with small American
flags poking from their breast pockets. First Lady Edith Bolling Galt
Wilson, "gowned in black" like at a funeral, took her seat just before the
president arrived.

The chamber was jammed. People sat on the stairs, in the aisles.

Wilson walked to the rostrum and looked out over a sea of faces, all
white, nearly all of them men. The 65th US Congress had one woman,
Jeannette Rankin (R-Montana), the first woman elected to Congress.*

---

* Rankin served two nonconsecutive terms in the US House, 1917–1919 and 1941–1943. By
odd chance, she was in office for both world war resolutions, and opposed both on principle.
She was the only member to reject going to war after Pearl Harbor.

There were no Black members. Secretary of State Lansing later wrote that Wilson had for so long resisted bringing America into the conflict because "he had been more and more impressed with the idea that 'white civilization' and its domination over the world rested largely on our ability to keep this country intact, as we would have to build up the nations ravaged by war."

No one made a sound while Wilson spoke. It was in this speech that he delivered the famous line "The world must be made safe for democracy." He ended the call for war this way:

> To such a task we can dedicate our lives and our fortunes, everything that we are and everything that we have, with the pride of those who know that the day has come when America is privileged to spend her blood and her might for the principles that gave her birth and happiness and the peace which she has treasured. God helping her, she can do no other.

Wilson sat down. Several seconds of silence stretched on, feeling to those who were there like an eternity, and then the chamber erupted in applause and shouts. The address was followed by four days of Congressional speechifying, and then the United States declared war on Germany.

It was the result Rathom had labored two years to bring about. Rathom praised Wilson's speech in a passionate editorial that sought to stiffen America for the hardships to come:

"Now welcome sacrifice, welcome the righteous appeal to arms, welcome the burden of human sorrow," Rathom wrote. "The flag whose birth was the hope of the world is raised from the dust of timidity, shame and selfishness." The piece was beautifully rendered for a topic so dark. One reader particularly moved by Rathom's words was the assistant navy secretary, a rising political figure, Franklin Delano Roosevelt.

"I appreciate the very excellent support that the Journal is giving, and especially your editorial," Roosevelt wrote to Rathom later that month. "I know how glad you must be, as I am, that at last we are definitely committed in the war and we must certainly use every effort to stimulate public opinion and public interest in the work of doing our share."

Stimulating public opinion had earned Rathom a nationwide following. He was not going to stop now. Through guts and guile and inexhaustible effort, the imposter had done more than any other individual to condition the American mind for war. At the same time he had elevated the invented character of John Revelstoke Rathom into the stratosphere of American civic life. He was an outcast no longer. *Stimulate public opinion? Use every effort?* For sure. In the coming months, Rathom would redouble his anti-German crusade in a relentless and reckless campaign. He would drive his national profile inexorably higher, gathering ever more attention, leaping into ever-brighter spotlights, soaring upward without regard, toward the scorching sun.

CHAPTER 15

Department of Judas

In the early evening of November 21, 1917, the elites of Boston society turned out in formalwear for a special banquet at the Boston City Club on Beacon Hill, next door to the dazzling golden dome of the Massachusetts State House. The Pilgrim Publicity Association, a trade group for the advertising industry, was sponsoring a dinner and speaking program headlined by the celebrity newsman and German spy hunter John R. Rathom.

Rathom's talk that evening was titled "Three Years of Germany's War against the United States." A cartoon printed on tickets to the event depicted Rathom chasing a wild boar that sported the ridiculous upturned moustache of Kaiser Wilhelm. Rathom's arm is cocked back in the drawing, and he is about to spear the pig with a giant fountain pen.

The granite and redbrick City Club building had never seen a dinner crowd so large; perhaps as many as a thousand attendees. People shut out of the sold-out talk were offering bounties of $50, about $1,000 today, to anyone interested in scalping their ticket, which had a face value of $2.50. The head of the Pilgrim Association claimed demand was so overwhelming the group could have sold fifty thousand seats.

Dinner started at 6:30. From the head table, Rathom peered through the haze of tobacco floating up to the high ceiling and looked across a sea of penguin suits, crammed around round tables packed wall to wall throughout the long and narrow ballroom. The Harvard Glee Club entertained with songs. Reporters from the major Boston newspapers had pencils ready to cover the newsman who was always good copy.

John Rathom was approaching a new summit of his celebrity.

His speaking tour, which had begun that June in Toronto with an explosion of lies and exaggerations, had been an absolute smash. The American public was enthralled with the idea that a newsman had run his own private counterspy ops against the Germans. Rathom had delivered a speech in Philadelphia in October that drew five hundred people, along with national news coverage of Rathom's alarming and entirely unsupported claim that "two officers of high rank" and "hundreds of men" in the US Army and Navy were known by the federal government to be spies for Germany. These men "are allowed their liberty," Rathom said, cryptically, "for reasons best known to the Department of Justice."

It was McCarthyism thirty years before McCarthy, and just as effective. The Philly crowd could hardly stop interrupting Rathom with applause, as he lied about how "a little group of common, garden-variety American reporters working for the Providence Journal outwitted the whole efficient Prussian secret service," as the *Philadelphia Inquirer* reported.

The week before his Boston engagement, Rathom had drawn "the largest group ever gathered" by the Canadian Club of New York, at the luxurious Hotel Biltmore on Madison Avenue in Manhattan. The major New York papers all covered the speech, and the newswires had seeded Rathom's spy mongering and heroic falsehoods around the world.

Invitations to speak were arriving faster than Rathom could respond. After Boston, he had major appearances planned for the Midwest.

And the capstone of his promotional tour was just becoming public.

Rathom had struck a deal with the prestigious New York magazine *World's Work*, to write exclusive stories about his battle against enemy spies, which would run as a series over several editions and then be published as a book. The series was due to start in January 1918. *World's Work* launched a subscription drive and national newspaper advertising campaign to pump the series. One ad showed a giant hand in the sky aiming a blinding flashlight on a German saboteur holding a bomb. The ad copy promised "The Biggest Story of the Year—John R. Rathom's exposé of Germany's plots."

Rathom *had* exposed German propaganda and espionage in his newspaper. But not in the field as the commander of a counterspy ring, as he claimed in his speeches. The imposter had edited the adventures of Emanuel Voska and others so that their thrilling stories starred John Rathom. Then he spun those yarns to the adulation of America.

The lies had started small, as they tend to do, with the occasional misdirection to protect his sources. Rathom believed lives would be at risk if his sources were revealed, and he may have been right.

But the imposter went further. He was playing a character, and nothing drives an actor like applause. Audiences lapped up his spy stories and begged for encores. A few tall tales were good for American morale, he told himself, so therefore good for the war effort. He was doing his part, as Franklin Delano Roosevelt had urged him.

It was all so reckless. So over-the-top. Rathom's falsehoods were like a Ponzi scheme. New ones had to be invented all the time to feed a hungry press. It was a dangerous game. He put his newspaper's reputation on a knife's edge. For an imposter with a secret to hide, the stakes were infinitely higher. But soon he was in too deep. With no way to step off his mountain of lies, he could only climb higher.

A former Massachusetts congressman introduced Rathom to the Boston crowd at 8:50 P.M. The audience erupted into "prolonged cheering," like they had just seen the last out of a no-hitter at the new ballyard across town, Fenway Park.

Dressed in a black tuxedo with wide lapels, a snowy white high-collared shirt, and a vest buttoned low around his bulging middle, Rathom took the podium.

"I feel as if the making of this little reputation was not half as hard as living up to it," he said, in a bit of false modesty recycled from other speeches. "I am delighted to be with you tonight and delighted, I am glad to say, for more than one reason." He looked down to several *Providence*

Journal reporters in the audience. "I was surprised and very glad when I saw at a table before me a group of my own men, men to whom the larger part of the glory for what we have done should descend. I am proud to stand here tonight before you and tell them to their faces."

The crowd burst into sustained applause.

Voices cried out, "Make them stand up!"

"Go ahead, stand up," Rathom commanded his reporters, who knew nothing of how their mysterious boss had landed his scoops.

The reporters rose. The audience rose with them in thunderous ovation.

When the hall had calmed, Rathom continued. "During the first year of our work we lived in a constant hell, knowing, as we did, where our material was coming from, knowing that it was absolutely true in every respect—knowing that 90 percent of those who read it did not believe it. And we were in a most disheartened frame of mind, and it took all of our energy and all of our mental qualities to understand that we had to *keep on*."

Over the next ninety minutes, the crowd hung on Rathom's words "with almost breathless interest," as he unfolded his greatest hits, the full portfolio of his inventions and exaggerations:

The *Providence Journal* intercepted and decoded German messages. The paper placed reporters undercover at jobs inside the German embassy. Karl Boy-Ed had assigned an undercover *Journal* reporter to secure the hotel rooms for the infamous Huerta conference, and that was how Rathom knew which room to bug.

Rathom's spy stories were intimately crafted, with quirky details that rang like real life. On this night he added a funny new tale about the Maine bridge bomber Werner Horn. *Journal* reporters under Rathom's command, he said, entirely making this up, shadowed Horn and his suitcase of dynamite from New York to Vanceboro, and then Rathom himself later debriefed the frostbitten German in jail.

In preparing for his attack,

> Horn went down to West Street, New York, and bought a four
> dollar suit of second-hand clothes and let his beard grow for a

week; cut off his military moustache and put on a filthy old cotton shirt and cotton coat; and in that disguise went about the Merchant's Limited train from New York to Boston. When they got his confession from him and I asked him why, after taking all these precautions he had come on the finest train in America, he said: "Sir, I am an officer and a gentleman, and I don't travel any other way."

The *Journal* outed spies, Rathom said, foiled bombings, uncovered passport fraud, gathered the evidence that led to the arrest of the Welland Canal plotters. Almost none of it was true, much of what he claimed was implausible, some hardly *possible*, and yet nobody seemed to question how the leader of such a busy counterspy operation could also publish two newspapers a day.

Rathom told the delightful "hearts story" in Boston. The "facts" were essentially the same as in prior speeches: Pretty young *Journal* woman shares lunch with Franz von Papen on a packing crate stuffed with secret documents. His arm slides around her waist and she, "in dreamy fashion," as if charmed by him, "took out of her hair a red crayon pencil and in a more dreamy way on the top of this box drew two large red hearts." Same punchline: "It was von Papen himself who put the arrow through the hearts." Pause for laughter. Then, Rathom said, in a new twist, after British authorities confiscated the crate they gave the documents to the US ambassador in London, and "the entire contents within three weeks found their way into our own State Department."

Hands mashed together in another deafening tribute from the crowd.

One man in the audience, though, was not clapping. This man discreetly scribbled notes. He was in the front row, table number C8, directly in front of Rathom and practically close enough to smell the cigar smoke on him.

Unbeknownst to Rathom, the scribbler, a specialist in taking shorthand, was an agent for Bruce Bielaski's Bureau of Investigation.

This agent had secret orders to create a verbatim transcript of Rathom's address.

Everything Rathom said would be used against him.

❖

By the second half of 1917, news coverage of Rathom's largely fictional escapades touched every corner of the country. America was at war and a hero-hungry press turned Rathom into a spy-hunting sensation.

The *Fort Worth Star-Telegram* called Rathom "one of the most remarkable men in America." In Vermont the *Express and Standard* said, "Mr. Rathom has performed a mighty big work for this country." In Nebraska the *Hamilton County Register* named Rathom "the man who more than anyone else has been responsible for the discovery of German official treachery." The *Chicago Tribune* beamed that "Mr. Rathom made famous the phrase, 'The Providence Journal tomorrow will say—.'" The *Detroit Free Press* proclaimed Rathom had "performed a tremendous patriotic service." In Utah the *Ogden Standard* declared that "this country owes Mr. Rathom a debt of gratitude."

Purple praise spilled across the *Boston Globe*: "John R. Rathom's name is known from the Atlantic coast to the Pacific as the man who alone and unaided . . . fought Germany's secret and diplomatic agents to a standstill, exposed their plots, intrigues and propaganda and finally drove the arch conspirators out of the country."

One story on the wires in late 1917 even bad-mouthed the rest of America for not being more like John Rathom:

> It is a sad commentary on American foresight and solidarity that of the 100,000,000 people of the United States, only one man was wise enough to see the menace of German autocracy to this country when the World War began in 1914, and that only one was loyally energetic enough to begin effective work in combatting the menace. John R. Rathom, editor of the Providence, R.I., Journal is that man, and the stupendous piece of constructive patriotism he has performed is destined for a permanent place in the history of these troubled times.

People could not get enough of the "spy hunter." Suddenly, reporters wanted Rathom's thoughts on all kinds of national issues. His opinions were printed with the solemnity normally reserved for senators and cabinet chiefs. When Rathom criticized the US secretary of war as a squishy "pacifist at heart," voters read his comments in Albuquerque. Rathom's call for a declaration of war on Austria made the front page in Chattanooga.

During this time, Rathom continued sending unpublished tips to Bielaski. In November 1917 he informed Bielaski that "German plotters" were assembling at a Brooklyn saloon near Vanderbilt Avenue. Meanwhile, "German propagandists" met every Sunday evening at 8 o'clock on East Fifty-Fourth Street. He advised Bielaski in another note, "You might suggest to your Columbus, Ohio, office that they keep an eye on one James Muller, 395 East 12th Ave., Columbus, whose propagandist activities are becoming more marked and bolder."

In each of these cases, Bielaski passed the tips to Bureau of Investigation field offices.

There was, however, a dark side effect of Rathom's new fame. He was an anti-German zealot. In his paranoia he sincerely believed that German spies had infiltrated every facet of American life. He spread that fear like a sick man shedding a virus. His celebrity was the wind that carried it across the nation.

Rathom warned the people of Boston in his speech:

> Along your docks, on your vessels, working as waiters in your clubs and restaurants, in several of your business houses, shipping concerns and factories in and about this city, are literally thousands of German and Austrian spies, who are ready and willing to go to any length to aid the cause of Germany and her allies in this war.

Rathom drove these fearful themes in other cities, in other speeches, and in widely quoted editorials. He printed an ominous warning in his pages every day during the war, which began: "Every German or Austrian in the United States, whether naturalized or not, unless known by years of association to be absolutely loyal, should be treated as a potential spy."

President Woodrow Wilson had set the tone for anti-immigrant fear-mongering in December 1915, when he declared "the gravest threats against our national peace and safety" were already inside America's borders.

"There are citizens of the United States, I blush to admit," Wilson said, "born under other flags but welcomed under our generous naturalization laws . . . who have poured the poison of disloyalty into the very arteries of our national life."

Wilson was talking about hyphenism, the suspicions that immigrants who identify with the Old Country, such as German-Americans or Irish-Americans, might be disloyal to the United States. These groups used the hyphen, Wilson said, "Because only part of them have come over." Their hearts still belonged to Europe.

In his 1916 reelection campaign, Wilson explicitly rejected votes from "the hyphenates." Part of his enmity may have come from the political actions of German-Americans, who hated his policies on arms sales to the Allies and opposed his reelection.

With the country at war, Wilson nationalized fear by creating a government agency, the Committee on Public Information, to market the war and anti-German propaganda like some new cola, with ubiquitous advertising in newspapers, posters, films, and public speeches by volunteers.

Americans began to turn on their neighbors in an epidemic of suspicion.

The federal government forced the registration of some five hundred thousand US civilians as "enemy aliens." Bielaski's Bureau of Investigation spied on many of these people, largely Americans of German background. Some six thousand were arrested and jailed in internment camps, not for crimes, generally, but for suspicion they might harbor disloyal thoughts. One famous internee was Karl Muck, conductor of the Boston Symphony Orchestra and the former head of the Royal Opera in Berlin, born in 1859 in Darmstadt, Germany.

Rathom contributed directly to Muck's internment, by accusing him in October 1917 of ignoring a request to play the "Star-Spangled Banner" at a Boston Symphony Orchestra concert in Providence. The charge was false. Muck, in fact, was unaware that a group of Rhode Island women's clubs had requested the song. Rathom lambasted Muck with the headline AMERICAN ANTHEM ENTIRELY IGNORED. He charged that Muck had rejected the "Star-Spangled Banner" in favor of "Russian, Hungarian, and German selections." Rathom's rage spilled onto the editorial page, where he demonized Muck as a "dangerous enemy alien" who had "grossly offended every patriotic American" and ought to be "placed where he belongs—behind bars in an internment camp."

Federal agents surveilled Muck for months. In March 1918 opponents organized against a planned Boston Symphony Orchestra concert at Carnegie Hall in New York. Muck was arrested as an enemy alien on March 25, and interned at Fort Oglethorpe, Georgia, for the offense of criticizing US policy in private notes to a woman.

Two decades later, in World War II, the United States interned about 120,000 Japanese-Americans in camps, including George Takei, the five-year-old future actor and helmsman of the starship *Enterprise*, who was deemed too dangerous to boldly go to kindergarten in his own hometown in California.

The United States has since stopped interning whole classes of blameless people whenever we become afraid, but we never stopped blaming our neighbors. Hate crimes against Muslim Americans increased by 1,600 percent after the 9/11 attacks. In 2020 anti-Asian hate crimes rose 149 percent in sixteen of America's largest cities, as frightened people lashed out over COVID-19, a virus first discovered in China.

❖

In the upper reaches of the Wilson administration, ire was fixed not on xenophobic targets but on one man in particular.

John Rathom had become a problem.

After two years of confidential collaboration with the editor, government men with unaccountable power decided that Rathom needed to be silenced. This policy reversal was not decided by Congress or through administrative hearings. The decision came out of clandestine meetings of Attorney

General Thomas Watt Gregory and an aide or two, hardly enough people for a decent poker game.

The reasons the Department of Justice turned on Rathom are many and cumulative. Rathom deserves plenty of blame. He toured the nation claiming credit for investigations performed in some cases by federal agents or by Voska's network, but certainly not by him. Stick out your chin that far and it shouldn't be a surprise when somebody whacks it.

In his Philly and New York speeches, Rathom accused the Department of Justice of allowing hundreds of foreign spies in the US military to walk free—and the public believed him. The way Rathom told it, every city he visited was a well-known hotbed of enemy agents. The *Boston Globe* got the message. After Rathom's City Club speech, the paper printed Rathom's photo and the shrieking page 1 headline: SAYS BOSTON IS FULL OF SPIES. Implicit in these sorts of headlines was an indictment of the Department of Justice. If a *newsman* knew where the spies were, shouldn't federal lawmen drop their cocks and do something?

There were also political motivations to knock Rathom off his pedestal. Politics then were not as blindly tribal as now, but these were partisan actors. As Rathom's fame grew, so did the volume of his personal megaphone. He leveraged his new public standing to criticize President Woodrow Wilson, Gregory's boss and friend. Wilson and Gregory were Democrats; Rathom was associated with a northeastern Republican newspaper. He had endorsed Wilson's Republican opponent, Charles Hughes, in the presidential election of 1916.

And so, beginning around November 1917, the full power of the US Department of Justice was secretly mustered at public expense to muzzle one loud newsman from Providence.

Bielaski ordered his agents in Boston to cover Rathom's City Club speech. "Get as full report of his remarks as possible without attracting his attention," Bielaski directed. The agents produced a verbatim stenographic transcript of Rathom's white lies and whoppers that ran more than twenty-five typewritten pages.

One week after the Boston event, Attorney General Gregory fired the first shot in the government's campaign to shut John Rathom's big mouth.

❖

The letter from the attorney general of the United States exploded like a panic bomb inside the offices of *World's Work* magazine.

World's Work was a serious, business-minded periodical. It was founded in 1900, under the editorship of Walter Hines Page, who left in 1913 to become US ambassador to England, a post he held through the war. Page left the magazine under the control of his son Arthur, an erudite, pipe-smoking, prep school, Harvard guy.

And so it fell to thirty-four-year-old Arthur Page to receive an ominous letter dictated personally by Gregory. The letter, dated November 28, 1917, said that the Department of Justice had seen *World's Work* advertising for its coming series by John Rathom, and the department was not happy.

"From the information in its possession, the Department believes that the statements which Mr. Rathom has made in his public speeches, and which it is believed will be repeated in the articles which your magazine will publish, are without foundation in fact," Gregory wrote. "The Department believes the publication of these articles would tend to interfere seriously with its work and would reflect improperly upon it."

The attorney general threatened to go public with this information, decimating not only Rathom's credibility but the magazine's, too.

The letter was unprecedented. The timing, horrendous. *World's Work* was just releasing its December issue, which contained a fawning article about Rathom by the magazine's managing editor, French Strother. Strother's article was headlined THE PROVIDENCE JOURNAL WILL SAY TODAY . . .

Strother was the son of a judge from Fresno, California. He worked in government for Republican officeholders, then moved to New York to chase a dream of getting into literature. He started on the administrative side of *World's Work*, and then moved to the news department around 1904.

He was a scrupulous, talented reporter, who climbed the organization to become managing editor and lead writer.

Strother's story in the December issue of *World's Work* recounted Rathom's major newspaper scoops. It was a curtain-raiser for Rathom's exclusive series, which was due to begin in January. The leaders of *World's Work* were understandably shaken by the attorney general's letter. The magazine quietly arranged with the Department of Justice to dispatch Strother to Washington for a confidential review of files related to Rathom's stories. In the meantime, the magazine bought itself some time by announcing that Rathom's first article was delayed to February.

Gregory sent Rathom a copy of his ominous letter to *World's Work*. Rathom was on a tour of the Midwest and probably did not see the letter for at least two weeks. He generated more sensational news coverage in Chicago on December 4 and in Detroit on December 8. His remarks in those cities were substantially the same as his Boston speech, suggesting he had no idea he had triggered Gregory and the Department of Justice.

He soon got the message.

On December 18, Rathom was in a desperate flap. He rushed to Washington by train to meet personally with Bielaski, at the Bureau of Investigation's new headquarters, in a dull, eight-story building at the corner of Vermont and K Streets that looked less like the home of a national counterspy agency and more like elderly housing.

Bielaski later noted that Rathom arrived "in a very crestfallen mood" and was not feeling well. With good reason: Attorney General Gregory had threatened to out him as a fabulist.

"Well I got out of bed to come down here," Rathom told Bielaski. "I am not in very good shape. I am very greatly worried about this thing."

He grumbled that the *Providence Journal* had worked incredibly hard on its revelations over the previous three years and spent a great deal of money reporting those stories.

"I began to talk unadvisedly and foolishly," Rathom admitted, "but my only motive in talking was to arouse the public in every case. . . . My only motive was to help in the public service."

Rathom thought the Bureau of Investigation chief was a friend. He thought he was confessing to Bielaski in confidence. What Rathom did not know, and likely never knew, was that Bielaski secretly recorded their conversation:

RATHOM: What does concern me and concerns me tremendously is this one thing: Anything in the way of publicity or otherwise which will cast a shadow on the *Providence Journal*'s work for the past three years. That is the only thing that amounts to anything and that is the only reason I came to Washington. And I want to know just how you people stand on that point.

BIELASKI: I stand just this way. We have received a copy of your remarks in Boston and somebody sent us a copy of your remarks in Philadelphia. [Gregory] said he would tell the *World's Work* that he understood that the articles were forthcoming, assuming they would be along the lines of those speeches, and that the information had by the department was that [the speeches were] inaccurate. And that information was available to them if they cared to have it. They immediately sent a man down here.

RATHOM: Yes.

BIELASKI: It seemed very much a surprise to these *World's Work* men. I don't know what they are going to do about it.

RATHOM: What the *World's Work* is going to do? It isn't the *World's Work*—I don't care. It is what the attorney general is going to do.

Rathom proposed two possible off-ramps from the predicament.

He could write "two or three" accurate articles for *World's Work* that excluded any falsehoods from his Boston speech, and submit them confidentially for Department of Justice review. Any material Gregory found objectionable, he could "blue-pencil"—meaning he could cut it.

The second option was to delay publication of the series indefinitely, and offer some vague excuse related to public policy—they would think of something.

Considering the first option, Bielaski could not imagine how Rathom could write accurate stories, given the way the articles were being promoted by *World's Work*.

> BIELASKI: I don't see how you can avoid getting in a jam. This is the story of the work of the employees of the *Providence Journal* . . .

> RATHOM: Of course, a number of our men have been engaged in the work; that is quite true. . . . We did not have a *Providence Journal* man in the embassy, of course, but we did get some stuff right out of the embassy itself.

Bielaski was skeptical, but he agreed to present Rathom's two propositions to Gregory, who happened to be "sick in bed" with a head cold.

> RATHOM: He is in bed. Well, I ought to be in bed.

Two days later, Rathom telephoned Bielaski at 7:25 A.M. Bielaski recorded the call. Rathom griped that so much effort had gone into promoting the *World's Work* articles that *something* had to be written. So the option of indefinite delay was unworkable.

Bielaski also had bad news: Gregory had no interest in reviewing stories before publication.

> BIELASKI: The attorney general said he did not think he could do it. It would place a certain responsibility on him.

RATHOM: On the other hand, we want to be in the position of doing everything we can to please the department. In order to be sure of that we just want a suggestion that anything the department feels improper we will be glad to eliminate.

BIELASKI: I am sure the attorney general would not listen or agree on that.

Rathom tried once more, asking if Bielaski would review the articles, "as an individual, without the knowledge of anyone except you and myself."

BIELASKI: No, I could not divorce myself from the department in this way.

RATHOM: Well that leaves it all up to us.

❖

By late 1917 something extraordinary was happening to the American press: It was sounding more and more like John Rathom.

AMERICAN INFESTED WITH GERMAN SPIES, read a headline in *Literary Digest*. The story quoted the assertions of the *New York Tribune*, which agreed that spies were "everywhere."

Editorial writers around the country adopted Rathom's imagery of a country overrun by a silent invasion. The "United States is infested with German spies," the *Birmingham News* declared. "Who will be the St. Patrick to chase the snakes out of America?"

In July 1917 the *Journal and Tribune* of Knoxville, Tennessee, proclaimed: AWAKE AT LAST! AFTER A RIP VAN WINKLE SLEEP UNCLE SAM SITS UP AND TAKES NOTICE OF THE GERMAN SPY SYSTEM.

In an advertisement, the Packard Motor Car Company of Philadelphia lamented "an America infested with spies and German-bought traitors working every minute to weaken our national structure." Former US president Taft urged that spies and "plotters" be shot. Teddy Roosevelt helped found the nationalist American Defense Society, which was something like a national neighborhood watch to police sedition.

Rathom's mindset had seeped into the national consciousness. People took it as a given that spies were boiling out of the ground like termites.

How much of this was Rathom's doing? A lot, in the judgement of the Department of Justice, which blamed Rathom for spreading spy panic that reflected poorly on the federal agency whose job it was to round up spies. In January 1918 Assistant Attorney General Charles Warren forwarded newspaper clippings from the *Boston Herald* to his boss, Attorney General Gregory, "in order to show that the remarks of Mr. Rathom find echo elsewhere."

"I call your especial attention," Warren wrote, referring to an editorial, "at the end of which mention is made of certain despicable German plots, very close to us here in Boston [that] have never seen the light of publicity, etc. etc."

On January 19, 1918, Rathom gave an ill-advised speech to the Society of the Genesee in New York. It was stupid of him. Rathom knew he had irritated Gregory with his lies and criticism of the Wilson administration. Yet he poked the bear. Not poked, he kicked it in the groin. Rathom charged that "German pacifists" held important posts in the US War Department. He said the Department of Justice "was undermanned and was working at cross purposes." He alleged that law enforcement was soft on spies, scouring law books for excuses *not* to arrest them.

It was too much for Gregory. Rathom had crossed his last line.

On January 29, the attorney general of the United States dictated secret orders, intending to shut Rathom down, shut him up, and, if necessary, destroy him:

> It occurs to me that this man Rathom should be jerked before the Grand Jury in Boston and thoroughly examined, and if he admits that what he has been telling are lies or that he has not the evidence, have the grand jury make a report to the court which in that way can be published.

The US attorney in New York, Francis G. Caffey, was at that moment pursing a similar strategy against an officer of the American Defense Society, C. S. Thompson, who had spoken out of turn and embarrassed the government. Thompson triggered a storm of breathless national news coverage with the stunning claim that the US government had secretly executed fourteen German spies.

When Thompson refused to divulge his confidential source, he was subpoenaed before a grand jury.

Thompson was flat wrong; the United States had not been secretly executing spies, though Thompson seemed to believe the claim. There is evidence that Thompson's source was a particular celebrity news editor from Providence. Fittingly, then, Thompson and Rathom would both be called before the same grand jury.

❖

The day after Gregory dictated his orders to proceed against Rathom, the telephone rang in the Bureau of Investigation field office in Providence, Room 301 of the stately granite Federal Building downtown. Special agent in charge Tom Howick took the call. An agent from New York was on the train to Providence, he was told, with a subpoena that "must be served that night."

Howick notified the US marshal, then arranged a car service. The agent from New York hustled off the train in downtown Providence at 10:55 P.M. The two Bureau of Investigation agents and the marshal hopped in the car together and made the steep drive up College Hill into the city's East Side, to a charming home on Brown Street, a few blocks from Brown University. The lawmen thumped up darkened steps to the wooden porch and banged the door until it opened.

They placed the subpoena into the hand of John R. Rathom.

Rathom was compelled to appear before the grand jury in New York that coming Friday. Rather than impanel a new grand jury in Boston, it had been decided to use the same investigative jury already sitting in the Thompson case in Manhattan. In his testimony, Thompson fingered Rathom as the source of his outrageous statement about the US government executing spies. He claimed Rathom told him he had heard it directly from President Woodrow Wilson.

Rathom appeared in secret before the grand jury on February 1, at the federal courthouse in Lower Manhattan, a billowing five-story monstrosity in Second Empire style in City Hall Park. Under questioning, Rathom denied he was Thompson's source and then "testified briefly" about statements from his Boston speech, according to Bielaski's notes.

Testifying under oath was odious for Rathom. He could see it was the path to his own destruction. During a recess, Rathom asked Bielaski, was there were some way he could avoid more testimony and, critically, a public report by the grand jury?

Yeah, maybe. Bielaski took Rathom's plea to the attorney general.

Gregory's terms were brutal. He would let Rathom out of the subpoena only if he made "a complete confession" in writing, to the lies, exaggerations, and inventions he had spread on the lecture circuit. This confession would remain secret, Gregory promised, unless he decided "the public good" required that it be released. And that would depend entirely "on Mr. Rathom's future conduct."

The price Rathom had to pay to avoid testifying was to sign what the Russians call a *kompromat*—a package of damaging information held for blackmail. Rathom would strap dynamite to himself and to his reputation, and the US government would forever hold the trigger. The price to avoid testifying was his freedom to speak freely.

Seeing no other path, Rathom agreed to be blackmailed.

On February 4, Rathom, Bielaski, and the president of the Providence Journal Company, Stephen O. Metcalf, conferred in New York. Rathom and Bielaski wrote Rathom's confession, "which was dictated in large part by Mr. Rathom and in part by myself," according to Bielaski's notes.

The confession was formatted as a letter from Rathom to Gregory. Bielaski was not altogether satisfied with the draft, and thought the confession contained too many vague statements, but on the whole it was devastating enough that Rathom would never want it released, and that was the point. Rathom took a copy home to Providence, where his signature was to be witnessed and co-signed by officers of the *Journal*. When the letter did not immediately make its way back to New York, Bielaski telephoned Rathom. The letter was coming by courier, Rathom promised. He mentioned he had made "one or two minor changes," of no consequence whatsoever.

No consequence? Hardly. Rathom had rewritten the letter. Bielaski unloaded on Rathom for trying to squirm out of the text they had written together. "I may state that the Department received within the last two days a suggestion from one of the ranking Cabinet officers that prompt steps should be taken to see you are exposed."

"The Attorney General is not in any mood to temporize with these matters," Bielaski warned. He directed Rathom to recast the confession again, using "plain unvarnished statements of the exact facts without any evasion," or else Gregory will "take drastic action as it within his power."

That meant Rathom would have to testify.

Rathom conferred with his lawyer and decided he could not sign his own kompromat. He would testify in New York on February 11.

❖

While John Rathom and the feds tangled in secret, the American public devoured the first of Rathom's widely hyped articles in the February edition of *World's Work*.

The editorial leaders of the magazine, Page and Strother, wanted to sell magazines, but they were journalists, men of truth, who would not knowingly print lies. Before they let Rathom anywhere near their presses, they investigated. They learned, in Page's words, that Rathom "had covered certain sources of information by assuming their activities for the *Providence Journal*." Page and Strother forced Rathom to reveal sources to them, probably Gaunt and Voska, and verified that the sources had provided information to Rathom for news stories. Strother spoke to Secretary of the Navy Josephus Daniels, who confirmed that Rathom "had been useful" in providing tips to the navy. Strother also verified that Rathom had been at the White House on a date he had claimed.

Feeling better about Rathom's credibility, and under tremendous pressure to deliver the articles they had promised the nation, Page and Strother gave Rathom the all-clear to write a new opening story of the series, so long as it "not be guilty of the faults which our investigation has shown were inherent in the initial article."

They still did not entirely trust Rathom. As a Plan B, Strother began work on his own set of articles, with Bielaski's assistance, on government actions against German spies in the United States.

Rathom's article, "Germany's Plots Exposed," was Rathom-lite. He attacked German diplomats with truth and libel, but with far less of his usual self-promotion. Newspapers across the United States reprinted the shocking main charge of the story: that the *Providence Journal* intercepted and decoded a German wireless message suggesting that Berlin had deliberately ordered the *Lusitania* to be sunk. The cipher was a series of numbers, which, Rathom claimed, corresponded to page and line numbers in shipping journals and popular magazines, which indicated words that spelled out a message.

The story was "clearly a manufactured one," the Department of Justice later concluded, "and is not founded upon facts."

With the success of his *World's Work* article, Rathom had never been bigger or more popular. Behind the scenes, though, the Department of Justice worked even harder to take him down.

On February 11, the day Rathom was due to resume his testimony, Bielaski brought French Strother from *World's Work* to the courthouse, to testify to the grand jury about false statements Rathom had made to him. While Strother was in the grand jury room, Bielaski and Rathom waited together for Rathom's turn in the box. Bielaski played it cool, making a point to chat about everything except the fact that Rathom was about to face a legal buzz saw.

The pressure was too much. Rathom cracked. He desperately did not want to testify. Was there any way to avoid it? He offered to write a new confession.

And so he did, on February 12, in the US attorney's office in New York, in the presence of his lawyer, a second lawyer representing the *Providence Journal*, and Bielaski. It was signed by Rathom and witnessed on the spot by the newspaper's lawyer, an assistant US attorney, and the department stenographer.

"While this letter is not altogether accurate," Bielaski wrote to his boss, the attorney general, "and still places Mr. Rathom in a more favorable position that he is entitled to, it seems to entirely destroy all of his principal claims and I believe it would be so regarded by the public generally should it be known."

The feds had their kompromat.

❖

The day Rathom signed his confession, a grim group of men gathered at 8:30 P.M. at the Prince George Hotel in New York, an upscale Midtown hotel with dark floors and lots of lacquered wooden walls. Rathom was there. So was French Strother, and another editor at *World's Work*, Herbert Houston. *World's Work* boss Arthur Page soon arrived. And at Rathom's invitation, Bureau of Investigation chief Bielaski joined the group.

Houston was red hot and went after Bielaski. The magazine had just stopped it press run to pull Rathom's second article out of the March issue. It was a huge embarrassment, and the magazine intended to print a note blaming the Department of Justice. The department had ruined the "greatest counter-propaganda stroke against the Germans that was possible," from the pen of a man "who had the ear of the people like no one else had." It was stinging black eye for *World's Work*. And to whose benefit? Only Germany's.

Bielaski pushed back. It was unfair to say the Department of Justice stopped the articles. The department had only offered evidence of Rathom's falsehoods. If the magazine was jammed up that was the fault of *World's Work* and John Rathom.

Strother took Bielaski aside. He had heard Rathom had written some sort of letter to the attorney general to get out of testifying and Strother wanted to see it.

Bielaski said he did not have the authority to show the letter, but Rathom did.

No, Strother said, Rathom had insisted he had not received his copy of the letter.

Actually, Bielaski corrected, Rathom took his copy with him when he left the courthouse.

Strother immediately confronted Rathom and insisted he cough up the letter.

Reluctantly, Rathom pulled several pages from his pocket and handed them over.

Strother, Page, and Houston together read Rathom's confession in silence. When they had finished, nobody said anything for a few moments. Then Arthur Page said, "Mr. Rathom, with that letter in existence I am unwilling to continue the publication of the articles in *World's Work*."

In its first test, the kompromat had demonstrated its destructive power.

Later that night in his hotel room in the Prince George, Rathom wet his pen and scratched a few pitiful lines to Bielaski:

> The World's Work people have just gone. I can't go to bed tonight without writing you a note to tell you how I greatly appreciate the way you handled a very difficult situation and to say to you that I am grateful for all your personal thoughtfulness for me.

Rathom still thought the Bureau of Investigation chief was his friend. Bielaski had conned the conman. And he was not done.

❖

Bielaski's agents continued to dig into Rathom's background in the spring of 1918. Agents ran down Rathom's claims about intercepting foreign wireless messages. They interviewed sources who claimed Rathom had connections with sketchy Russian agents. They staked out events at which

Rathom was rumored to be speaking. The feds even shattered the "hearts story." They asked the State Department about any German documents captured by Britain in a crate marked by two red hearts. A spokesman for the department responded that no such box ever arrived from London. "I have not been able to confirm the statement that such a box was intercepted by the British Control Office," the spokesman said. [*]

In March a Bureau of Investigation special agent called on a New York law firm that had conducted a private investigation into Rathom's background, around 1913, on behalf of an aggrieved client who had been on the sharp end of Rathom's writing. A partner in the firm, John Crim, turned over a file thick with sworn affidavits from former Rathom coworkers and acquaintances, trashing him in British Columbia, Oregon, and San Francisco, about unpaid debts and allegations of extortion. Crim had collected letters from schools Rathom claimed to have attended, but which never heard of him. He had affidavits from records clerks saying there was no marriage license for Rathom and Florence. He had documents from Australia confirming there was no birth certificate for a John R. Rathom in Melbourne.

With this information, it dawned on top figures in the Justice Department that John Rathom was not who he said he was. He was an imposter.

Rathom's signed confession was one half of the kompromat. It could destroy his reputation. The personal file acquired by the Bureau of Investigation was the second half. If the public ever saw the contents, Rathom's very identity would be annihilated.

"Unless a halt is called on Mr. Rathom by the government of the United States, he will go down in history as one of the leading publicists in this war," Crim wrote to Bielaski, when he gave his secret Rathom file to the feds. Crim warned that the United States would be humiliated if her enemies were to expose John Rathom. He urged: "I hope that you will do it first."

---

[*] Rathom heard the hearts story from Voska, who later claimed the accurate version involved a Czech stenographer undercover at the Austrian consulate, who had charmed the consul general. Who knows? It might be too good a story to be true.

CHAPTER 16

The Only Thing We Have to Smear

In February 1919, just three months after the armistice that ended the war—John Rathom's war—a petty naval officer holding the rank of chief machinist's mate transferred from a post in San Francisco to a busy naval base in Rhode Island, Naval Station Newport. Machinist's Mate Ervin Arnold, who was forty-four years old, arrived in Newport while suffering a flair-up of rheumatism, and was immediately sent to the base hospital for treatment.

While hospitalized, Arnold began to surreptitiously monitor other people in the ward. How they walked. How they spoke. He noted their mannerisms and their diction. He eavesdropped on conversations. He engaged others in leading dialogues, earning their confidence and drawing out information.

And from his hospital bed, Arnold began to make careful notes about who around him might be gay.*

Arnold was a fifteen-year navy veteran. Before his service he worked for nine years as a Connecticut vice cop. As a detective, Arnold had gathered evidence against "sexual perverts," as gay Americans were known in this

---

* I use the modern term *gay*, which Arnold would not have understood in this context. The term *homosexual* was not yet in wide use in his day, a time when gay Americans were prosecuted as sex criminals.

primitive era. He had heard rumors while on the West Coast that Newport was teeming with gay sailors, and he quickly convinced himself that the gossip was right.

"What Arnold discovered during the ensuing days," wrote author John Loughery in his book on early gay history in the United States, *The Other Side of Silence*, "was the eclectic world of fairies and trade, of cross-dressers and party-givers, cocaine addicts and heavy drinkers, for whom mobilization had been a wildly social experience."

Arnold was fixated on rooting homosexuality out of the navy, with "an anxiety bordering on obsession." He claimed he had the world's greatest gaydar: He said he could identify a gay man nine times out of ten by the way he walked. Arnold was not very bright, but he got things done. He was "aggressive, uneducated and the bulldog type," a US Senate subcommittee would later conclude, after an investigation into the wreckage Arnold's fixations created in Newport.

Arnold's fear of homosexuality is at the center of one of the most humiliating episodes in US naval history. The scandal he set into motion would taint the reputation of a rising political star, Franklin Delano Roosevelt. It would lure Rathom from Department of Justice exile, back into the spotlight, and into a public dogfight with the young Roosevelt.

Roosevelt and Rathom had something in common—both were ruthless political knife fighters not above playing dirty to win.

❖

Throughout the Gilded Age, Newport, Rhode Island, was the summer playground of the Astors and the Vanderbilts and other lesser mogul families, who hosted elegant lawn parties at their grandiose getaway mansions along Belleview Avenue. The moguls are gone, but their mansions survive, now drawing sunbaked sightseers for ticketed tours through glittering interiors that can feel like 3-D snapshots of vintage wealth porn.

Newport has also long been a navy town. Before World War I, Naval Station Newport typically hosted some two thousand new recruits, who rotated through the station to learn seamanship and naval practices before being assigned to a ship or another base. Beginning in the summer of 1917, after the United States entered the war, new recruits flooded into Newport. Housing on the base was swamped. The overflow had no option but to spread into the community. Sailors found quarters in cheap private apartment buildings, in homes as boarders, and at the downtown YMCA. The city swarmed with twenty thousand young sailors, many of whom lived in off-base housing with little or no supervision. These young bell-bottoms let loose. Newport trembled with a party-town vibe. Liquor, cocaine, and prostitutes were conveniently at hand.

Within this thrumming community, gay sailors drafted from around the country, many of whom probably grew up thinking they were alone in the world, began to find each other. They built their own thriving underground social scene, connecting for camaraderie, romance, or just sex at the YMCA or along the Newport Cliff Walk, a seaside strolling path between the rolling ocean and the backyards of the millionaires' mansions. Civilian authorities were alarmed by rumors of drugs, sex parties, and gay hookups in Newport. Officers at all levels of the navy wanted to clean up the town.

In March 1919 Arnold persuaded his superiors to sign off on a cleanup plan that in hindsight is almost too stupid for words.

Arnold's plan was to recruit a team of navy sailors to conduct an undercover sting operation to take down the "cocksuckers and rectum receivers" whom Arnold believed were undermining the morals of community.

Under Arnold's plan, his recruits, chosen for their youthful good looks, were the bait. These covert operatives were assigned "to go forth into Newport and vicinity and associate and mingle with the alleged sexual perverts." Released into the wild, the handsome young operatives, some still in their teens, made themselves available to be picked up by gay men. They "loitered at the YMCA, made dates, attended parties, went strolling with new acquaintances after dark by the beach and in the cemetery."

The difficulty with a sting of this sort is acquiring ironclad proof of sexual criminality—not something an operative could get in a conversation.

To surmount this problem, the members of Arnold's covert team "were to allow certain immoral acts to be performed on them for the purposes of securing evidence," a US Senate investigation found.

The navy wanted to identify "perverts" in uniform giving head to other men.

So they sent Arnold's volunteers to get head from those men.

In short order, the covert operatives enjoyed a "fairly staggering amount of oral sex" in the line of duty.

"In their pursuit of the 'cocksuckers' Arnold had charged them to find," Loughery reported, "this group of young men was all but tireless."

The operation was a success—sort of. It led to mass arrests in April 1919. Working with local police, Arnold raced around Newport camouflaged in an ambulance, rounding up suspects. More than twenty navy men were nabbed in the sting, accused of immoral acts, and jailed in deplorable conditions on an old ship. More than forty members of the US Navy ultimately would take part in Arnold's covert unit over the next several months; a quarter were between the ages of sixteen and nineteen.

In the spring of 1919, the sting expanded and began entrapping the general public. Arnold's secret sodomy squad became known as Section A of the Office of the Assistant Secretary of the Navy.

And who was the assistant secretary? That would be Franklin Delano Roosevelt.

Much of the public blame for Section A would ultimately fall on Roosevelt. Roosevelt authorized a continuation of the cleanup operation and oversaw the transfer of Arnold and another leader of the operation, Lieutenant Erasmus Hudson, to the Office of Naval Intelligence. How much Roosevelt knew about the vice squad's tactics is disputed. He would later claim he knew nothing of how Section A gathered evidence of sex crimes. It is hard to believe Roosevelt was completely ignorant of what the navy was doing with its seamen.

At the time, Roosevelt was thirty-seven, baby-faced, and dashing. This was before the presidency and the New Deal. Before four national election wins. Before his governorship of New York. Before polio. In 1919 Roosevelt, was 6'2", trim and athletic, the rising star of a wealthy Hyde Park family, a sportsman, golfer, tennis player, and sailor. In 1912 Roosevelt had been a mere New York state senator when he backed Woodrow Wilson's bid for the Democratic Party's nomination for president. Wilson repaid the favor by appointing Roosevelt assistant navy secretary, under Secretary Josephus Daniels, a North Carolina newspaperman and another loyal Democrat.

How Arnold and Hudson persuaded top navy leaders to back their sting is hard to fathom. Sending teenaged recruits into a community of strangers to get blown and take names is a depressing low point in the history of the US military.

The navy's oral sex scheme soon blew up in its face.

❖

John Rathom survived his *World's Work* crisis of early 1918. The magazine replaced his articles with a series on government counterspy operations, authored by managing editor French Strother. Strother wrote the first piece in a fevered twenty-four hours, so the magazine could be printed on time. Bureau of Investigation chief Bruce Bielaski gave Strother access to closed case files, agent reports, and witness statements. The series began with a note acknowledging the bureau's help, and promising: "The facts and documents published in these articles are verified."

Newspapers across the country speculated on why Rathom's series had been pulled. The *New York Tribune* reported blindly sourced information that the stories had been withdrawn under pressure by the Department of Justice. Rathom issued such a severe denial that nobody knew what to believe and the controversy faded away.

In May 1918 American troops launched their first major offensive of World War I, at the Battle of Cantigny, in northern France.

Four months later, that New Brunswick farm boy in the Canadian infantry, Henry Arsenault, was shot through the leg but evacuated to a field hospital in time to save his life, his future, the future of the five Joes, my family, and me.

World War I ended in Allied victory on November 11, 1918, about nineteen months after the United States declared war on Germany.

"Everything for which America fought has been accomplished," President Woodrow Wilson proclaimed, amid delirious national celebration that spilled into the streets.

Nearly five million American troops served in World War I, and 116,516 died in combat or from disease, including from the 1918 influenza pandemic.

Back home, events tumbled swiftly upon the conclusion of the war.

It was less than twelve weeks after the armistice that anti-gay zealot Ervin Arnold transferred to Newport and began his covert investigation. That same month, February 1919, Bruce Bielaski left the Bureau of Investigation for private law practice. And in March another Rathom nemesis, Attorney General Thomas Watt Gregory, resigned his post in Wilson's cabinet.

Under new leadership, the Department of Justice conducted an internal scrub of its Rathom files, scrutinizing the department's confidential communications with the editor prior to his speaking tour as well as the kompromat material assembled after the department turned against Rathom in late 1917. It was a cover-your-ass exercise by an agency concerned about its exposure for trading information with Rathom for years. "The suppressing of Rathom's articles in the 'World's Work' has removed any trace that the Department of Justice assisted this man in perpetuating his false stories," concluded a summary of the internal review. "It is unfortunate he was never publicly denounced and that he still retains his elevated position of an editor of a newspaper from which pedestal he can maliciously manufacture false criticisms against private citizens of the United States, the Government and the present Administration."

Rathom kept a modest (by his standards) profile in 1919. He ran the *Providence Journal*, wrote songs and poems, attended World War I victory celebrations, and rallied his readers against a new threat to the pursuit of happiness—Prohibition. In February, Rathom gave a speech to educators at the Brooklyn Training School for Teachers. With the Germans defeated, the Communists were the next villain up. "Bolshevism is largely a mental attitude," Rathom thundered. "Unfortunately, a great many people of high ideals and high standing have been bitten with that disease." It was a safe topic; the Department of Justice was never going to be offended by attacks on the Reds.

The kompromat remained locked away. For Rathom, the passing of time and the exit of Bielaski and Gregory from government may have eased his fears of being exposed. Or maybe one year out of the limelight was all Rathom could stand.

In January 1920 Rathom dipped his poisoned pen and wrote a blistering editorial that would signal his return to the national stage and into a new conflict with the US government.

❖

Nobody had ever seen a federal criminal trial like the one unfolding in US District Court in downtown Providence. The newspapers had no idea how to cover sexual accusations too lewd to be described in print, and so hardly any journalists wrote about the trial over four days of testimony in early January 1920.

At the defendant's table: the Reverend Samuel Neal Kent, age forty-six, an Episcopal priest and navy chaplain. Kent was 5'11" and a slim 170 pounds. He had been described as "extremely bald," with "a sallow complexion, round face rather full. Hair grayish tint. Walks with a quick step, very erect." He wore tiny round wire eyeglasses without temples, known as nose glasses because they sat perched high on the bridge of the nose.

Kent was by many accounts a good priest. He was also, the evidence shows, a gay man during a time when homosexuals were branded as perverts and routinely jailed.

The Reverend Kent was the most prominent civilian pinched in the Section A sting in Newport. He faced charges of moral depravity.

In the witness box testifying under oath: Charles B. Zipf, an operator for Section A, a square-skulled sailor, with wide-set eyes, heavy dark eyebrows, and a high forehead. Zipf was from Freeport, Illinois. He had studied medicine at the University of Michigan before joining the navy. He was about twenty-two years old.

Under cross-examination by Kent's lawyer, Zipf described the navy's sting operation, which astonished onlookers in court found almost too bizarre to believe. Zipf confirmed he received a directive to infiltrate Newport's underground gay social scene from Ervin Arnold.

"You received your instructions from him?" Kent's lawyer asked.

"Yes, sir," Zipf said.

"Did Arnold tell you that you were obliged to perform this duty?"

"Orders were orders in the navy."

"Then you understood you were under compulsion to accept this appointment to proceed under this investigation of vice conditions in Newport?"

"No," Zipf corrected. "I imagine I could have gotten out of it if I really tried."

"Then you didn't want to get out of it?"

"Not particularly so."

"You liked it? You liked the work?"

"No," he corrected again. "I liked the principle of the thing."

"Were you told that it was your duty to allow your penis to be held?"

"Not as a duty. We were to obtain evidence."

"And if necessary to obtain evidence you were to allow your penis to be handled?"

"Yes, sir."

"And you were to allow that handling to continue until there was an erection?"

"Yes, sir."

"And an emission?"

"Yes, sir."

"And that you were to suck parts or allow yourself to be sucked?"

"No sir—not to suck parts."

"Were you not told that you were to allow yourself to be sucked—your instrument to be sucked, if necessary?"

"If necessary—yes, sir," Zipf confirmed.

Zipf testified that he went to bed with Kent one night the previous March. He was among four operators who testified to having sexual relations with the Reverend Kent. The accusations were probably accurate; Section A entrapped its victims but there is no evidence it framed them.

Samuel Kent was raised in Lynn, Massachusetts, and educated at the prestigious Boston Latin School. His family was poor, so instead of attending college Kent got a job at a shoe factory. He was a good employee, but the shoe business was dull. He tried working as an event promoter, and then in 1908 at age thirty-five Kent entered the Episcopal Theological School in Cambridge, Massachusetts. He was ordained in 1911, and soon became assistant rector of New York's Church of the Holy Communion, where he built a fine reputation. His boss later recalled Kent as "a perfectly splendid manly man."

Kent moved to Pennsylvania and became school chaplain at Lehigh University. After the United States entered the First World War, Kent served as chaplain at Fort Niagara, and then in 1918 took a post at a small US Army facility in Newport.

At the time, the Great Influenza epidemic was ravaging nearby Naval Station Newport. The naval base did not have enough clergy for so many sick sailors, so Kent volunteered. "He comforted as many of the sick as possible," wrote Lawrence R. Murphy, who authored a definitive history of the Newport scandal, "talking gently, writing letters, or providing spiritual assurances to the dying," while putting himself in constant jeopardy of infection and death. By late autumn 1918 the influenza pandemic ebbed. Kent continued ministering to military men in Newport, responsible for holding services, visiting men in the stockage, and guiding young souls around the falling pianos of life.

Kent's defense in court was to deny everything and offer character witnesses. This defense worked. Or perhaps the twelve men on the jury could not bring themselves to reward the tactics Section A had used the collect the evidence. Either way, the jury deliberated for three hours on January 8 and found Kent not guilty.

The drama may have ended there but for John Rathom.

Rathom played the story of Kent's acquittal on the front page. More provocatively, he blasted the Navy Department in a blazing editorial, blaming Navy Secretary Daniels, "who, through this entire case, deliberately employed every bestial and degrading scheme he could utilize to bring everlasting shame to an innocent man." Nowhere did Rathom detail exactly what degrading schemes the navy had employed.

After Kent's acquittal, a group of Rhode Island ministers complained to President Woodrow Wilson of "the deleterious and vicious methods" of entrapment the Kent trial had exposed. Such methods "cannot fail to undermine the character and ruin the morals of the navy men so employed." The press got a copy of the letter and quoted from it. The wires spread the complaints around the country.

Navy Secretary Daniels felt the heat. He responded by naming a court of inquiry to investigate Section A and its methods. Admiral Herbert O. Dunn would oversee the inquiry. The Dunn court spent months taking testimony from witnesses. It produced thousands of pages of evidence, a record sociologists have mined for decades for clues about gay life in America prior to the Stonewall riots in 1969, the unofficial kickoff of the gay rights movement.

Rathom was unsatisfied with the navy's promise to investigate itself. On January 18 he sent explosive telegrams to each member of the US Senate Committee of Naval Affairs, alleging that top navy brass knew that "many seamen of the Navy have been used for the most vile and nameless practices in order to entrap innocent men."

Rathom called for a Congressional investigation, and he got one. The Committee of Naval Affairs designated three of its members—Republicans Lewis H. Ball of Delaware and Henry Keyes of Vermont, and Democrat William King of Utah—to investigate allegations raised by Rathom and the local ministers.

Rathom never explained why he pursued the scandal with such ferocity. It was a great story, of course, which for a journalist is usually enough. It is also easy to imagine Rathom's pent-up rage at the Wilson administration and everyone associated with it. To get Rathom to sign the kompromat, the administration had done the legal equivalent of dangling him upside down off a balcony. Rathom also had a powerful moral compass for other people's missteps, if not his own, and a hatred of sex crimes dating back to his early days in Victoria. The imposter had also developed a taste for applause. More than a year into his government-imposed sabbatical from rabblerousing, Rathom saw the Newport scandal as a return to the stage.

Roosevelt belittled Rathom's attacks on navy leadership as "a deliberate and malicious attempt to create trouble, in addition to being false." Rathom issued a tart response. Reporters fanned the prickly little conflict into a conflagration.

ROOSEVELT DENIES RATHOM CHARGES, read a headline in the *New York Times*, as if the two men were of equal stature and neither needed any more introduction.

Navy Secretary Daniels was Rathom's top target when the Newport scandal first broke. But after his public tiff with Roosevelt, the celebrity journalist turned his acid pen on Roosevelt.

It was the biggest mistake of Rathom's life.

❖

In early July 1920 Democratic Party delegates from around the forty-eight states poured into Civic Auditorium, in downtown San Francisco, to nominate new candidates for president and vice president. This was back when convention delegates actually chose candidates in smoke-filled rooms, rather than just feted them on television. The incumbent, Wilson, was unwell, recovering from a stroke. Legally, Wilson was eligible for a third term, but the party was in the mood for a new standard-bearer. A dozen or more affluent white guys entered the convention as plausible nominees to run against the GOP ticket of Warren G. Harding, a US senator from Ohio with a deep soothing voice and shaggy black eyebrows, and his running mate, Massachusetts governor Calvin Coolidge.

After forty-four ballots, the Democratic delegates selected as their presidential candidate Ohio governor James M. Cox, a handsome, clean-shaven, fifty-year-old with short hair severely parted to the side. Cox was an accomplished politician and entrepreneur. His business legacies survive to this day—there likely are Americans right now waiting on hold to speak to a service representative for Cox Communications. Once the Democrats had selected Cox, the party needed someone to balance the ticket as the vice presidential nominee. A Cox delegate had an inspired idea, and entered into nomination the name of the assistant secretary of the navy.

Shouts rang out throughout the hall seconding the nomination of Franklin Delano Roosevelt for vice president.

"Cox and Roosevelt!" the delegates hollered, as if stress-testing the sound of the ticket. The Democrats liked the sound. The room erupted into cheers. Roosevelt was from New York, the biggest prize in the Electoral College. If the ticket could take Roosevelt's home state, it would be well on its way to winning. Other vice presidential hopefuls recognized the rolling bandwagon for Roosevelt and jumped out of its way, pulling their names from contention. FDR was nominated for vice president by acclamation.

The presidential campaign of 1920 was waged in an uneasy time of labor strikes, fears of "radials" and "Reds," a sharp postwar recession, and bitter partisan argument over Wilson's plan to establish a League of Nations for the international community to resolve disputes.

The Newport scandal was low static in the background, audibly popping up on occasion. In May, Navy Secretary Daniels testified before the naval inquiry into Section A, explicitly denying Rathom's charge that top navy officials knew of and permitted "vile and nameless methods" to gather evidence. "That is absolutely false," Daniels insisted, in widely reported comments. "There is not a scintilla of truth in it."

Rathom also appeared before the court of inquiry. During his testimony, on May 27, in Westerly, Rhode Island, the navy lobbed a shot across his bow. A judge advocate alluded to a letter Rathom wrote in 1918 to former Attorney General Gregory—Rathom's confession—and asked, "Is it not a fact that many of the war stories in which the *Providence Journal* claimed credit for unearthing German spy systems were false?"

Rathom exploded. The very question "is a deliberate, willful and absolute falsehood in all that it says and all that it implies." He ranted that he could not comment on any confidential communication between himself and the former attorney general "without a release from Mr. Gregory," as if Gregory were the one with something to hide. Rathom angrily accused Daniels and Roosevelt of planting the question to "injure and degrade" him.

The bluster worked. Rathom slipped out of the noose. But it was clear from the close call that Roosevelt knew about the kompromat.

The 1920 presidential race was mercifully short by today's standards. Harding, the GOP nominee, ran what is known as a front-port campaign. Instead of barnstorming the country kissing hands and shaking babies, he stayed home in Marion, Ohio, a town of twenty-nine thousand, and let interested parties come to him. Business leaders, office holders, hacks and lobbyists, journalists—they all paraded through Harding's charming upper-middle-class home, meeting with Harding or scribbling down the remarks he delivered each day on his big circular porch.

In July, Rathom and his boss, *Providence Journal* president Stephen O. Metcalf, trekked to Ohio to meet privately with Harding. There appears to be no record of what they spoke about. Rathom told the newsmen hanging around Harding's porch that the visit was just a social call. There was no question that the Republican-leaning *Providence Journal* would support Harding in the 1920 presidential election. The newspaper praised Harding's "character" and "great experience," while linking Cox to the "the baleful theories that the present Democratic administration has disastrously promulgated."

As Election Day approached, Rathom's support of Harding and his rage at Roosevelt came into perfect alignment, like the solstice sun at Stonehenge. In reckless inspiration Rathom prepared a bombshell designed to destroy Roosevelt. He timed its release for maximum effect, in the final days before the vote, what is now known in political jargon as an October surprise.

❖

It was October 23, 1920, a Saturday, ten days before the presidential election. Vice presidential nominee Franklin Delano Roosevelt arrived in Newburgh, New York, on the Hudson River, south of Roosevelt's home in Hyde Park. He was staying at the Hotel Palatine, a handsome redbrick building that looked like a municipal armory that went way over its construction budget. At the hotel, Roosevelt was surprised by one of John Rathom's reporters. The man placed a sealed envelope in Roosevelt's hand. The reporter said he did not know what was in it. He excused himself, duty done, and left Roosevelt with the envelope.

Inside Roosevelt found a letter addressed to him from Rathom, thirteen typewritten pages, excoriating Roosevelt in nearly every paragraph in unusually personal terms. The letter opened by recounting the fact Roosevelt and his boss, Daniels, had appointed the former warden of New York's Sing Sing state prison, Thomas Mott Osborne, a friend of Roosevelt's from New York State politics, to run Portsmouth Naval Prison, a dreary concrete castle on an island in the mouth of the Piscataqua River in Maine.

Roosevelt could sense where this was going. For months he had been in a low-wattage public quarrel with a navy captain named Joseph K. Taussig, about the naval prison and Osborne's leadership. Osborne believed in returning rehabilitated men to service after they completed their sentences. It was controversial. In early 1920 Taussig called for a court of inquiry to investigate the records of more than two thousand prisoners returned to military service during the war, including, it was alleged, men who had been imprisoned for sex crimes. Returning these men to duty had undermined morale and military discipline, Taussig said. Roosevelt, in response, argued that the vast majority of the men "returned to the service had made good."

Taussig had evidently brought his complaints to Rathom.

Rathom alleged in the letter that Osborne had turned the Portsmouth prison into "a joke" by softening its approach with reduced sentences, movies for the inmates, boxing and wrestling matches, and little or no work for those incarcerated. From there, the letter claimed the *Providence Journal* had acquired evidence proving two alarming charges against Roosevelt:

1. That Roosevelt approved Osborne's practice of returning to naval duty "men who have been convicted of crimes involving moral turpitude," in violation of longstanding rules and practices.
2. That Roosevelt destroyed official records related one of those convicted sailors.

"You have been going about the country," Rathom wrote, "denying that you or Mr. Daniels ever returned a man to active duty who had been convicted of a crime involving moral turpitude. You expect the people of this country to believe that statement because you, Franklin Roosevelt, make it—therefore it must be true."

"You, even more than Josephus Daniels, have been the evil genius of [the navy] and you have earned the detestation and contempt of every patriotic and skilled naval officer with whom you have come in contact."

These were serious charges. *Destroyed records?* That was a felony. Roosevelt got in touch with Osborne, who reported back with a mortifying bit of intelligence. A Republican-leaning newspaper in Osborne's hometown of Auburn, New York, had received a posted copy of Rathom's letter, dated for public release in the morning paper—Monday, October 25—eight days before the election. Osborne also heard that the letter had been posted from 18 West Forty-Fourth Street in New York City, an address used by the Republican National Committee.

Rathom's October surprise was already in the hands of editors across the land.

Roosevelt sprang into action. He wrote to Francis Caffey, the US attorney for the Southern District of New York, pleading for Caffey to do *something*. "The circulation of charges of this character would obviously blacken my character as a candidate for the office of Vice-President of the United States," Roosevelt wrote. He said Rathom's letter was "criminally libelous," and urged the Department of Justice prosecute him.

Next, Roosevelt sent a blanket notice to a mass of newspaper editors, warning that he intended to sue Rathom for libel immediately upon the letter's publication, and that any newspaper that printed it also risked a lawsuit. Within days, Roosevelt made good on the threat. He filed suit in the Supreme Court of New York against John Rathom and two GOP operatives who allegedly helped spread the letter. Roosevelt's lawsuit sought a staggering $500,000 in damages. The suit generated sensational headlines, of course. Who had ever seen a vice presidential candidate sue a celebrity journalist the week before a national election?

US Attorney Caffey saw no prosecutable crime in Rathom's letter. But he had another idea to defang John Rathom.

The kompromat.

"I suggest that as soon as possible your personal counsel get in touch with me and let me make him some suggestions," Caffey wrote to Roosevelt.

Here, I have to pause the story to consider Rathom's position.

Rathom is on the precipice of ruin. His heels hang over the edge, yet still he swings and spits and fights on. Why? Why risk everything to go after Roosevelt days before an election most experts expected the Democrats to lose?

Clearly, the imposter was passionate in the pursuit of justice, despite his own moral elasticity. He also had a blind spot for personal consequences that bedeviled him his whole career. And of course, Rathom could not have imagined he was tangling with the preeminent American politician of the twentieth century, and may have seen Roosevelt as a lightweight riding high on his connections.

Of all the possible reasons, I choose to think Rathom just said *fuck it*. The government had bullied him into signing away his freedom to speak. Without that, what is a journalist? Or an American? Faced with the choice of timid silence, or free speech and a fiery death, Rathom chose to fly into the sun.

He spoke out and dared government officials to do their worst.

And they did.

US Attorney Caffey leveraged the US Department of Justice in a purely partisan defense of Roosevelt and the Democratic presidential ticket. He sought permission from the new attorney general, A. Mitchell Palmer, a former Democratic congressman from Pennsylvania, and then released a public statement:

> In the interest of the public good, as well as in fairness to Mr. Roosevelt as a former officer of the United States, I think I ought now to say that I do not believe any attack by Mr. Rathom would be given credence by anyone who knows his record.

With that brief announcement, Caffey released the first half of the kompromat—Rathom's confession—to the press.

CHAPTER 17
Kompromat

CONFIDENTIAL
February 12, 1918
[To]: Hon. Thomas W. Gregory, Attorney General of the U.S.,
Washington, D.C.
Sir:

My attention has been called to the embarrassment which your department has been occasioned by the popular impression which prevails that I or the Providence Journal should be credited with the work which has been accomplished since the outbreak of the European War in the suppression of activities of German agents in the country, which impression has arisen not from publication of matter in the Providence Journal, but from speeches which I have made on a few public occasions, and from statements which I may have made of similar character to private individuals.

So begins the secret confession of John R. Rathom.
It continues:

I feel that the general opinion, which has rather unfortunately credited us with the actual bringing to justice of German spies and malefactors,

has been misdirected to the extent that our only possible claim to valu-
able constructive work in the past 3-1/2 years ought in fairness to be
restricted to the educational value of our continued efforts, and to
the newspaper enterprise which produced a great number of stories
printed in our newspaper.

The belief that the Providence Journal has specifically brought to
justice any of these individuals creates an unjust impression, and does
take away from the Department of Justice the full credit to which it
is entitled for this work. We sincerely regret that this situation has
arisen . . .

In his confession, Rathom disclosed that the *Providence Journal* did not intercept any German messages with its own wireless station. He conceded "it is not true that the Providence Journal's own representatives ever occupied positions" inside German and Austrian consulates. His enchanting tale of the inept saboteur Werner Horn was "practically correct," though "any suggestion that the material was gathered by, or that Horn was arrested at the instigation of, any Providence Journal representative, is not true."

On and on it went for pages. Gaston Means was Rathom's source on the Canadian Parliament fire, even though Rathom knew Means was working for the Germans and was unreliable. The *Journal* "did not have any representative" in Consul General Bopp's office in San Francisco, as Rathom had claimed, "nor did the information furnished by us, as far as we know, figure in Bopp's conviction." Rathom knew of no German spies in Detroit "beyond those which have become public property through the newspapers and court proceedings in that city."

The document disavowed Rathom's sensational Huerta story, about the New York conference between Karl Boy-Ed and the exiled Mexican dictator Victoriano Huerta, after Department of Justice officials cast doubt that such a meeting ever happened. The information "came to our men second hand," Rathom wrote. More than a decade later, the German spy Franz Rintelen acknowledged meeting with Huerta in New York, but it was too late to help Rathom.

Even Rathom's greatest hit, the hearts story, was put to rest. There never was any pretty young *Journal* woman in the consulate:

> *My source of information with respect to the "hearts" story was a set of circumstantial reports made to me . . . and the person referred to who made the markings on the box was a young Croatian woman, a stenographer in the employ of Consul-general von Nuber, who was secretly aiding the British government.*

The confession rightly credited Voska's Bohemian National Alliance for providing the newspaper confidential information from the consulates. Rathom also acknowledged that a "major part of the documentary evidence" he received for his stories was from British, Canadian, and US government sources.

He admitted he covered up where he got his information "by intentionally suggesting sources which did not actually exist."

Near the end of the document, Rathom pleaded for mercy for his newspaper work, which "only in an infinitesimal degree" contained the fantasies he spun in his speeches, he wrote. Rathom foresaw that his speeches would taint the revelations published in his pages, many of which were developed from knowledgeable sources. On this point, his fears were exactly right. Newspaper editors around the country, many of whom had eagerly printed Rathom's stories before and during the war, were outraged by the confession, believing they had been duped.

The *New York Herald* reported on the confession with a towering six-deck headline:

BIG SPY SYSTEM OF PROVIDENCE "JOURNAL" MYTH

RATHOM, EDITOR, HAD TO ADMIT CAMOUFLAGING WAR TIME
"NEWS" SOURCES

CONFESSION GIVEN OUT

RHODE ISLAND MAN COMPELLED BY U.S. TO TELL WHERE TIPS
CAME FROM

KEPT SECRET TWO YEARS

ATTACK ON F. D. ROOSEVELT RESULTS IN CAFFEY SHOWING
RECORD HELD IN ABEYANCE

The lede of the *Herald* story was a devastating distillation of the drama:

> There never was such a thing as an elaborate spy system of the
> Providence Journal whereby that newspaper through agents in
> German and Austrian diplomatic offices claimed it was enabled
> to get all the inside facts on German spy and destruction systems
> in this country.

The *Boston Globe* printed long sections of Rathom's confession, broken
up with helpful little subheads, such as NOT TRUE HE HAD OWN AGENTS and
DID NOT USE OWN WIRELESS. The *New York World* could barely comprehend
the full depth of Rathom's fabrications, opining that the confession is "one
which for comprehensive avowals of downright falsehood has few parallels
in the annals of mendacity."

A few writers wading through the wreckage of Rathom's celebrity tried
to see what his confession said about America.

"When newspapers bear false witness at times of great national excitement, they can do incalculable amount of harm," read a solemn column
in the *Montgomery Advertiser*, of Alabama. Novelist and journalist Upton
Sinclair wrote sarcastically about the outgoing Wilson administration,
"which in its last days of collapse appears to have taken up blackmail."

Said Sinclair:

> The British government wanted to get us into the war, and to
> stir us up against the Germans in this country, and so it turned

over all this stuff to Rathom, and Rathom embellished it and turned it into a first-class detective thriller. The only trouble was, it made the American Secret Service men mad, because it made them out to be a lot of dubbs. So they had a showdown with Rathom and made him sign a confession. But did they tell you and me? No, they did not! They were afraid it might injure our morale during the war.

The *Nation* magazine blasted Rathom as a tool of the British and lamented that his "dime-novel clap-trap was the sort of propaganda with which the whole country was drugged." The magazine was equally hard on federal officials who sat on Rathom's confession for two years: "The Government which suppressed this important information, contributing in that way—among others—to war hysteria and terrorism, and publishes it only to aid the political ends of one of its henchmen, is an accessory after the fact to Mr. Rathom's malfeasance."

A haunting editorial on Rathom in the *Minneapolis Star* could be written today:

> A great newspaper, not scrupulous in regard to its news, may inflame public opinion to the extent of making a nation want war, make it violate its own instincts toward tolerance, and drive it to fear and desperation. There can be no law until news comes clean. In first and last analysis, nations are the creatures of propaganda.

In America, we are what we read, what we see on television, what we post, what we tweet.

Historians who published books about the war before Rathom's confession were generous to the editor, if not always accurate. "It is hardly too much to say that the course of the war might have been different, and with it the whole future of the United States, but for the remarkable achievements of the Providence Journal in deciphering German codes," reads a passage in *The World War and Its Consequences*, a book by University of Michigan professor William Herbert Hobbs published in 1919.

Post-confession mentions of Rathom usually came in condemnation. Walter Millis's influential 1935 history *Road to War* dismissed Rathom's scoops as "figments of a romantic imagination." That was not accurate, either. Millis conflated Rathom's speeches with his newspaper stories.

The lies poisoned everything Rathom had ever done. Soon, history would forget him. Was it fair? Not entirely. But public figures once paid excessive costs for lies. It was a sort of rough justice. America barely punishes public liars anymore. And now the country hardly knows whom to trust.

❖

With the grand cathedral of his reputation crashing down around him, Rathom responded with as much bluster as he could manage. He denied, falsely, that he signed the confession to get out of testifying to the grand jury. He insisted the "few entirely superficial matters touched on by this letter" did not diminish the work the newspaper had done during the war. He printed his own confession in the *Journal*, which he called a "statement," under the headline CAFFEY'S ATTACK ATTEMPT TO TURN ATTENTION FROM ROOSEVELT'S RECORD.

Bombast aside, Rathom was embarrassed and deeply hurt. He shared his feelings with his friend Adolph S. Ochs, the publisher of the *New York Times*, with whom Rathom served on the executive committee of the Associated Press. "I have been assailed by papers of the caliber of the New York *American* as a 'British agent,'" Rathom wrote to Ochs a week after his confession went public. "This of course is a wicked and willful falsehood." He laid out, in a general way, the breadth of his sources, as if begging Ochs not to think of him as a spy. "In every case we received our information from these channels in an entirely legitimate manner . . . I do not need to prove to those among my colleagues in the newspaper profession who know me that I have never stooped to improper or dishonorable methods."

One thing working in Rathom's favor was that his confession lacked context. Most of the text would make little sense to anyone without working knowledge of the original stories, claims, and controversies. For that reason, and because the confession followed in the wake of electrifying headlines about Roosevelt's $500,000 lawsuit, the story of Rathom's duplicity did not penetrate as deeply with the general public as it might have. Rathom was ruined as a dinner speaker, he was a laughingstock at highbrow publications, such as the *Nation*. But there were no prominent calls for his head, and he kept his job as editor of the *Providence Journal*.

His problems, though, were far from over.

Franklin Delano Roosevelt was not done with John Rathom.

❖

On November 2, 1920, voters across the United States surged to the polls for the first presidential election after the Nineteenth Amendment granted suffrage to American women.

Voters were in the mood for change. The Republican ticket of Harding and Coolidge laid an historic beatdown on the Democrats, Cox and Roosevelt. Harding won more than 60 percent of the popular vote to Cox's 34 percent, and annihilated Cox in the Electoral College 404–127. Harding won Roosevelt's home state of New York, along with the entire northeast and Midwest, and everything west and north of Texas.

Maybe had he become vice president, Roosevelt would have shrugged off his rocky history with the wounded Providence editor and dropped his $500,000 lawsuit. But after such a crushing defeat, Roosevelt's political future needed triage. His determination hardened. He would either force Rathom to retract the allegations in his October surprise or he would stomp what was left of John R. Rathom deep into the earth.

Roosevelt had his own surprise.

Three months after the election in February 1921, Roosevelt called on an assistant US attorney general overseeing criminal matters. Roosevelt somehow had learned, maybe from US Attorney Caffey, that Rathom's confession was only half of the kompromat the Department of Justice had assembled against the editor. Roosevelt persuaded the official to permit a peek at the department's confidential Rathom file.

Roosevelt did not go to see the file himself. He sent a trusted friend, Charles H. McCarthy, a lawyer who had served as his aide in the Navy Department. Roosevelt explained that he was hopeful he could pressure Rathom into issuing a retraction, "However, I want to be fortified in case the suit against Rathom should ever come to trial."

Roosevelt told McCarthy to hire a stenographer and make a copy of the full Rathom kompromat ASAP, "before any change in administration will bring in people who are unfamiliar with the circumstances of the controversy between Rathom and the government."

"There is probably a lot of irrelevant material in the file," Roosevelt advised his friend. "What we want are the main facts, showing that Rathom's life has been a thoroughly disreputable one in almost every part of the globe; that he has left a bad reputation behind him in every place, and that he is in no way to be believed."

"The documents in the Department of Justice, of course, could not be used in a civil suit, but they would form the basis for cross-examination," Roosevelt wrote.

Having already blown apart the editor's credibility, Roosevelt intended to obliterate Rathom's very identity.

It was a dirty job, but we know McCarthy did it because a detailed abstract of the kompromat sits today in the archives of the Franklin D. Roosevelt Presidential Library and Museum in Hyde Park, New York. It contains affidavits from people in Victoria, Oregon, California, and Chicago, chockablock with sordid accusations about Rathom's bad debts, theft, and extortion. It has letters from schools Rathom claimed to have attended but in fact had no record of him; documents that suggest Rathom was using a false name and that he wasn't really married to Florence as well as a history of his adultery in the poisoned cherries fiasco.

Roosevelt's loyal henchman scooped it all up.

As McCarthy reported to Roosevelt, "You have Rathom where the hair is short."

❖

Post-confession John Rathom was a pale copy of his former self, fated to an early grave. In May 1921 Rathom was among the speakers at an America Day meeting of the American Defense Society, at Carnegie Hall in New York. Rathom was deep into his anti-hyphen shtick—"There are hundreds of thousands of Irish in the country who are not loyal, not American, and never will be American"—when he was interrupted by a petite woman in a brilliant green hat.

The heckler shouted at Rathom: "Prove your statement!" When Rathom ignored her, she yelled, "What about the hyphenated press? What about British propaganda?"

The disruption hijacked news coverage of Rathom's speech. The *New York Herald* headlined its story "IRISH HYPHENS" STIRS WOMAN IN GREEN HAT. The celebrity editor accustomed to holding audiences breathless had been upstaged by a random critic whom the reporters on hand did not even bother to track down for her name.

Things were going no better for Roosevelt. It was as if the lives of the two adversaries were intertwined in misery. The US Senate subcommittee investigating Section A and the Newport scandal released a scathing report in July 1921, largely substantiating Rathom's original allegations after the Reverend Kent trial.

The committee found that Ervin Arnold, the homophobe who launched a thousand headlines, lacked "any sense of moral obligation" to the young men on his team and should never have been put in charge of anyone under any circumstances.

Young men on the undercover vice squad "not only permitted one act to be performed upon them, but returned time after time to the same suspect and allowed a number of acts to be performed," the senators noted in horror, perhaps not entirely grasping that situation.

In blistering summation, "It is doubtful, in the minds of the committee, if such an immoral condition as presented can be found in the annals of the United States Navy."

The committee's Republican majority dumped the greatest portion of this steaming pile of blame onto Roosevelt, still a rising Democratic politician and possible presidential contender. The GOP majority charged that Section A was "under the immediate direction of Franklin D. Roosevelt." They ridiculed Roosevelt's claim that he knew nothing of how Section A gathered evidence of sex crimes despite having met with Arnold and Hudson, the local officers in charge of the sting. "Franklin D. Roosevelt," the committee wrote, "was a man of unusual intelligence and attainments, and after three days of conversation on the subject must have known the methods used and to be used to secure evidence."

In his defense, Roosevelt issued a long statement accusing the Republicans on the committee of partisan games. "It rather amuses me to know that these Republican Senators consider me worth while attacking so maliciously and savagely." Roosevelt said. "Perhaps they may later on learn what a boomerang is."

News coverage of the Senate report battered Roosevelt, though the stories left most readers wondering what exactly it was all about. The *New York Times* headlined its article LAY NAVY SCANDAL TO F. D. ROOSEVELT, with the subhead DETAILS ARE UNPRINTABLE. The *New York Tribune* tiptoed a little closer to the truth, blaming Daniels and Roosevelt for "permitting men of the enlisted personnel to go to unwarranted lengths" to gather evidence.

In less than one terrible year, Roosevelt had suffered an election blowout and saw his name linked to a national disgrace. And in both of these disasters, one man was out in public stirring the pot.

John Rathom.

Roosevelt's legal team performed meticulous research for his civil suit against Rathom. McCarthy, Roosevelt's friend and lawyer, was convinced Rathom could not substantiate his allegations that Roosevelt recklessly permitted men convicted of moral turpitude to remain in the service. Convicted sailors who were returned to work included petty thieves, drunks, and a man accused of having pornography. Just one of the cases troubled Roosevelt's legal team—that of a chief electrician named Clarence Parker. Parker had been convicted of sodomy, a serious offense at the time. The testimony against him had been dubious, however, and Roosevelt's team believed there was a good argument that Parker had deserved leniency. The problem was, Parker's file was missing, just as Rathom had charged. Rathom publicly accused Roosevelt of destroying the file. In fact, it was only "misplaced." It was later discovered locked in the desk of a navy commander whose father had been a *Providence Journal* reporter.

Roosevelt believed he was certain to win the libel case. And with the second half of the kompromat, Roosevelt was going to close the casket on Rathom's career. He was going to destroy him personally and permanently.

Until fate intervened.

❖

Three weeks after the release of the Senate report on the Newport scandal, in August 1921, Roosevelt took some vacation in eastern Canada. He had for many years summered at his family's cottage on Campobello Island, a narrow splatter of land, part of New Brunswick, off the US town of Lubec, as down east as it gets in Maine. Roosevelt spent a long day sailing and swimming. Soon he felt exhausted and feverish, like he was coming down with something. He legs grew weaker by the hour. The symptoms worsened. By the third day of his illness, he could no longer stand.

Doctors were stumped. Was it a blood clot? A spinal lesion? They could not say. Finally, on August 25, 1921, a specialist named Dr. Robert Lovett diagnosed Franklin Roosevelt with infantile paralysis. That was the old-fashioned name for polio. The diagnosis was a blow and a shock. Roosevelt was in his prime at thirty-nine years old. It was unusual, though not unheard of, for someone of his age to contract the dreaded childhood disease.

Roosevelt withdrew from public life to concentrate on recovering whatever health he could. His long years of rehabilitation included hot baths and swims, and practice with a set of metal braces that locked his paralyzed legs straight and permitted him to stand and shuffle short distances with crutches. Mostly he used a wheelchair. It would be seven years before Roosevelt was ready to run again for office, this time as an American with a disability. He won the governorship of New York in 1928, and then the presidency in 1932, again in 1936, and an unprecedented third term in 1940. The day after the Japanese attack on Pearl Harbor, he propped himself up before Congress and declared December 7, 1941, "a date which will live in infamy." He guided the United States through war and unbearable sacrifice, was reelected in 1944, and died in office on April 12, 1945. America has just about run out of ways to memorialize Franklin Delano Roosevelt—parks, stamps, buildings, a massive walk-through memorial in Washington, DC, have been made or renamed for him. In 1946 the US Mint put Roosevelt's profile on the front of the dime, where it remains.

Roosevelt's civil case against Rathom never came to trial. Stricken with paralysis, seeing his dreams—his entire life—upended in a few cruel summer days, Roosevelt let the lawsuit die for lack of action. He had more pressing problems.

With no trial, the rest of the Rathom kompromat stayed locked away, untouched for decades. Without Roosevelt, there was no one to publicly challenge the imposter's fake identity.

❖

In 1922, while Roosevelt was still in the early days of his fight with polio, Rathom faced an even harsher diagnosis—ulcers and cancer after a lifetime of fine meals and fat cigars. The newswires carried a small item in August reporting that surgeons at the Homeopathic Hospital in Providence had operated on the famous editor.

One month after his operation, Rathom was too weak to write his friend Adolph Ochs of the *New York Times*. Instead, Florence penned Ochs a letter, in rounded script that flattened as her hand grew tired. "I have John home with me now—almost two months," she wrote. "The great problem is to nourish him when no food appeals and he only takes it as he would medicine. Day by day we try to see a little improvement, but progress is very slow. At times he feels very much discouraged and dispirited." She thanked Ochs for his kindness toward "my dear husband," and signed the note "Florence M. Campbell Rathom."

That same year, Rathom sent Ochs a book of verse by T. E. Brown, a nineteenth-century British poet. Rathom marked his favorite poems for Ochs in the table of contents. The imposter may have seen something of himself in Brown's poem "Old John."

> *You were not of our kin nor of our race,*
> *Old John, nor of our church, nor of our speech;*
> *Yet what of strength, or truth, or tender grace*
> *I owe, 'twas you that taught me.*

In January 1923 the *Providence Journal*'s board of directors gave Rathom an indefinite medical leave with pay. Rathom improved enough to sail with Florence to the south of France and then to England, hoping a seven-month vacation would improve his health. He wrote Ochs in June from aboard the ocean liner *Aquitania*, on his way home from Europe. He advised Ochs against opening a London newspaper, as Ochs had considered, arguing that the *New York Times* had become too important. The *Times* "demands and should receive the unswerving devotion and attention of everybody connected to it."

Rathom spent summer and autumn of 1923 convalescing at his camp on Kennebago Lake in Maine, and then in October returned home to the east side of Providence.

America's fallen celebrity editor died on the sofa in his home study, on December 11, 1923, surrounded by books and old newspapers. He was fifty-six. He left no known children.

The newspaper owned by his friend Adolph Ochs did Rathom a favor upon his death. Rathom's obituary in the *New York Times* repeated much of the editor's fake biography and saluted his service to the *Providence*

Journal, without mentioning his fight with Roosevelt or the publication of his humiliating confession just three years earlier. A *Times* editorial lauded Rathom as "a vivid and rugged character."

"He loved to fight," the editorial read. "He was not without a certain spirit of mischief. Hate him or like him—and it made no particular difference to him which you did—John Rathom never failed to be interesting."

The Associated Press, which Rathom served as an executive committeeman, also gave Rathom a soft sendoff. Most newspaper readers in the United States saw the wire version of Rathom's obituary, which omitted his freefall from his high public pedestal.

The editors of the *Nation* were among the few that spoke ill of the dead: "The death of John R. Rathom of the Providence Journal recalls one of the most despicable episodes of the entire war period—the wholesale lying of that newspaper as to its alleged discoveries of unwanted activity by the German representatives in this country." Rathom's heroic tales, the magazine groused, "are doubtless still believed by multitudes."

Rathom was buried in Swan Point Cemetery, Providence, the state's most prestigious graveyard, like a gated community of affluent dead. Swan Point is wooded and gorgeous, covering rolling hills along the Seekonk River, open for visitors on banker's hours. More than twenty governors are buried there, sharing the ground with Civil War veterans, people who earned the Congressional Medal of Honor, industrialists, abolitionists, suffragists. Horror writer H. P. Lovecraft joined Rathom in Swan Point in 1937.

For many years after Rathom's death, the woman who was his wife in every sense except under the law, Florence Campbell, often appeared at Rathom's gravesite at noon, a lone, slender figure speaking aloud to the flawed and interesting man she loved for a quarter century. Florence remained in the house on Brown Street she had shared with Rathom. After Florence died in 1956, at age eighty-three, a lawyer in charge of emptying her house found Rathom's study untouched, just as it was when he died thirty-three years earlier. The book he had been reading lay open on the desk. His cigars had turned to crumbs. Sun-bleached curtains dangled in tatters.

There is no headstone carved with the name John Rathom. His bones and his secrets were buried in an unmarked grave. I don't know why.

Perhaps the imposter preferred not to rest forever beneath a lie.

Perhaps he chose a memorial of emptiness to honor a vital piece of himself sacrificed to become someone new.

CHAPTER 18

Out of Character

Two horses pulled the funeral carriage, thumping their solemn four-beat gait against the streets of Adelaide, South Australia, on the afternoon of August 30, 1880, still the chilly season this far below the equator. A procession of fifty carriages followed, riding west, dragging long shadows into a low winter sun.

The earthly remains of a prominent South Australian, Judah Moss Solomon, lay upon the carriage in a humble, unadorned casket, in keeping with the tradition of Australia's small but devout Jewish community. The shops along Rundle Street, where Solomon and his fellow Jewish settlers had built a synagogue, were shuttered that afternoon so everyone could attend the services for the first president of the Adelaide Hebrew Congregation and a former mayor of the city.

There are two kinds of successful mayors: the lofty thinkers and the urban mechanics; Solomon had been the latter. In office he had buried himself in the dull details of drainage and sewers and weeding diseased meats out of the food chain. He had given much of his adult life to his adopted city. In addition to his time as mayor, he served in the South Australian Parliament, and had worked as city auditor and even as the coroner. By the time of his death from stomach cancer at age sixty-one, he was one of the best-known men of business and government in all of South Australia.

"No matter what position he undertook, he devoted himself heart and mind to the mastering of its requirements, and he was never satisfied till he had investigated even to the minutest detail," the local newspaper wrote of the late Judah Moss Solomon. He was also famously muleheaded, the paper reported with some tact: "Indeed, he might have been more successful in his Parliamentary career had he been less independent and not held so consistently to those sentiments which he believed correct."

Among the mourners in the funeral procession were a former premier of South Australia, five sitting members of Parliament, and a number of former MPs. Adelaide's current mayor was on hand to pay tribute to the man who held the office a decade earlier.

In life, Solomon had been painfully familiar with the route to Adelaide's West Terrace Cemetery. Many times he had made this mournful ride; he buried two wives and eight of his fifteen children.

Solomon's surviving offspring were in their father's procession, of course, including Vaiben Louis Solomon, easy to pick out by his wiry rectangle of soot-black beard. Vaiben Louis, then twenty-seven, named for a famous uncle, was a gold hunter and serial entrepreneur. He would later rise to become the first Jewish premier of South Australia.

Also in attendance but overshadowed by all the bigwigs, was a twelve-year-old boy, another son of the deceased. The boy's name was John Pulver Solomon. He was the eleventh child of Judah Moss Solomon, born in 1868.

Like his father, the boy had made many trips to the cemetery. Three siblings born after John Pulver were already dead. Just two months earlier, John Pulver's half-brother Samuel died at age thirty-two. John's mother, Adela Pulver, was also in the ground, having died in 1875 from childbirth complications the day after delivering her second stillborn baby in two years. John was seven years old when he lost his mum.

With his father now dead, John Pulver was an orphan, no longer tied to Adelaide by his parents.

Perhaps he was already dreaming of sailing far away and making his own legend in America.

The road to the graveyard was as straight as a yardstick. Adelaide was a planned community, built on a stretch of flatland carefully surveyed and chosen for soil quality and convenience to fresh water. The heart of the city was laid out in the 1830s, first on paper, as a rigid grid of right-angled streets. The outer rectangle was encircled by a cocoon of green parkland, beyond which lay farms and, by 1880, the early signs of sprawl. The city is near the southern coast of Australia but on the east side of a deep gulf, so the closest navigable water is due west.

At the cemetery, the coffin was lowered into the grave. It would be marked with a narrow stone slab with a rounded top. A line from a traditional Jewish song is carved in Hebrew at the top of the headstone: "The dead will live in His grace, welcome to the name of His glory." The stone has some typos, common on Jewish graves outside Israel, especially old ones made when Hebrew was essentially a dead language.

Rabbi Abraham Tobias Boas of Adelaide stepped forward to address the mourners. The man in the grave was not just a member of his faith, he was family; Boas was married to Solomon's cousin.

The rabbi spoke:

> The Jewish community has lost in him a worthy member, for in both his public and private career he maintained in its truest sense its dignity and good name by his integrity, honesty, intelligence, truthfulness, and liberality—bright stars in the firmament of our holy religion . . . You will be comforted by the fact that he has left a name worthy of a Jew.

The Solomons of Australia were a rugged family of warriors, adventurers, gold hunters, pioneers, and outlaws. They were born with the bold blood of entrepreneurs and wheeling deal-makers with the stomachs for big risk.

And when beaten down, the Solomons had a knack for remaking themselves. It started with Judah Moss's uncles, Vaiben and Emanuel Solomon, the first of the Solomons to make their fortunes in Australia. The vibrant

Solomon family of the late nineteenth century owed an enormous debt to Vaiben and Emanuel, who had been cast across the sea as boys, and dropped friendless in prison costumes onto a wild and foreign land. Alone and penniless, they built wealth and stature and political and social influence, creating these things from nothing.

Vaiben died before John Pulver was born, but Emanuel lived long enough to see the child. John Pulver may even have remembered the craggy-faced old man with kind eyes, a shock of black hair, and bone-white muttonchops. Emanuel Solomon died in 1873, when John Pulver was about five.

Vaiben and Emanuel Solomon made compelling models for John Pulver—the uncles showed it was possible to reinvent yourself on another continent.

❖

August 6, 1817
Durham, England, some 260 miles north of London.

The clatter of iron keys sounded through the stone halls of the ancient Durham County Gaol. Guards pulled prisoners from their cells, clamped them into chains, hauled them squinting into the daylight, and loaded them onto a horse cart for the bouncing ride to court.

The prisoners were about to face what passed for justice under the ruthless penal codes of early nineteenth-century Britain.

Among the prisoners were a pair of young Jewish street peddlers from London, the Solomon brothers. They were teenagers, born around 1800. Sources differ on which brother was older. Neither had received much education. The brothers were short and slightly built, between 5'2" and 5'4". Each had "rounded faces with large dark black eyes and prominent noses," pale complexions and long black hair to their necks, wrote their distant relative, Trevor S. Cohen, in a richly drawn article published in 2000 in the *Journal of the Australian Jewish Historical Society*. I have leaned heavily on Cohen's account.

The Solomon boys had spent the past ten months in custody awaiting trial, jailed in a four-hundred-year-old dungeon that reeked of human waste and dank, wet rock. They slept on piles of dirty straw, in an isolating silence broken by the hurried footsteps of rats. The devout Jews gritted their teeth through the Christian services they were forced to attend, in a jail that mixed accused prisoners of all ages and backgrounds with hard-boiled criminals.

Vaiben and Emanuel were sons of Samuel Moss Solomon, a Jewish tradesman in London who eked out a living as a pencil maker. Times were difficult for Solomon's family. A war with France had just ended; Napoleon Bonaparte's reign had crumbled with his defeat at Waterloo. But the British economy had not recovered and Europe was falling into recession. Emanuel and Vaiben worked as peddlers to help support the family. It was a discouraging occupation. The streets were thick with vendors shouting over each other for attention, and profit margins in pencil sales were paper thin.

In 1816 the boys had volunteered to go on the road with a supply of pencils to sell, along with whatever knickknacks and cheap jewelry their father could acquire. They would travel hundreds of miles north into the English countryside, where they anticipated less competition.

"They had not left home for the traditional objective of seeking their fortune," Cohen wrote. "Theirs was an exercise in family survival with the hope that their luck might change for the better."

By the autumn, with the days growing shorter and winter on the way, Emanuel and Vaiben were making their way south again toward home, buying and selling items, working each transaction for a little profit. On October 15, they found lodging for the night in the village of Northallerton. That evening, an angry farmer and a local constable came knocking, to inquire about some stolen clothing.

When the brothers came out to meet them, Emanuel was wearing the farmer's coat.

Now, after nearly a year waiting for their trial, the brothers were led into a courtroom stuffed with spectators and jurors and witnesses. At the head of the solemn proceedings, the "elderly, grim-faced Lord Chief

Baron, resplendent in his robes" presided over the trial. The court was a busy verdict mill, churning out rulings all day long. *Guilty! Guilty! Guilty!*

The charges against Emanuel and Vaiben were read into the record. They were accused of breaking and entering and stealing. They pleaded not guilty. The prosecutor laid out the evidence.

In October 1816 the boys were working their business on the streets of Heyington, when a farmer named Thomas Prest spotted them heading toward his house. That evening, Prest came home to learn he and his wife had been robbed of some clothing. He immediately suspected the two teens he had seen that morning. A neighbor told Prest he had noticed the boys heading south, each carrying a bundle. Prest pursued the boys to Northallerton and notified the authorities. A search of the brothers' lodging house turned up several more items belonging to Prest and his wife: another coat, a jacket, stockings, and a muff.

In their defense, Emanuel and Vaiben claimed they had bought the items on the road from some other traveler, in exchange for jewelry. They could not afford a lawyer, and with no witnesses to support their story, the jury did not believe them. The excessively heavy hammer of justice fell upon the Solomon boys. Convicted of taking clothing valued at five pounds, the teenagers were sentenced to seven years banishment at hard labor, far away from home, across two oceans, in a penal colony in Australia.

❖

A few decades before the Solomon boys were busted, British authorities faced a growing social crisis. The Industrial Revolution had forced many laborers out of work, leading to high unemployment and enormous suffering. Crime rates were rising. Penal codes were merciless and prisons were dangerously overfilled. England had customarily rid itself of convicts by sending thousands across the Atlantic to the American colonies. But the colonies started to act up in the 1770s, some tea was ruined in Boston, and things got out of hand. By 1783 the independent American states were not accepting imports of British criminals.

As an alternative, beginning in 1788, England transported its prisoners more than ten thousand miles away to undeveloped Australia. British colonization of the continent would be driven over the next eighty years by the use of penal colonies, which were established alongside free communities built by settlers. Murderers and rapists, for the most part, were still hanged locally in England, but for many other criminals, including the pettiest thieves, courts commonly imposed sentences of seven or fourteen years hard labor in Australia. Just sailing there took at least several months. For some convicts, banishment across the seas was a death sentence; crammed belowdecks in unsanitary conditions, many never lived to touch land. Once in Australia, convicts with useful expertise, such as masonry or agriculture, were often assigned jobs in their field. The unskilled could be stuck with chain gang work, clearing land or building roads. Guards enforced the rules with medieval-style corporal punishment.

Eventually, when a convict's time had been served, he or she received a "certificate of leave," ending their forced labor and permitting their return to England. Many stayed, however. They moved to one of the free Australian settlements, got jobs, opened businesses, married, and raised children. About 160,000 convicts were shipped to Australia before the practice stopped in 1868. Twenty percent of modern Australians can trace their lineage to these prisoners. People used to be embarrassed about it. Now it's cool to discover a transported criminal in your family story.

Emanuel and Vaiben Solomon were assigned to the prisoner transport ship *Lady Castlereagh*, which departed England in late December 1817. Six months later in June 1818, the brothers came ashore in Hobart, on Tasmania, a large island about the size of West Virginia, 150 miles south of the Australian mainland.

They were taken to George Town, a remote penal settlement, and put to work under the watch of overseers. The brothers frequently clashed with authority and endured vicious retribution. Two years into their sentence, Emanuel made a run for freedom. The secluded colony was not fenced like a traditional jail, but was hard to escape because there was almost no place else to go. He was recaptured and punished with fifty lashes with a cat-o'-nine-tails, a nine-headed whip that split the skin in parallel wounds across a prisoner's bare back. The lashes were "administered to the roll of drums" over a span of about half an hour. After the first twenty-five lashes the overseers called in a relief whipper with a fresh arm.

In 1821 Emanuel and Vaiben were hauled before a panel of magistrates to face an accusation of stealing clothing. Yes, the exact crime that had put them in the penal colony to begin with. They were transferred to a colony for repeat offenders at Newcastle, on the southeast coast of the Australian mainland. Newcastle was "hard, tedious and monotonous," according to Cohen. They worked between seven and ten hours a day, depending on the available daylight, probably toiling as laborers, constructing "public works buildings . . . loading and unloading government vessels, repairing roads and drains." Twice a week they were issued salted beef or pork and four pounds of wheat.

In August 1824, seven years after their trial and nearly eight since their arrest, Emanuel and Vaiben Solomon completed their sentence and were freed. Now in their midtwenties, they set out to rebuild lives so brutally interrupted. Seeing opportunity in their land of exile, they moved to Sydney, a city of some twelve thousand people, and opened a business. As Cohen wrote:

> From the time of their release the brothers survived by trading. At first they dealt in "slops" [loose sailors' outfits] and cheap clothing, but gradually they diversified, buying and turning over anything that would give a quick profit. The relished the *laissez-faire* spirit that prevailed and found no situation for which their experiences had not prepared them. They speculated and won. With nerves of steel toughened from years of deprivation, and an eye for a bargain in the cutthroat, fickle colonial market, they were a success.

By the 1830s the brothers were well-established Sydney businessmen. The held auctioneering licenses and conducted sales of their own goods and disposed of merchandise for clients. News of their success thrilled family members in London. A new wave of Solomons, along with other Jewish settlers, migrated to Australia—voluntarily, this time. This new group docked in Sydney Harbor in 1833.

Among the new arrivals was Vaiben and Emanuel's nephew, the future mayor of Adelaide, Judah Moss Solomon. He was then a boy of twelve.[*]

Judah Moss completed his education at Sydney College and then joined his uncle Emanuel in Adelaide around 1840 as an apprentice in the family business. He was "enterprising and enthusiastic and displayed rare commercial skills," Cohen writes. Soon, he struck out on his own, becoming a government auctioneer, and then settled down in Adelaide in 1846 to run an auctioneering firm associated with his uncle. He became a big portly guy, who wore his hair swept back, with a set of muttonchops, droopy mustache, and a shaved chin.

Judah Moss married his first wife, Rachel Cohen, in 1842. Over the next two decades, the couple had ten children, though several died. One daughter died at four months, another at eleven months. Two babies were stillborn. Six days after the birth of her second stillborn baby, in 1864, Rachel died at age forty-four.

Three years after losing his wife, Judah Moss remarried at age forty-nine. His new bride was Adela Pulver, then twenty-six. Adela was born in England, the daughter of a "Jewish minister," the Reverend Isaac Pulver. Ten months after their wedding, Judah Moss and Adela were about to have a baby. Adela's family was from Melbourne, and it appears she went home to deliver her first child, her husband's eleventh.

It was a boy, born on July 4, 1868. They named him John Pulver Solomon—though he would later rename himself in North America.

John Pulver was followed by a brother, Elias, in 1870; a sister, Rosetta, in 1871, who would die at age six; and two stillborn infants, in 1873 and

---

[*] The Solomons recycled names. They are a nightmare to keep straight. In addition to sons Vaiben and Emanuel, Samuel Moss Solomon had a son named Moss, who was the father of Judah Moss. Judah Moss named his eldest son Moss Judah. He also raised sons named Vaiben and Emanuel, who were the half-brothers of John Pulver.

1875. Weakened by bronchitis, Adela died the day after the birth of her second stillborn child, on September 21, 1875.

Amid all this staggering heartbreak, John Pulver immersed himself in sports, books, and the performing arts. He was schooled at Whinham College in Adelaide—not a "college" like we commonly think of higher education, but a boarding and day school for boys. The college was housed in a stately Elizabethan-style complex made from cut bluestone and brick, with a tall narrow clock tower.

Few references to school-aged John Pulver survive. The local newspapers recorded that he won awards in English literature in 1882, when he was fourteen, and then again the next year. He was honored at school for writing the best original poem, and he would remain a poet—and writer—the rest of his life. John Pulver was an excellent public speaker even then, delivering lines of verse before audiences and acting in plays. One reviewer who saw teenaged John Pulver deliver the long Scottish poem "The Execution of Montrose" called him "an elocutionist of passable merit."

In 1884 John Pulver starred in a Whinham College production of the one-act farce *A Regular Fix* by the English writer John Maddison Morton. He played Mr. Surplus, a lawyer, and the straight man in a series of snappy Abbott and Costello exchanges with the protagonist, Mr. De Brass:

DE BRASS: "As I said before, he died."

SURPLUS: "Very well."

DE BRASS: "No he was very ill."

SURPLUS: "No matter; he died. I presume with a will."

DE BRASS: "No, very much against his will."

John Pulver's father, Judah Moss, was a rare politician: He actually liked the press. Judah Moss articulated his profound respect for reporters at a banquet in 1872, celebrating South Australia's anniversary as a colony. The event was a boisterous, boozy affair, sponsored by an aging Emanuel Solomon for several hundred longtime colonists. Judah Moss rose from his seat, shouted above the noise, and urged men raise their glasses to "the press."

The *South Australian Register* summarized the gist of his toast:

> It had fallen to his lot [J. M. Solomon] to propose [a toast to] the Press of South Australia, and in doing so he would remark that though as a public man he had not escaped castigation by the Press, he did not allow that fact to trouble him. . . . The press has been called the Fourth Estate but, as he had heard remarked by a distinguished member of the Press the previous evening, "it ruled the other three." He quite concurred in that opinion. When it was fairly and properly conducted and did not attempt to injure private individuals, but aimed at the promotion of the public good, the Press was of great advantage and importance to the community.

After Judah Moss's death, when the time came for John Pulver to choose a career, he picked one his late father would have liked.

He became a journalist.

In early 1887, at age eighteen, John Pulver left Adelaide, sailed around the Australian continent, and landed on February 18 in Port Darwin, a city in the Northern Territory where his half-brother Vaiben Louis Solomon had established himself as a budding politician and publisher.

John Pulver lived in the town of Palmerston and worked as a news reporter, likely for his brother's paper, the *Northern Territory Times and Gazette*. Vaiben Louis owned the *Gazette* from 1885 to 1890 and was its editor most of that time.

Vaiben Louis was then in his midthirties. He was the most accomplished of Rathom's half-siblings. V. L., as he was called, was a stocky man with a dense black beard it would have taken a machete to tame. He was born in

Adelaide and educated at Scotch College, Melbourne, one of the schools Rathom would later claim, falsely, that he attended. V. L.'s nickname was "Mr. Everything" because there were few ventures he would not try. He opened businesses in mining, agriculture, and construction, among others. For the year they were together in the north, the brothers were close. They played on the same team in the Port Darwin Cricket Club. John Pulver continued to deliver poems before audiences, including at a banquet V. L. attended.

V. L. Solomon left the Northern Territory in February 1888, on an extended trip to the other side of the continent. He was already dabbling in politics and would be elected to Parliament in 1890. In 1899 he became opposition leader in Parliament, and led a political movement that brought down the sitting government. In the wake of the collapse, V. L. Solomon became premier of South Australia. One week later, his administration also fell, going down in history as South Australia's shortest-lived government, and earning him another nickname: Sudden Solomon.

Without V. L., the Northern Territory had nothing to anchor John Pulver or to quench his enormous ambitions. The month after his half-brother sailed away in 1888, John Pulver also departed. In March he booked space on the *Tsinau*, a steamship carrying twenty-three Chinese passengers and a cargo hold packed like a macabre Noah's ark: stacks of animal hides, two tons of severed animal horns, casks of tallow, and bags of sea cucumbers.

The steamer's destination was British Hong Kong.

John Pulver was nineteen. He had decided to repeat the feat of Emanuel and Vaiben, by dropping himself with nothing onto a foreign land across the sea. He would walk the high wire without a net and build his own life—re-create himself afresh—as his famous uncles had done.

The *Tsinau* left Australia on March 27, 1888. As the ship vanished below the horizon, John Pulver Solomon vanished from the records of history.

❖

Rathom's identity was not widely in doubt for most of the twentieth century. In the 1970s two former *Providence Journal* editors, Garrett Byrnes and Charles Spilman, fell into the Rathom vortex while working on a company history project. They repeated some of the Rathom investigations done in the early 1900s by private detectives, by contacting schools and newspapers mentioned in Rathom's biography, and which, in fact, had never heard of him. They concluded that much of Rathom's biography was fake. "Just who was this man who called himself John R. Rathom?" they wrote. "It is almost a certainty that he was not born to that name."

In 1979 Byrnes and Spilman learned from a librarian at the State Library of Victoria, Australia, of a baby born in Melbourne on the day and year Rathom had claimed as his birthday. The baby was John Pulver Solomon. It was "intriguing speculation," they wrote, whether J. P. Solomon could have been John Rathom.

Now we can stop speculating. With help from the modern-day extended Solomon family in Australia, I have assembled the key pieces of evidence that together confirm that John Revelstoke Rathom was John Pulver Solomon:

1. Same birthday and birthplace

Byrnes and Spilman got this far in the 1970s. Rathom was consistent that he was born on July 4, 1868, in Melbourne. John Pulver Solomon was born on that date in Melbourne, according to Australian birth records. With modern databases, we can go further: There are no records of anyone named John Rathom born on that date or any date within years, anywhere in Australia.

2. The obituaries

In 1880 John Pulver Solomon, age twelve, is listed in press reports among the mourners at his father's funeral. He is not listed as present for the funerals of his half-brothers Vaiben Louis, in 1908, and Benjamin, in 1922, when Rathom was in Providence, nor is he listed among surviving relatives.

John Pulver was gone.

3. Steamship *Abyssinian*

In his 1905 application to become a US citizen, Rathom reported that he had arrived in the United States in April 1889, landing in Los Angeles. None of that is true.

In 1913 Rathom offered a different story. He swore on a passport application that he had originally sailed to the United States from Hong Kong in February 1889, aboard the ocean liner *Abyssinian*. Again, Rathom engaged in a little casual perjury, for the *Abyssinian* did not land in the United States at the time. But the fact that Rathom named the ship on which he emigrated—and I confirmed it was a real ship—was intriguing. The *Abyssinian* sailed the Hong Kong to Vancouver, British Columbia, route in 1889. We know from the public record that John Solomon went to Hong Kong after leaving Australia, and that Rathom first surfaced in British Columbia. So, I thought, perhaps the name of ship and the date of arrival, if nothing else, were legitimate? Were these breadcrumbs of truth dropped by Rathom?

Turns out they were. I could not find the ship manifest, but God bless the old shipping reporter for the *Vancouver Daily World*. The day the *Abyssinian* lumbered into Vancouver Harbor on February 9, 1889, a short article on her arrival appeared on page 2, under the headline FROM THE ORIENT. The story listed all white adult passengers by honorific and last name. There were eighteen of them.

And there it was: *Mr. Solomon*.

It remains unknown where he got the name *Rathom*, but it appears John Solomon departed Hong Kong under his real identity.

This is how it lines up:

- In March 1888 an athletic Australian newspaper reporter named John P. Solomon sails to Hong Kong.
- Ten months later, Mr. Solomon sails from Hong Kong to Vancouver. Solomon then promptly vanishes. He is never heard from again.
- Right after Solomon disappears, an athletic Australian newspaper reporter named John Rathom, with the exact

same date of birth as John Solomon and no prior documentary evidence of ever existing, makes his first appearance in
the public record, in British Columbia.

4. The marriage license

This was Solomon's one sentimental mistake, early in his long career
playing the character J. R. Rathom.

By the time Rathom moved to Providence, Rhode Island, he had decided
his father's name would be Harold Revelstoke Rathom and his mother
would be Dora Adelaide (Hamilton) Rathom. Lies, of course. Those people
never existed, and we can see Rathom winking at us in his mother's middle
name, Adelaide, the name of the city in which he grew up and of which
his father, Judah Moss, had been mayor.

Rathom's 1890 application for a license to marry his sweetheart Mary
Crockford in British Columbia still exists. It is a one-page, fill-in-the-
blank document, and as far as I know the first time Rathom had to create
an official government record under his fake identity. Rathom listed his
father as Harold Robert Rathom, close to the fake paternal name he would
use later. But as a young man about to take a wife, Rathom cannot bring
himself to entirely erase his late mother, Adela Pulver, from his past. On a
wedding license loaded with lies, he told a truth. His put down his mother's
name as *Adela*.

He later renamed his fictitious mum to obscure the connection. But too
late! Got you, John Solomon!*

---

* The ten months J. P. Solomon spent in Hong Kong are still a mystery. It is likely he was
reporting. In the early 1900s, Rathom published a couple of pieces about life in China, likely
based on his recollections. In 1917 he told *Printer & Publisher* that he freelanced in China in
1888–1889 for the *New York Herald*. That is plausible. The *Herald* included dispatches from
around the world, and we know Rathom later did work for the *Herald* in Victoria. The *Herald*
did not use bylines in that era, so identifying his stories is all but impossible. The *Herald* may
even have inspired the made-up biography of John Rathom. The paper sponsored the adventures of explorer/journalist Sir Henry Morton Stanley—"Dr. Livingstone, I presume?"—the
closest real-life model for the swashbuckling Rathom character.

❖

So J. P. Solomon became J. R. Rathom.

Why, though?

Why did a bright young man from a prosperous and influential family invent a new identity to wear as a costume every day for the rest of his life?

CHAPTER 19
Genesis of a Lie

n 1872, when John Pulver Solomon was just a four-year-old ankle biter growing up in Adelaide, his father became desperate to break up the engagement of John Pulver's half-brother, Vaiben Louis.

How desperate? Not only did Judah Moss Solomon forbid V. L. from going through with the marriage, he placed a classified advertisement in the *South Australian Register* to warn everyone in town with the legal authority to conduct a wedding:

> MINISTERS of RELIGION and REGISTRARS of MAR-
> RIAGES, are CAUTIONED AGAINST MARRYING my
> SON, VAIBEN LOUIS SOLOMON, he being a Minor.
> J. M. SOLOMON, Adelaide
> October 8, 1872.

To V. L.'s credit, he did not immediately keel over dead in embarrassment. The Solomon family dispute was not really about V. L.'s age; he was a strapping young man of nineteen. The issue was that V. L. had fallen in love with a Gentile, Mary Wigzell. Mary was about sixteen, from Adelaide, and probably not wealthy as the daughter of a Rundle Street fruit vendor. Records show she was baptized as a Christian at St. Paul's Church in Adelaide.

That Mary was not Jewish was a big problem for Judah Moss Solomon. *His own son marrying outside of the faith?* Over his cold corpse. Traditional Judaism is matrilineal—the religion is passed down through the mother. Judah Moss was the first president of the city's Hebrew Congregation, but if he wanted Jewish grandchildren, his sons had to marry Jewish women. It was not unusual back then, and even now in some cases, for parents to disown an offspring who "married out."

"One can imagine the raising of eyebrows in Adelaide's strait-laced Anglo Jewish community when the news broke of this engagement of the son of its leading citizen," wrote Trevor S. Cohen, V. L.'s distant relation, in 1977, in the *Journal of the Australian Jewish Historical Society*.

Vaiben Louis somehow learned about his father's newspaper ad in advance, because V. L. had time to place his own classified response in the same edition of the paper, saving what little face he had left:

> MINISTERS of RELIGION and REGISTRARS of MAR-
> RIAGES are respectfully informed that the undersigned has not
> the least intention of requiring their services at present, and that
> when he has he will not advertise his family affairs through the
> medium of the public Press. The advertisement which referred
> to me is a deliberate attempt to mislead my many friends.
> VAIBEN LOUIS SOLOMON.

Judah Moss had won. There would be no wedding. Vaiben Louis left town. He joined a gold-hunting expedition to Australia's Northern Territory, where he settled down as a bachelor.[*]

---

[*] Meanwhile, V. L.'s sweetheart, Mary, married some other bloke, had a baby, and then lost her husband to a fatal bout of pneumonia. Vaiben Louis remained single until his father died in 1880. Three months after the undertaker put Judah Moss Solomon in the ground, V. L. married the woman he never stopped loving, Mary Wigzell.

This was the upbringing of the young Jewish boy John Pulver Solomon, raised under the strict tutelage of his devout father, one of the most prominent Jews in the South Australian colony, head of the synagogue he helped to erect, and a man fanatical about the preservation of his faith.

With this in mind, imagine the alarm five years later—in the Solomon household and throughout the wider Adelaide Jewish community—when Australia's premier newspaper of record reported in 1877 that influential factions in the United States were turning against American Jews. The US correspondent for the Melbourne *Argus* wrote:

> NEW YORK, July 9—In default of any more exciting topic for popular discussion, the people of the United States have recently been working themselves into a general agitation over a rather vulgar quarrel between [a] hotel manager and a Jewish banker.

The story was already a consuming topic of debate in the United States. A Saratoga, New York, resort had denied accommodations to a rich New York City banker and businessman because he was Jewish. The banker was Joseph Seligman, the last person anyone would expect to be banned from a hotel. He was wealthy, influential, and wired into the power structure of the United States. Multiple US presidents considered him a friend. Seligman was a rags-to-riches story straight out of a Horatio Alger novel: the young immigrant who emigrates to the Unites States with nothing, and by his own sweat and smarts became a wild success. So much of a success, in fact, that Seligman paid the real Horatio Alger to tutor his kids.

Seligman's background was part of what made the story so riveting. He was among the best-known, most influential Jewish Americans of his day. And a hotelier would not take his money.

South Australian Jews reading this news alert at the time probably had no equivalent lived experience in their young colony, where "the general atmosphere was extremely progressive for its times, and Jews were vested with full civil and political rights and opportunities from the start," wrote

E. S. Richards, a lecturer at the Flinders University of South Australia, for the Australian Jewish Historical Society.

Historian Suzanne D. Rutland, professor emerita in the Department of Hebrew, Biblical and Jewish Studies at the University of Sydney, told me in an online interview that Australian Jews of the era faced what she calls "gentleman's anti-Semitism"—exclusion from certain tony sporting clubs and the like, but little social discrimination in business or politics. "Australian Jewish history is very, very different than Jewish history in the United States."

Why? For one, there were just not enough Jewish settlers in Australia to intimidate anybody. In 1871 there were about 6,900 Jews on the continent, making up about 0.42 percent of the population. The United States received waves of Eastern European Jewish immigrants in the mid- to late nineteenth century, while Australia, a longer, more dangerous trip, received far fewer. Many Australian Jews were also British or had emigrated through Great Britain. They shared a national bond with most other settlers, and seemed less foreign.

It is impossible to know how the Seligman incident specifically affected Rathom, then not quite ten years old and still known as J. P. Solomon. It was a worldwide news story and Solomon may have heard it discussed at home, among his father and brothers, or other members of the Adelaide Hebrew Congregation. The Seligman affair is more important to the Rathom narrative for what it represents: The normalizing of anti-Jewish discrimination in late nineteenth-century America.

❖

A tradition at the Touro Synagogue in Newport, Rhode Island, is the annual public reading of President George Washington's 1790 letter to the "Hebrew Congregation in Newport." The text is short; it is more of a thank you note than a formal letter, dashed off by the president after a trip to Rhode Island. But in a few spare words, Washington laid out the guiding doctrine for religious freedom in the United States: a recognition that "all possess alike liberty of conscience."

"May the children of the stock of Abraham who dwell in this land continue to merit and enjoy the good will of the other inhabitants—while every one shall sit in safety under his own vine and fig tree and there shall be none to make him afraid," he wrote. Washington loved the "vine and fig tree" imagery from the Bible. He quoted it often. The character George Washington sings that line in the musical *Hamilton*. The president's guarantee of "liberty of conscience" was a relief to Jewish Americans scattered throughout the United States. A tiny religious minority could have easily been legislated underground or out of existence by a Christian majority.

For the next several generations, Jewish residents "occupied a secure, stable and untrammeled place in American society," wrote historian John Higham, for the American Jewish Historical Society. There were not enough Jews in early 1800s America to be threatening to the white Christian majority. One estimate suggests that in 1826, the US Jewish population was about six thousand.

Things began to change in the 1840s, amid a large wave of German Jewish immigration. These new Americans spread across the country. Many earned a living as traders and peddlers. Higham traces a rise in "anti-Jewish feelings" in the United States to this wave of immigration.

In 1862, during the Civil War, Union general Ulysses Grant lost his patience with price-gouging black-market profiteers. He blamed the practice on Jewish peddlers, who "come in with their carpet sacks in spite of all that can be done to prevent it." Over the objections of a top aide, who knew a disaster when he saw one, Grant issued General Order No. 11. The order banned Jews from the war zone, which included parts of Kentucky, Mississippi, and Tennessee. All Jewish residents were supposed to pack up and bug out. "It was the most sweeping anti-Semitic action undertaken in American history," wrote Ron Chernow in his 2017 biography *Grant*.

President Abraham Lincoln recognized the unfairness and the potential political damage and reversed Grant's order before many Jews were forced from their homes. Grant ultimately came to recognize he had done something evil and stupid, and was haunted by regret; "even on his deathbed" he lamented that he had unfairly wronged American Jews.

After the war, questions about the patriotism of American Jews briefly waned—until the 1870s, when "a pattern of discrimination began to take root," Higham said.

By 1877 the number of Jews in the United States topped a quarter million, driven largely by German and Polish immigration. Jews weren't so rare anymore. Meanwhile, some Americans were beginning to taste the prosperity of the coming Gilded Age. Jewish people matriculated to college, rose in business, entered professional jobs. New millionaires emerged among first-generation Jewish immigrants, including the banker Joseph Seligman.

Suddenly, it seemed, Jews were plentiful and doing well for themselves. And so rose another caricature, of a peacocking people "glittering with conspicuous and vulgar jewelry" and "always forcing his way into society that is above him."

Several years before Seligman was barred from the Grand Union Hotel, a New York National Guard regiment banned Jews from its ranks. In 1876 a Jersey shore hotel advertised itself as Gentile-only. The Seligman incident in 1877 may have been the most famous of the antisemitic sensations of the period, but it did not unleash anti-Jewish feelings in the United States. It only revealed them.

❖

Joseph Seligman was a thick, prosperous-looking man, with deep-set eyes, wavy gray hair brushed back, and a salt-and-pepper Vandyke. He was born in 1819 to Jewish parents in Bavaria. Seligman was an excellent student at the University of Erlangen and could have had a career in medicine or theology. Instead, he chose a risky new beginning in the United States. At age seventeen, he sailed steerage class to New York. His timing was terrible; he arrived as the US economy was cratering in the wake of bank failures known as the Panic of 1837. He moved to Pennsylvania and took a job as a cashier. He invested a portion of his wages on merchandise that he could resell at a profit as a traveling peddler.

By 1839 Seligman had made enough money to send for some of his brothers to come to America. The enterprising Seligman boys opened their own dry goods store. From this shallow toehold in the US economy, the Seligmans climbed relentlessly upward. They opened additional stores, started an import and clothing business in New York, and organized a banking firm that would make them very rich. "The mastermind of Joseph Seligman directed the vast operation with such success the business expanded so they had branch houses in London, Frankfort and Paris, as well as in the larger cities in the United States," reads one Seligman biography from 1893.

Seligman opposed slavery and was an early member of Lincoln's Republican Party. He was friendly with the president and "was among those who urged Lincoln to name Grant to the high command" of the Union army. After Grant became president in 1869, he offered Seligman the job of Secretary of the Treasury, but the banker demurred and remained with his own businesses.

"In 1877, he was at the height of his career," wrote the historian Lee M. Friedman of Seligman. "Financially successful, socially recognized, politically powerful, he ranked among the nation's great—concededly the country's outstanding Jew."

For years, Seligman had vacationed with family at the Grand Union Hotel in Saratoga, New York, about two hundred miles north of Manhattan. At the time, Saratoga was among America's premier summertime hot spots. It was full of bankers, politicians, railroad barons, showing off lady friends who never wore the same outfit twice. The city was known for its enormous hotels, which featured covered piazzas for strolling like an early Las Vegas strip. "Up and down these piazzas, daytime and nighttime, paraded the fashion show in all its pomp and vainglory," Friedman wrote.

The Grand Union was "the very center" of the summertime circus. It was a monstrous, six-story luxury complex done in French Second Empire architectural style, which gave it the look of a Parisian art museum in a neighborhood that needed stricter zoning. The resort was run by lawyer and former New York judge Henry Hilton, a son of a Scotch immigrants.

In June 1877 Hilton, then age fifty-two, ignited a national firestorm. On his orders, hotel staff turned away Joseph Seligman and his family because Seligman was Jewish. This was not just Seligman's aggrieved interpretation of what happened. Hilton was frank about it in an interview with the *New York Times*. Business had been soft the year before, Hilton argued, because Christian customers did not want to mingle with Jews. So no more Jews. It was a business decision.

Jews, Hilton told the *Times*,

> are not wanted any more at any of the first-class summer hotels. They have brought the public opinion down on themselves by a vulgar ostentation, a puffed-up vanity, an overweening display of conditions, a lack of those considerate civilities so much appreciated by good American society, and a general obtrusiveness that is frequently disgusting and always repulsive to the well-bred.

Seligman was incensed. He clapped back with an acerbic open letter to the hotelier, which warned it was a grave error to ban "a large class of people . . . merely to pander to a vulgar prejudice under the mistaken notion that by doing so you will fill the house with other nationalities. You will find yourself mistaken. You are no judge of American character."

Press coverage of the affair whipped around the world—through Europe, Australia, and rural American hamlets that may never have seen a Jewish traveler. The dispute was litigated in newspaper columns, in letters to the editor, by customers in taverns and diners, and neighbors over fences. Much of the initial coverage condemned Hilton's Jewish ban as bigoted and un-American. But Hilton was a better judge of the dark impulses of the American character than Seligman realized. Reporters who interviewed hotel keepers for follow-up stories found some who agreed with Hilton, even if they insisted their names stay off the record.

Even some newspapers friendly to Jews offered bad takes that were deeply harmful. The *Brooklyn Daily Eagle*, for instance, opined that hotels exist to make money, and that people in the hotel industry operate in their own financial self-interest. So if Hilton says Jews hurt his bottom line, who could argue? "Having found the Israelites unprofitable customers, Mr. Hilton will have no more of them," the paper reported. "How a people so remarkedly level-headed as the Israelites should deem this an insult or an outrage, we cannot understand."

Two years later in 1879, the Manhattan Beach Hotel on Coney Island emphatically banned Jews as a marketing ploy, adding new fuel to the national debate. The hotel's president, Austin Corbin, a developer and railroad baron, told the *New York Daily Herald* that he would not rent to Jews because their presence discouraged visits from highbrow customers.

Corbin's comments read like a stump speech in a campaign for Grand Dragon. "I never knew but one 'white' Jew in my life," he said. "The rest I found were not safe people to deal with in business."

While insisting he "did not like the Jews as a class," Corbin for some reason volunteered one weird line of faint praise for Jews. "There are some well-behaved people among them," he said. If that line rings queasily familiar, Donald Trump summoned the same dark spirit in 2015, after suggesting Mexicans were drug mules and rapists: "And some, I assume, are good people."

❖

Social discrimination against Jews spread at a ferocious pace in the United States through the 1880s. Some East Coast private schools "began as a matter of policy to reject applications from Jewish children." Social clubs blackballed Jewish applicants. "By the end of the century Jewish penetration into the most elite circles in the East became almost impossibly difficult," Higham wrote.

These were the grim facts that greeted John Pulver Solomon.

The young Jewish journalist sailed the Pacific in 1889, with aspirations to not just penetrate the elite circles of the United States but to conquer them, to stand beneath hot lights on the brightest stages of American civil life.

He took a hard look at the barriers to Jewish advancement and made a business decision.

On the altar of ambition, John Solomon sacrificed his Jewish identity.

He became John Revelstoke Rathom, the persona of a Gentile.

On his 1890 marriage license, Rathom listed his religion as the Church of England, common enough among Australians at the time, socially neutral throughout the United States. Once he stepped into that character, he never stepped out. Not even in death—his funeral in 1923 was held at Grace Episcopal Church, Providence, in the soft filtered light of the risen Christ appearing in stained glass.

This is the foundational lie of the Rathom story. The character of John Rathom was created to hide the fact that its creator was a Jew. It is why John Solomon could never go home. How could he face his devout family? Or the ghost of his father around every corner in Adelaide?

For very good reasons, some Jews throughout history have disguised themselves behind other religions to avoid bigotry or persecution. There is even a name for them: Crypto-Jews. In the thirteenth and fourteenth centuries, for instance, Jews in Spain were forced to convert to Catholicism. Some only pretended to convert. They knelt before the cross in public, then continued their Jewish traditions in secret in their sheds and cellars.

Learning this made me think: What if Rathom never entirely gave up his Jewish identity? What if he only hid it?

Could Rathom have been a Crypto-Jew?

One piece of evidence makes me wonder. On November 12, 1918, the day after the armistice to end the First World War, Rathom published the text of Psalm 100 on his editorial page. The scripture appeared in the paper with no explanation; it would seem none was needed on the first day of peace:

MAKE a joyful noise unto the LORD, all ye lands.
2 Serve the LORD with gladness; come before his presence with singing.

3 Know ye that the LORD he is God; it is he that hath made us, and not we ourselves; we are his people, and the sheep of his pasture.

4 Enter into his gates with thanksgiving, and into his court with praise: be thankful unto him, and bless his name.

5 For the LORD is good; his mercy is everlasting; and his truth endureth to all generations.

When I first discovered this passage years ago in the *Providence Journal* archives, it struck me as thoroughly Christian. It is the King James translation of the Bible. But Psalm 100 is an ancient Hebrew poem, and a Jewish prayer of thanks. It is recited by devout Jews nearly every day as part of the introduction to morning prayers. Rathom would have recited the psalm as a boy hundreds or thousands of times. Would he not have done so as a man?

It was not hard to imagine Rathom, alone in his study in Providence, hunched over a tattered prayer book, mumbling aloud the verses. I like the image. The man without the lies. It makes him seem less of an outcast. An imposter to the world, but his true self before God.

Acknowledgments

This book grew out of a journalism project I co-wrote as a reporter at the *Providence Journal* in 2004, commemorating the newspaper's 175th birthday. That was how I first learned of John Rathom and fell under his spell. Thanks to everyone at the *Journal* who nurtured my interest in narrative storytelling, especially Joel Rawson and Tom Heslin, and thanks to my co-writer on the history project, Paul Edward Parker, from whom I learned a lot about historical document sleuthing.

For years, the notion of a Rathom book idled in my head, taking up brain space that I really could have used elsewhere. Then in 2018 I wrote a short piece on Rathom for Globe Live, an in-person *Boston Globe* storytelling event before a theater audience. The *Globe*'s omnitalented Scott Helman helped develop the piece, coached my live performance, and ignited my pursuit of the Aussie imposter.

Somebody has to be the first person outside an author's family to fully believe in a book idea. That was my agent, Michael Signorelli. Thanks, Michael. Thanks also to Jessica Case and the folks at Pegasus Books, for their faith in the story and my ability to deliver it.

I've never more appreciated people who are passionate about helping writers dig out obscure facts. I got invaluable assistance from staff at the Providence Public Library, the New York Public Library, the Chicago Public Library, the Toronto Public Library, and the State Library of South Australia.

Author Heribert von Feilitzsch was generous to a stranger writing out of the blue with esoteric questions about long-dead spies.

Thank you to my consultants on all things Jewish: Rabbis Roderick Young and Andy Kahn—they are true teachers—as well as Gal Tziperman Lotan and old friend S. I. Rosenbaum.

I connected with Rathom's distant relatives in Australia mostly by luck, and now they're my mates for life. Jenny Cowen's book on Solomon family genealogy was an island of calm in a raging storm. Trevor Cohen's exquisite articles were like a lighthouse.

My old colleague and sounding board Scotty MacKay has helped me a hundred ways. Next round is on me, bud.

And, of course, thank you to my wife, Jennifer Levitz, an inspired journalist who can make a front-page story out of damn near anything, who read my drafts and radiated encouragement and joy.

NOTES

CHAPTER ONE

Three days after Christmas [Boy-Ed departs]: "Boy-Ed Departs, Attacking Press," *New York Times*, Dec. 29, 1915; "*Boy-Ed Sails for Home, Assailing Free Press*," *Standard Union* (Brooklyn), Dec. 28, 1915; "Boy-Ed at Sea, So Is Col. House," *New York Tribune*, Dec. 29, 1915; "Boy-Ed, Departing, Defends His Acts," *Sun* (New York), Dec. 29, 1915, 2; "Capt. Boy-Ed Sails; Blames U.S. Press." *Evening Star* (Washington, DC), Dec. 28, 1915.

An apartment on Monroe Street: Hoboken Historical Museum, "Francis Albert Sinatra (1915–1998)," https://www.hobokenmuseum.org/explore-hoboken/historic -highlights/frank-sinatra-the-voice/; Matt Micucci, "The Traumatic Birth of Frank Sinatra," *Jazziz*, Dec. 5, 1915, https://www.jazziz.com/the-traumatic-birth -of-frank-sinatra/.

Most outrageous story: "Says Germany Used Huerta against US," *New York Times*, Aug. 4, 1915.

A paper that has brought to light: "History-Making Editor is Rathom of Providence Paper Which Lands War Scoops," *Province* (Victoria, BC), Mar. 4, 1916.

Wilson scoured cover-to-cover: Kevin J. O'Keefe, *A Thousand Deadlines: The New York City Press and American Neutrality, 1914–17* (The Hague: Martinus Nijhoff, 1972), 11.

Had such a profound effect: French Strother, "How John R. Rathom Exposed Hun Spies," *Vancouver Sun*, Feb. 10, 1918.

Called himself John Rathom: Garrett D. Byrnes and Charles H. Spilman, *The Providence Journal—150 Years* (Providence: Providence Journal Company, 1980), 261, 267.

He could be deeply serious: *A Hundred Years of The Providence Journal 1829–1929* (Providence, Providence Journal Company, 1929), 23.

A bio he submitted: "History of the State of Rhode Island and Providence Plantations: Biographical." American Historical Society, 1920,

Once penned a poem: "Rathom, John Robert Revelstoke 1917, 1920–1923." New York Times Company Records, Adolph S. Ochs Papers, Box 32, Folder 36, Manuscripts and Archives Division, New York Public Library.

Boy-Ed grew up: Heribert von Feilitzsch, *The Secret War on the United States in 1915: A Tale of Sabotage, Labor Unrest and Border Troubles* (Amissville, VA: Henselstone Verlag, 2015), chap. 2.

In January 1915: von Feilitzsch, *The Secret War on the United States in 1915*, chap. 1.

To build a memorial: Livia Gershon, "How D.C.'s Newly Unveiled WWI Memorial Commemorates the Global Conflict," *Smithsonian Magazine*,

Apr. 20, 2021, https://www.smithsonianmag.com/smart-news/world-war-i
-memorial-unveiled-180977551/.

No other man in the world: "An Editor Who Exposed the Hun," *Vancouver Daily World*,
June 25, 1917.

No journalist on this continent: "Civic Welcome to Providence Editor," *Toronto Daily Star*,
June 13, 1917.

The new Central Technical School: Architectural Conservancy Ontario, https://www.
acotoronto.ca/show_building.php?BuildingID=3420.

We have been aided in this work: "How German Secret Plots Were Exposed," *Printer &
Publisher*, July 1917.

The hearts story: "Three Years of Germany's War on the United States," *Empire Club of
Canada Speeches, 1916–1917* (Toronto: Empire Club of Canada, Toronto), 570–87.

Blew out its front page: "Amazing Tale of How Rathom's Staff Outwitted the Hun Spies
and Plots," *Toronto Daily Star*, June 15, 1917.

A spontaneous singing: "The C.P.A. Gets a Gavel," *Printer & Publisher*, July 1917.

CHAPTER TWO

For the narrative of Franz Ferdinand's assassination, I leaned heavily on these four
texts:

Margaret MacMillan, *The War that Ended Peace: The Road to 1914* (New York: Random
House, 2013).

Greg King and Sue Woolmans, *The Assassination of the Archduke: Sarajevo 1914 and the
Romance That Changed the World* (New York: St. Martin's Press, 2013).

Charles River Editors, *The Assassination of Archduke Franz Ferdinand: The History and
Legacy of the Event that Triggers World War I* (Scotts Valley, CA: CreateSpace,
2014).

G. J. Meyer, *A World Undone: The Story of the Great War 1914 to 1918* (New York:
Bantam Dell, 2006).

OTHER SOURCES AND SPECIFIC CITATIONS:

A curious mixture: King and Woolmans, *The Assassination of the Archduke*, chap. 15.

They rode in the back: King and Woolmans, *The Assassination of the Archduke*, chap.16;
Benjamin Preston, "The Car That Witnessed the Spark of World War I," *New
York Times*, July 10, 2014.

Imagine the German empire: RadioFreeEurope/RadioLiberty, "Europe before
World War I vs Today," https://www.rferl.org/a/world-war-i-map-
europe-1914-2014/25427811.html.

Nerve damage in his left arm: "Treating the Kaiser's Withered Arm," *Untold Lives*,
Feb. 28, 2014, https://blogs.bl.uk/untoldlives/2014/02/treating-the-kaisers
-withered-arm.html.

Without the hard work: MacMillan, *The War that Ended Peace*, chap. 3.

Resemblance is uncanny: Miranda Carter, "What Happens When a Bad-Tempered
Distractible Doofus Runs an Empire?" *New Yorker*, June 6, 2018.

Cobbled-together assortment: Meyer, *A World Undone*, chap. 2.

Aggressively building their armies: Bill Price, "Mobilizations," in *The Unprevented War: Why the First World War was Fought* (New York: RW Press, 2014).

About 45 percent: Price, "Cultural and Religious Differences," in *The Unprevented War.*

Slight, introverted, and sensitive: MacMillan, *The War that Ended Peace,* chap. 18.

Idolized Nietzsche: King and Woolmans, *The Assassination of the Archduke,* chap. 14.

Serve the larger goal: King and Woolmans, *The Assassination of the Archduke,* chap. 14.

Threw the weapon out a window: Charles River Editors, *The Assassination of Archduke Franz Ferdinand,* chap. 3

Agreed to "sacrifice their lives": King and Woolmans, *The Assassination of the Archduke,* chap. 14.

The Battle of Puebla: William Booth, "In Mexico, Cinco de Mayo Is a More Sober Affair," *Washington Post,* May 5, 2011.

In no way did the subjects: "Maximillian's Reception," *New York Herald,* reprinted in *Soldier's Journal,* June 29, 1864.

Not in the least a comic-opera prince: Robert Payne, "Mayerling Remains a Mystery," *New York Times Magazine,* Jan. 26, 1964.

Passed the succession rights: "The Crown Prince's Successor," *New York Times,* Feb. 2, 1889.

Drank from the river: George F. Shrady, M.D., ed. *Medical Record: A Weekly Journal of Medicine and Surgery, Volume 49* (New York: William Wood and Company, 1896).

Heir consumptive: "Austria Crown Prince Dead," *Seattle Post-Intelligencer,* May 20, 1896.

Printed his premature obituary: "Archduke Franz Ferdinand Dead," *St. Louis Globe-Democrat,* Feb. 2, 1896.

Very big man: "Throne for a Woman," *Boston Globe,* June 27, 1900.

A one-man extinction event: Talia Mindich, "8 Things You Didn't Know about Franz Ferdinand," PBS NewHour, June 27, 2014, https://www.pbs.org/newshour/world/8-things-didnt-know-franz-ferdinand.

Hoped to pair one off with Franz: King and Woolmans, *The Assassination of the Archduke,* chap. 3.

Was forced to swear: Meyer, *A World Undone,* chap. 1

The morganatic wife: "Somewhere in Bohemia," *Pall Mall Gazette,* June 27, 1900.

Dispatched Franz Ferdinand to Bosnia: MacMillan, *The War that Ended Peace.*

High-ranking Serb nationalist officers: King and Woolmans, *The Assassination of the Archduke,* chap. 19.

Became known as the "blank cheque": Price, "The Blank Cheque," in *The Unprevented War.*

Beginning August 1: Library of Congress, "World War I Declarations," https://guides.loc.gov/chronicling-america-wwi-declarations.

Duty of an impartial neutrality: President Woodrow Wilson proclamation, printed in *State Press* (Muncie, IN), Aug. 5, 1914.

CHAPTER THREE

His name was Werner Horn: Werner Horn statement to A. Bruce Bielaski, Feb. 7, 1915, Machias, Maine, Investigative Reports of the Bureau of Investigation 1908–1922, https://www.fold3.com/image/1717348; Horn statement, June 17, 1917, Boston, https://www.fold3.com/image/1717380; Bielaski's report to Attorney General T. W. Gregory, Feb. 13, 1915.

A case of syphilis: National Archives, Department of Justice letter, Capt. George Threlkeld to Frank Burke, assistant director of the Bureau of Investigation, Aug. 1, 1919, Investigative Reports of the Bureau of Investigation 1908–1922.

Ulysses S. Grant had visited: "Celebration of the Formal Opening," *Bangor Daily Whig and Courier*, Oct. 19, 1871.

Hundreds of German-born men: "Germans Parade Here," *New York Times*, Aug. 5, 1914.

The cry resounds: "Watch on the Rhine," LyricsTranslate, https://lyricstranslate.com/en/rein-rein.html.

The sea blockade: Paul C. Vincent, *The Politics of Hunger: The Allied Blockade of Germany, 1915–1919* (Athens: Ohio University Press, 1985), 21.

National health office estimated: Vincent, *The Politics of Hunger*, 145.

A two-front war: Bill Price, "Plan for War," in *The Unprevented War: Why the First World War was Fought* (New York: RW Press, 2014).

More than six hundred German steamers: Vincent, *The Politics of Hunger*, 36.

He was a disciple: Richard W. Rolfs. *The Sorcerer's Apprentice: The Life of Franz von Papen* (Lanham, MD: University Press of America, 1996), 2–5.

"When the war broke out": "Nationalversammlung (1919–1920) Untersuchungsausschuss über die weltkriegsverantwortlichkeit," *Official German Documents Relating to the World War* (New York: Oxford University Press, 1923) 1310–13.

Plot to dynamite the locks: "Dynamite Plot Bared in Detail by Von Der Goltz," *New York Times*, Apr. 21, 1916.

The general staff is anxious: Mixed Claims Commission, *Opinions and Decisions in the Sabotage Claims Handed Down June 15, 1939, and October 30, 1939, and Appendix* (Washington, DC: Government Printing Office, 1940).

Two years on a coffee plantation: Werner Horn statement to A. Bruce Bielaski, Feb. 7, 1915.

Not a particularly intelligent piece of work: Franz von Papen, *Memoirs of Franz von Papen* (New York: E. P. Dutton, 1953), 62.

Caught up with the stranger: Statement of Carr G. Horn, Feb. 8, 1915, National Archives, https://www.fold3.com/image/1717368

Too heavy to lift: Statement of Aubrey Tague, Feb. 8, 1915, National Archives, https://www.fold3.com/image/1717361.

A thunderous boom: Statement of Aubrey Tague, Feb. 8, 1915.

His so-called escape plan: Bielaski's report to Gregory, Feb. 13, 1915.

Began his investigation: Statement of George Ross, Feb. 8, 1915, National Archives,https://www.fold3.com/image/1717371.

Teenaged newsreel photographer: Raymond Fielding, *The American Newsreel: A Complete History, 1911–1967* (Jefferson, NC: McFarland & Company, 2006).

Would ultimately be indicted: "Werner Horn Only Man Indicted," *Boston Daily Globe*, Mar. 3, 1915.

Bielaski biographical information: James S. Pula, "Bruce Bielaski and the Origin of the FBI," *Polish American Studies* 68, no. 1 (2011): 43–57.

They spoke for three hours: Bielaski's report to Gregory, Feb. 13, 1915.

CHAPTER FOUR

Circulation was modest: N. W. Ayer & Son. *N. W. Ayer & Son's American Newspaper Annual and Directory* (Philadelphia, N. W. Ayer & Son, 1915), 660, 674, 874–75.

More than an office building: *Providence Journal*, June 12, 1905.

Eighteen thousand moving pieces: Bob Greene, "Team Spirit Faded when Linotype Left," *Chicago Tribune*, Nov. 14, 1989.

Complicated love affair: Sal Robinson, "The (Other) Eighth Wonder of the World: Linotype," Melville House, Oct. 6, 2014, https://staging.mhpbooks.com/the -other-eighth-wonder-of-the-world-linotype/.

Rathom's blockbuster to the New York Times: "Boy-Ed Found the 'Plot,'" *New York Times*, Apr. 7, 1915.

A shady private detective: Edwin P. Hoyt, *Spectacular Rogue: Gaston B. Means* (Indianapolis: Bobbs-Merrill Company, 1963), 16, 36, 106, 306.

"Newspaper capital": Walter Millis, *Road to War: America 1914–1917* (Boston: Houghton Mifflin, 1935), 42–43.

Experienced communication professionals: Herbert von Feilitzsch, "Operation Perez: The German Attempt to Own American Newspapers in World War I," *FCH Annals: Journal of the Florida Conference of Historians*, 2015, 87–88.

Office at 1123 Broadway: von Feilitzsch, "Operation Perez," 89–90.

Placed a long op-ed: Bernhard Dernbug, "Germany and England—The Real Issue," *Saturday Evening Post*, Nov. 21, 1914.

"White" propaganda: "Types of Propaganda," *Encyclopedia of American Foreign Relations*, https://www.americanforeignrelations.com/O-W/Propaganda-Types-of -propaganda.html.

United Muslims of America: *United States of America v. Internet Research Agency LLC*, US District Court for the District of Columbia, Feb. 16, 2018.

William Bayard Hale: "Wm. Bayard Hale Dies in Bavaria," *Boston Globe*, Apr. 10 1924.

Bernstorff's idea resurfaced: von Feilitzsch, "Operation Perez," 95.

Lips pressed into thin lines: Robert Lansing, *War Memoirs of Robert Lansing* (Indianapolis: Bobbs-Merrill Company, 1935), 356–57.

Honorary Doctor of Laws: Brown University, https://www.brown.edu/Administration /News_Bureau/Databases/Encyclopedia/search.php?serial=H0200.

Permission to buy a newspaper: von Feilitzsch, "Operation Perez," 96–97.

Gave the job to his associate: Hoyt, *Spectacular Rogue*, 35.

British warships were lurking: Hoyt, *Spectacular Rogue*, 36–39.

Newswires led the story this way: "British Cruisers Coal from US Ports Claims Collector," *Tennessean*, Apr. 6, 1915.

Unpublished 1938 interview: Vernon Cordry, "John R. Rathom and the *Providence Journal* in the Years Preceding the Entry of the United States in the World War," Stanford University Division of Journalism of the School of Social Sciences, Stanford University archives.

Means's brother, Frank: Hoyt, *Spectacular Rogue*, 19.

Operation began to unravel: Hoyt, *Spectacular Rogue*, 40.

Flood the zone with shit: Michael Lewis, "Has Anyone Seen the President?" *Bloomberg Opinion*, Feb. 9, 2018, https://www.bloomberg.com/opinion/articles/2018-02-09 /has-anyone-seen-the-president.

A famous opening line: "Lays Harbor 'Plot' to German Embassy," *New York Times*, Apr. 12, 1915.

CHAPTER FIVE

Ocean liner Abyssinia: "From the Orient," *Vancouver Daily World*, Feb. 9, 1889.

A boat race: "The Oar," *Victoria Daily Colonist*, June 7, 1889.

A clever journalist: *Victoria Daily Times*, Aug. 28, 1889.

Rathom had many creditors: "Rathom, John Robert Revelstoke 1917, 1920–1923," New York Times Company Records, Adolph S. Ochs Papers, Box 32, Folder 36, Manuscripts and Archives Division, New York Public Library. This and other sworn statements about Rathom's background were collected around 1914 by New York investigator Thomas Keith. The documents were merged later with the product of a second investigation, largely of Rathom's Chicago years, by lawyers for a Rhode Island politician Rathom had enraged. The US Department of Justice later acquired the material as part of the *kompromat* the DOJ assembled against Rathom. I know of three copies of the material: the DOJ files, the Franklin Delano Roosevelt Presidential Library, and the papers of Adolph Ochs, former publisher of the *New York Times*.

A plum freelance assignment: *Victoria Daily Times*, Aug. 28, 1889.

Rathom would be very contrite: Statement of Edward W. Wright, Adolph S. Ochs Papers.

About as unscrupulous: Statement of L. H. Ellis, Adolph S. Ochs Papers.

To arrange a 1:00 a.m. meeting: Statement of L. H. Ellis, Adolph S. Ochs Papers.

Police arrested John Rathom: "What Next?" *Victoria Daily Colonist*, Dec. 5, 1891.

No privileges whatsoever: "The Rathom Case," *Victoria Daily Colonist*, Dec. 6, 1891.

A slim, severe-looking man: "Henry W. Sheppard, Gaoler for the Victoria Police Department," Royal BC Museum Archives, https://search-bcarchives. royalbcmuseum.bc.ca/henry-w-sheppard-gaoler-for-victoria-police-department.

Discoveries ran on the front page: "This Is Shameful Crime," *Victoria Daily Colonist*, Nov. 29, 1891.

Rathom's trial: "The Rathom Case," *Victoria Daily Colonist*, Dec. 6, 1891.

Mary Crockford: Obituary, "Mrs. Mary Rathom Claimed by Death," *Daily Colonist*, Nov. 30, 1943.

William Crockford: Obituary, *Nanaimo Daily News*, July 26, 1884.

William De Veulle: Obituary, *Nanaimo Daily News*, Jan. 10, 1889.

Never had any respect for John R. Rathom: Statement of Jane A. De Veulle, Adolph S. Ochs Papers.

They got hitched: Wedding announcement, *Victoria Daily Times*, July 7, 1890; marriage registrations, British Columbia Division of Vital Statistics, GR 2962, vol. 093.

Prosecuted Rathom for assault: "A Reckless Reporter," *Victoria Daily Times*, June 9, 1892.

Demanded…a bribe: Statement of Yip Wing, Adolph S. Ochs Papers.

Indicted for criminal libel: *State of Oregon v. John R. Rathom*, Circuit Court of the State of Oregon, Feb. 29, 1893. . National Archives, https://www.fold3.com/image/5225339.

Jury deadlocked: "The Criminal Libel Suit," *Daily Astorian*, Mar. 11 1893.

Doing almost anything for pay: Statement of Watson J. Binder, Adolph S. Ochs Papers.

A goddamn crook: Statement of C.G. Fulton, Adolph S. Ochs Papers.

Tried to take his own life: Affidavit of Frank Patton, National Archives, https://www.fold3.com/image/5200504.

Entitled 'The Suicide': *San Francisco Call*, Jan. 21, 1900.

To cover a prizefight: John R. Rathom, "A Blow That Won a Championship," *San Francisco Chronicle*, Mar. 18, 1897.

Exposed a bribery scheme: John R. Rathom, "Monster Steal to be Boodled through the State Legislature," *San Francisco Chronicle*, Dec. 28, 1898.

Fire began to smolder: Louis Fisher, "Destruction of the *Maine* (1898)," Law Library of Congress, Aug. 4, 2009, http://www.loufisher.org/docs/wi/434.pdf.

Had indeed been destroyed by a mine: Fisher, "Destruction of the *Maine*."

Coal fire was more likely: Fisher, "Destruction of the *Maine*."

The Chronicle *feted*: "'Chronicle' War Correspondents Will Leave for the Front To-Day," *San Francisco Chronicle*, Apr. 23, 1898.

Joined US troops in New Orleans: John R. Rathom, "John R. Rathom, a 'Chronicle' War Correspondent, Tells of the Enthusiasm Shown in the Crescent City," *San Francisco Chronicle*, Apr. 30, 1898.

Media sensations: John R. Rathom, "Twenty Thousand Men Will Go to Cuba," *San Francisco Chronicle*, June 4, 1898.

Elected him chairman: Fred W. Stowell, "Presidio Boys the First to Embark," *San Francisco Chronicle*, June 12, 1898.

Say boys, I can't stand this: "Newspaper Life at the Seat of War," *San Francisco Call*, July 3, 1898.

The Negro cavalry: John R. Rathom, "Saved the Tampa Camps," *San Francisco Chronicle*, May 16, 1898.

Every man that hears it: John R. Rathom, "How Invading Army Sailed," *San Francisco Chronicle*, June 15, 1898.

The typical Cuban sky: John R. Rathom, "Under the Red Cross," *San Francisco Chronicle*, July 24, 1898.

Rathom ran off into the woods: "Told by a War Correspondent," *Arizona Republican*, Sept. 5, 1898.

In search of his friend John Rathom: "The Last Man on the Beach," *New York Sun*, Aug. 6, 1898.

Money had burned up in a fire: Statement of John Young, Adolph S. Ochs Papers.

CHAPTER SIX

Door was unlocked: Emanuel Voska and Will Irwin, *Spy and Counterspy* (New York: Doubleday, 1940), 21.

Voska was born: Voska and Irwin, *Spy and Counterspy*, ix–xii; Brendan McNally, "E. V. Voska: The U.S. Army Captain Who Founded Czechoslovakia," Defense Media

Network, Sept. 26, 2017, https://www.defensemedianetwork.com
    /stories/e-v-voska-the-u-s-army-captain-who-founded-czechoslovakia/.
Was relaxing on a train: Voska and Irwin, *Spy and Counterspy*, 6–20.
Informal committee of ethnic journalists: Voska and Irwin, *Spy and Counterspy*, 20.
Guy Reginald Archer Gaunt: "Admiral Sir Guy Reginald Archer Gaunt,"
    Royal Australian Navy, https://www.navy.gov.au/biography/
    admiral-sir-guy-reginald-archer-gaunt.
Two weeks before Christmas: Anthony Delano, *Guy Gaunt: The Boy from Ballarat who
    Talked America into the Great War* (Melbourne: Australian Scholarly Publishing,
    2016), 83–88, 97–100; David C. Wendes, *South Coast Shipwrecks: East Dorset and
    Wight 1870–1979* (Privately published, 2006), 62–63.
Park him out of sight: Delano, *Guy Gaunt*, 1.
Played to America's sense of right: Admiral Sir Guy Gaunt, *The Yield of the Years: A Story
    of Adventure Afloat and Ashore* (London: Hutchinson & Co., 1940), 137. Gaunt's
    memoir is hard to find. I paid hundreds of dollars for membership to a highbrow
    private library to see a copy. It is fairly awful, poorly written, and polluted with
    racist terms. And the memoir says nothing of Gaunt's later scandals, such as when
    he ran off with the wife of the royal ophthalmologist in London.
Polled newspaper editors: "American Sympathies in the War," *Literary Digest*, Nov. 14,
    1914, 939–41, 974–78.
Gaunt and I realized: Voska and Irwin, *Spy and Counterspy*, 24.
Strolling through the British embassy: Gaunt, *The Yield of the Years*, 137–38.
Briefly told story: Gaunt, *The Yield of the Years*, 138.

CHAPTER SEVEN
Leon Thrasher: "Family Appeals to Washington," *Boston Daily Globe*, Mar. 31, 1915; US
    Department of State, passport applications, Roll 0137, Certificates 52366-53265,
    May 25, 1911–June 2, 1911.
An undistinguished British steamer: *Shipping Casualties: Report on the Loss of the Steamship
    'Falaba,' Court to Investigate Loss of Steamship 'Falaba'* (London: His Majesty's
    Stationery Office, 1915), 3, https://archive.org/details/shippingcasualti00grea
    /page/3/mode/2up; Gerald Maurice Burn, *Falaba* (painting), 1908, National
    Museums Liverpool, https://www.liverpoolmuseums.org.uk/artifact/falaba.
Ship left England for Africa: Alastair Walker, *Four Thousand Lives Lost: The Inquiries of
    Lord Mersey* (Stroud, Gloucestershire, UK: History Press, 2012), 78.
Reports of German U-boat activity: "*Lusitania* Sails under American Stars And Stripes,"
    Portage (WI) Daily Register, Feb. 8, 1915.
Ruse became international news: "On Her Way from Queenstown to Liverpool,"
    Montreal Gazette, May 8, 1915.
Cruiser rules: Walker, *Four Thousand Lives Lost*, 30–32.
February 18 deadline arrived: "German Blockade Is On," *Brooklyn Times Union*, Feb. 18,
    1915.
Officers on the Falaba: Walker, *Four Thousand Lives Lost*, 79–80.
Sank in eight minutes: *Report on the Loss of the Steamship 'Falaba,'* 5.

One-hundred four people: *Report on the Loss of the Steamship 'Falaba,'* 7.

I do not like this case: John Milton Cooper Jr., *Woodrow Wilson: A Biography* (New York: Alfred A. Knopf, 2009), chap. 13.

Was Bryan's sincere belief: Robert Lansing, *War Memoirs of Robert Lansing* (Indianapolis: Bobbs-Merrill Company, 1935), 29.

Insisted to the international press: Ed L. Keen, "England Fears Germans May Torpedo Other Liners," *Evening Journal* (Wilmington, DE), Mar. 30, 1915.

Overweening confidence: Randy Dotinga, "*Dead Wake* Author Erik Larson Talks about History, Hubris, and the *Lusitania*," *Christian Science Monitor*, Apr. 10, 2015.

Among her cargo: Erik Larson, *Dead Wake: The Last Crossing of the Lusitania* (New York: Broadway Books, 2015), 182–83.

Bitter hindsight: "The 'Armed Lusitania' Myth," *Saskatoon Phoenix*, May 15, 1915.

An unusual warning: Advertisement, *New York Times*, May 1, 1915.

Six big liners: "Six Liners Leave New York," *Buffalo Commercial*, May 1, 1915.

George Sylvester Viereck: Niel M. Johnson, "George Sylvester Viereck: Poet and Propagandist," *Books at Iowa* 9, no. 1 (1968): 22–36, https://doi.org/10.17077/0006 -7474.1312.

His 1929 profile: "What Life Means to Einstein," *Saturday Evening Post*, Oct. 26, 1929.

Wilson hosted Rathom: "Image 814 of Woodrow Wilson Papers: Series 1: Diaries and Diary Material, 1876–1924; Appointment Books; 1904– 1915," Library of Congress, https://www.loc.gov/resource/mss46029. mss46029-002_0444_1282/?sp=814.

Laid out an incredible story: John R. Rathom, "Germany's Plots Exposed," *World's Work*, Feb. 1918.

Wrote the president for a favor: "Image 542 of Woodrow Wilson Papers: Series 2: Family and General Correspondence, 1786–1924; 1915, Apr. 13– June 2," Library of Congress, https://www.loc.gov/resource/mss46029. mss46029-070_0018_1139/?sp=542.

Now became ultimatums: Gerald H. Davis, "The 'Ancona' Affair: A Case of Preventive Diplomacy," *Journal of Modern History*, Sept. 1966, Vol. 38, No. 3,269.

Germany blinked: Lansing, *War Memoirs of Robert Lansing*, 48.

Assigned body number 248: Larson, *Dead Wake*, 305.

As one went westward: Lansing, *War Memoirs of Robert Lansing*, 22–27.

CHAPTER EIGHT

The liner Antonio Lopez: "Gen. Huerta Here, Vows He'll Be Good; May Stay," *New York Tribune*, Apr. 13, 1915; "Huerta Arrives in New York and Gets a Real 'Bomb Scare,'" *Bridgeport (CT) Times and Evening Farmer*, Apr. 13, 1915.

No bigger character than Huerta: George J. Rausch, "The Exile and Death of Victoriano Huerta," *Hispanic American Historical Review* 42, no. 2 (1962): 133–51, https://doi .org/10.1215/00182168-42.2.133.

Cloud upon our horizon: "No Peace until Huerta Lets Go Usurped Power," *Davis (OK) News*, Dec. 4, 1913.

Huerta's forces detained at gunpoint: Robert E. Quirk, *An Affair of Honor: Woodrow Wilson and the Occupation of Veracruz* (New York: W. W. Norton, 1967), 20–27.

Mexico has yielded: Associated Press, "Huerta's Foreign Minister Offers Compromise," *Inter Ocean* (Chicago), Apr. 20, 1914.

Obtain from General Huerta: "President Wilson Explains in His Message That the United States Seeks No War with Mexico," *New York Times*, Apr. 21, 1914.

Military losses: Jack Sweetman, "'Take Veracruz at Once,'" *Naval History Magazine* 28, no. 2 (2014).

German interests were trying to buy control: "Accuse Germans of Plots to Buy up War Plants Here," *New York Times*, June 9, 1915.

Wall Street Journal *responded*: "No Sign That Bethlehem Steel Will Pass to Germans," *Wall Street Journal*, June 10, 1915.

von Bernstorff wrote after the war: Johann Heinrich Graf von Bernstorff, *My Three Years in America* (New York: Charles Scribner's Sons, 1920), 95.

Remarkably like a bomb: *Bridgeport Times* story.

Dodging their dogged attempts: "Dodges Questions of Future," *Star-Gazette* (Elmira, NY), Apr. 16, 1915.

Rintelen was clean-shaven: Reinhard R. Doerries, Introduction to *The Dark Invader* (Portland, OR: Frank Cass, 1998), ix–xxxii.

Muscles of his jaw: John Price Jones, *The German Secret Service in America, 1914–1918* (Boston: Small, Maynard & Company, 1918), chap. 8.

Man of limited intelligence: Franz von Papen, *Memoirs of Franz von Papen* (New York: E. P. Dutton, 1953), 79.

Run like a lunatic asylum: Franz Rintelen, *The Dark Invader: Wartime Reminiscences of a German Naval Intelligence Officer* (New York: Penguin Books, 1938), part 2.

Chemical firebomb operation: Heribert von Feilitzsch, "The German Sabotage Campaign of 1915–1916." *Journal of the Florida Conference of Historians* 26 (June 2020): 1–6; Emanuel Voska and Will Irwin, *Spy and Counterspy* (New York: Doubleday, 1940), 122–23.

Antiwar political and trade group: Rintelen, *The Dark Invader*, part 2; "Peace Agitators Want to Keep Ships at Home," *Washington Herald*, July 7, 1915.

Man was a plant: Voska and Irwin, *Spy and Counterspy*, 192–95.

$900,000 was deposited: Michael C. Meyer, "The Mexican-German Conspiracy of 1915," *Americas* 23, no. 1 (1966): 84, www.jstor.org/stable/980141.

Weapons would be accumulated: Rausch, "The Exile and Death of Victoriano Huerta," 137.

CHAPTER NINE

A dangerous shopping list: "Futile Search for the Person who Filled the Cherries with Poison," *San Francisco Examiner*, July 8, 1899; "Candied Cherries Were Full of Arsenic," *San Francisco Examiner*, July 7, 1899; "Mystery Fades into Domestic Scandal," *San Francisco Call*, July 8, 1899; "Florence Campbell Confesses," *Los Angeles Daily Times*, July 29, 1899; "Strange Poison Plot," *Saint Paul (MN) Globe*, Aug. 20, 1899; "Poisoned Candy and a Family Skeleton," *San Francisco Call*, July 7, 1899.

A week's vacation to Santa Cruz: "Yesterday's Hotel Arrivals," *Santa Cruz Sentinel*, Nov. 13, 1897.

Pacific Ocean House: Geoffrey Dunn, "Celebrating Santa Cruz's 150th Anniversary," *Good Times*, Sept. 28, 2016, https://goodtimes.sc/cover-stories/celebrating-santa-cruzs-150th-anniversary/; Margaret Koch, "An Old Tree with a Story," *Santa Cruz Sentinel*, July 15, 1979.

West Virginia delegation: "Sight Seers," *Los Angeles Herald*, Sept. 10, 1897.

Struck up a quick friendship: "An Appreciative Visitor," *Evening Sentinel* (Santa Cruz, CA), Oct. 13, 1897.

Irish writer Sarah Grand: Greg Buzwell, "Daughters of Decadence: The New Woman in the Victorian Fin de Siècle," British Library, 15 May 2014, https://www.bl.uk/romantics-and-victorians/articles/daughters-of-decadence-the-new-woman-in-the-victorian-fin-de-siecle#footnote2.

John Dunning and the Botkin affair: Katie Dowd, "Murder by Mail: The Story of San Francisco's Most Infamous Female Poisoner," SFGATE, Oct. 10, 2016, https://www.sfgate.com/bayarea/article/San-Francisco-murder-poison-Cordelia-Botkin-9880884.php; Paul Drexler, "Candy from a Stranger: The Gifts of Cordelia Botkin," *San Francisco Examiner*, July 5, 2015, https://www.sfexaminer.com/news/candy-from-a-stranger-the-gifts-of-cordelia-botkin/.

A doctor visiting: "On This Evidence Mrs. Botkin Will Be Tried," *San Francisco Call*, Sept. 15, 1898.

CHAPTER TEN

Afternoon of July 24: Sydney Roberts, "Retirement of Famous Secret Service Man Recalls Capture of German Secret Papers from N.Y. Train," *Sunday News* (Lancaster, PA), July 19, 1942; Frank Sauliere, "Miami Visitor Blasted German Plot," *Miami News*, May 3, 1942; W. H. Houghton, "The Albert Portfolio," *Saturday Evening Post*, Aug. 17, 1929; Ernest Wittenberg, "Spy and the Subway Saga," *American Heritage Magazine*, republished by *Quad-City Times*, (Davenport, IA) May 22, 1966; "How Frank Burke Stole Albert's Brief Case," *Press and Sun-Bulletin* (Binghamton, NY), June 1, 1932.

Spent thirty million: John Price Jones, *The German Secret Service in America, 1914–1918* (Boston: Small, Maynard & Company, 1918), chap. 1.

Albert's jobs involved: George Sylvester Viereck, [presumed author], "War Propaganda: By One of the War Propagandists," *Saturday Evening Post*, June 22, 1929, 12.

Would later ruefully recall: Viereck, "War Propaganda," 161.

Train rattled north: Speed Graphic Film and Video, "A Ride on the Sixth Avenue Elevated, 1916," YouTube, Mar. 30, 2018, https://www.youtube.com/watch?v=A_3F32mPZvY.

German-owned wireless station: "*Providence Journal* Says it Gave Proof of Breeches of Neutrality," *New York Times*, July 1, 1915.

Navy Department is convinced: "Daniels Acts on Evidence of Newspaper," *New York Tribune*, Aug. 19, 1915.

A blistering attack: "Bryan Pledged Wilson to Yield?" *New York Times*, July 3, 1915.

Bribe labor leader Samuel Gompers: "Offer Gompers Big Bribe to Agitate Munitions Strikes," *Bridgeport (CT) Times and Evening Farmer*, July 21, 1915.

Threatening the banks: "Says German Agents Seek to Awe Banks," *New York Times*, July 29, 1915.

Huerta made his move: George J. Rausch, "The Exile and Death of Victoriano Huerta," *Hispanic American Historical Review* 42, no. 2 (1962): 138–39, https://doi.org/10.1215/00182168-42.2.133; see also "Huerta Arrested as He Nears Border," *New York Times*, June 28, 1915.

Published his Mona Lisa: "Says Germany Used Huerta against Us," *New York Times*, Aug. 4, 1915.

Allegations did seem ridiculous: Editorial, *Wilkes-Barre Record*, Aug. 5, 1915; Herman Ridder, "Sir Cecil or 1776," *Buffalo Times*, Aug. 9, 1915.

Desperate to protect his superior: "Horn Denies Charges Against Von Papen," *New York Tribune*, Aug. 18, 1915.

Rathom slashed back: "Defends Horn Story," *New York Times*, Aug. 19, 1915.

Albert was incredulous: Viereck, "War Propaganda."

von Feilitzsch summarized: Heribert von Feilitzsch, *The Secret War on the United States in 1915: A Tale of Sabotage, Labor Unrest and Border Troubles* (Amissville, VA: Henselstone Verlag, 2015), chap. 12.

First major wartime speech: *Toronto Daily Star*, June 15, 1917.

Deploy the Secret Service: Wittenberg, "Spy and the Subway Saga."

CHAPTER ELEVEN

James Francis Jewell Archibald: "War Writer was Acquainted with Nations' Secrets," *Leavenworth (KS) Weekly Times*, Sept. 16, 1915; Sylvester Scovel, "Fight on Cuban Soil," *Chicago Tribune*, May 14, 1898.

Iill-fated mission: Spencer C. Tucker, ed., *The Encyclopedia of the Spanish-American and Philippine-American Wars* (Santa Barbara, CA: ABC-CLIO, 2009), 269.

Five months with the German army: Advertisement, *Buffalo Courier*, Apr. 1, 1915.

Cosplaying wannabe: Emanuel Voska and Will Irwin, *Spy and Counterspy* (New York: Doubleday, 1940), 76.

An amateur magician: Constantin Dumba, *Memoirs of a Diplomat* (Boston: Little, Brown and Company, 1932), 260.

Cache was for Archibald to carry: Voska and Irwin, *Spy and Counterspy*, 77–84.

To provoke strikes at US factories: "Papers Archibald Carried," *New York Times*, Sept. 6, 1915.

Idiotic Yankees: "Capt. Von Papen Calls Us 'These Idiotic Yankees,'" *New York Times*, Sept. 22, 1915.

Stories made a sensation: Voska and Irwin, *Spy and Counterspy*, 89.

Eugene von Tomory: "Providence Journal Says Austrian Captain Carried Our Defense Plans," *New York Times*, Oct. 16, 1915; Voska and Irwin, *Spy and Counterspy*, 155–56. Voska's version of the story is confused. Writing twenty-five years after the events, he suggested that the British captured Tomory. Gaunt's contemporaneous report said the courier escaped.

British missed the courier: Report of Special Agent William R. Benham, Oct. 19, 1915, National Archives, Investigative Reports of the Bureau of Investigation 1908–1922, Roll boi_german_257-850_0056, https://www.fold3.com /image/1709538.

Bielaski gently rebuked: Bruce Bielaski, Letter to William M. Offley, Nov. 20, 1915. National Archives, https://www.fold3.com/image/5225221.

Rathom sent Bielaski a list of employees: John R. Rathom, Letters to Bielaski, Nov. 18 and 20, 1915, National Archives, https://www.fold3.com/image/5222994; https://www.fold3.com/image/5225219.

Five typewritten names: John R. Rathom, Letter to Bielaski, Dec. 15, 1915, National Archives, https://www.fold3.com/image/5225192.

Franz Bopp: "German Agent Name Figures in 'Exposé,'" *Minneapolis Star Tribune*, Dec. 15, 1915; "US Indicts Bopp," *San Francisco Examiner*, Feb. 9, 1916; "Journal's Disclosures," *Fall River (MA) Daily Globe*, Feb. 9, 1916.

Joseph Goricar: "Former Austrian Consul Exposes Spy Work Here," *Providence Journal*, Nov. 12, 1915; Voska and Irwin, *Spy and Counterspy*, 33–34. Interestingly, Voska describes but does not name Goricar in one part of his memoir, and later mentions Goricar offhandedly by name, as if he had already introduced him; "Every Outrage Planned in Advance, Says Goricar," *Providence Journal*, Nov. 14, 1915.

Story went national: "Consul Resigned; Wouldn't Spy on Us," *New York Times*, Nov. 12, 1915; "Wilson and Cabinet Confer over Reports on Bomb Plot," International News Service, printed in *San Francisco Examiner*, Nov. 17, 1915.

Was eager to interview Goricar: "Officials Take Up Goricar Charges," *New York Times*, Nov. 13,1915; Bruce Bielaski telegram to Rathom, Nov. 12, 1915, and to US Attorney's Office, Providence, RI, Nov. 13, 1915, National Archives, https://www .fold3.com/image/5200546 and https://www.fold3.com/image/5223682; John R. Rathom telegram to Bielaski, Nov. 12, 1915, https://www.fold3.com /image/5223678.

Bielaski's notes from the conference: Bruce Bielaski, memorandum, Nov. 18, 1915, National Archives, https://www.fold3.com/image/5200157 (the dates of the conference are transcribed incorrectly in this memo).

Ambassador complained bitterly: Johann Heinrich Graf von Bernstorff, *My Three Years in America* (New York: Charles Scribner's Sons, 1920), 110.

Rathom published an explanation: "Boy-Ed and von Papen Dismissed," *New York Times*, Dec. 4, 1915.

von Papen departed: "Von Papen, Sailing, Scores Newspapers; 'Not Bitter,' He Says," *Brooklyn Daily Eagle*, Dec. 22, 1915.

Paperwork included: *Selection from Papers Found in the Possession of Captain Von Papen* (London: His Majesty's Stationary Office, Harrison and Sons, 1916), https:// archive.org/details/selectionfrompap00unse/mode/2up?view=theater.

The Italian liner Ancona: Gerald H. Davis, "The 'Ancona' Affair: A Case of Preventive Diplomacy," *Journal of Modern History*, Sept. 1966, Vol. 38, No. 3, 267–77.

Published a story about the Ancona*:* "Goricar Says a German U-Boat Sank *Ancona*," *New York Sun*, Dec. 16, 1915.

CHAPTER TWELVE

A cold night in Ottawa: Report of the Royal Commission appointed to investigate the
origins of the Parliament Buildings fire, Printed by J. de L. Tache, Printer to the
King's Most Excellent Majesty, Ottawa, 1916; "Main Building Laid in Ruins"
Star-Phoenix (Saskatoon, SK), Feb 4, 1916; "Premier Escaped without Hat or
Coat and with Difficulty," *Ottawa Citizen*, Feb. 4, 1916; "Parliament Fire Still a
Mystery after 40 Years," *Ottawa Citizen*, Feb. 3, 1956; "Six Known to Be Dead,"
Star-Phoenix, Feb. 4, 1916; "Twenty Members Trapped in Commons Chamber
Fought Their Way to Safety," *Ottawa Journal*, Feb. 4, 1916; "Fall of the Great
Tower Is Watched by Many Thousands," *Ottawa Citizen*, Feb. 4, 1916; "Saved
Themselves by Rope Made of Towels," *Ottawa Journal*, Feb. 4, 1916; James Powell,
"Remember This? Sabotage on Parliament Hill?" City News, Jan. 28, 2019,
https://ottawa.citynews.ca/remember-this/remember-this-sabatoge-on-parliament-
hill-1215987; Jennifer Ditchburn, "US Historian Says It's Possible German Agents
Caused 1916 Parliament Fire," *Toronto Star*, Feb. 3, 2016; various stories, *Ottawa
Evening Journal*, Feb. 3, 1916.
Notified the Department of Justice: "Warning Given of Ottawa Plot," *Washington (DC)
Herald*, Feb. 5, 1916.
Furious telegram to Attorney General Gregory: John R. Rathom, telegram to Gregory,
Feb. 5, 1916, National Archives, https://www.fold3.com/image/5225120.
Outed H. Snowden Marshall: "Gregory Denies Warning," *New York Times*, Feb. 5,
1916.
An undercover sting: John R. Rathom, letter to Bielaski, Feb. 7, 1916, National Archives,
https://www.fold3.com/image/5224869.
Harry Perissi: Bruce Bielaski, letter to Rathom, Jan. 3, 1916, National Archives,
https://www.fold3.com/image/5223051.
Request was personal: John R. Rathom, letter to Bielaski, Jan. 4, 1916, National
Archives, https://www.fold3.com/image/5225169.
Sent a coded telegram: Bruce Bielaski, telegram to special agent in charge, Boston,
National Archives, https://www.fold3.com/image/1919617.
Interview with one of Bielaski's investigators: F. P. Schmid, interview report, Jan. 10,
1916, National Archives, https://www.fold3.com/image/1919622.
A suspicious package: W. L. Furbershaw, report, Jan. 25, 1916, National Archives,
https://www.fold3.com/image/1919641.
You might have a spy: Bruce Bielaski, letter to Rathom, Feb. 4, 1916, National Archives,
https://www.fold3.com/image/5225146.
Austrian government bribe: "Baron Zwiedinek Continues Austro-German Propaganda
under Direction of Bernstorff," *Providence Journal*, Feb. 27, 1916.
Burning up is a death too sweet: G. M. Murdock, Bureau of Investigation report, Mar.
18, 1916, National Archives, https://www.fold3.com/image/5224697.
A sketch of him from 1903: "Dr. Frank Iska Lectures Here," *The Gazette* (Cedar Rapids,
IA), Nov. 16, 1903.
Analyzed by a typeface expert: Letter to W. M. Offley, Bureau of Investigation, May 1,
1916, National Archives, https://www.fold3.com/image/5224653.

Duties as a paid German agent: Bruce Bielaski, memo to the attorney general, Feb. 17, 1916, National Archives, https://www.fold3.com/image/5224846.

Went hard at Agent E-13: Transcript, conversation between John Rathom and Gaston Means, Providence, Feb. 6, 1916, National Archives, https://www.fold3.com/image/5225058.

Royal commission investigated the blaze: Report of the Royal Commission, various pages.

Hand-deliver the transcript: Department of Justice letter to Frank Polk, counselor for the Department of State, Feb. 12, 1916, National Archives, https://www.fold3.com/image/5225080.

Bielaski answered on February 8: Bruce Bielaski, letter to John Rathom, Feb. 8, 1916, National Archives, https://www.fold3.com/image/5224857.

Will see what I can do: John R. Rathom, letter to Bruce Bielaski, Feb. 9, 1916, National Archives, https://www.fold3.com/image/5224854.

CHAPTER THIRTEEN

The brisk afternoon of Dec. 30, 1903: Francine Uenuma, "The Iroquois Theater Disaster Killed Hundreds and Changed Fire Safety Forever," *Smithsonian Magazine*, June 12, 2018, https://www.smithsonianmag.com/history/how-theater-blaze-killed-hundreds-forever-changed-way-we-approach-fire-safety-180969315/; http://www.iroquoistheater.com/; D. B. McCurdy, *Chicago's Awful Theater Horror* (New York: Memorial Publishing Company, 1904); "The New Iroquois Theater, Chicago," *Daily Chronicle* (De Kalb, IL), Nov. 18, 1903; "Gorgeous Stage Production," *Champaign (IL) Daily News*, Dec. 27, 1903; Bob Secter, "The Iroquois Theater Fire," *Chicago Tribune*, Dec. 19, 2007.

A deadline news lede for the ages: "More Than 600 People Killed by Fire in New Iroquois Theater," *Chicago Record-Herald*, Dec. 31, 1903.

A letter to Florence: Garrett D. Byrnes and Charles H. Spilman, *The Providence Journal—150 Years* (Providence: Providence Journal Company, 1980), 470–71.

Booker T. Washington: "Booker Washington," *Daily Morning Journal and Courier* (New Haven, CT), Oct. 28, 1901.

Created a lecture: "Absentees Were Losers," *Decatur (IL) Herald*, Mar. 23, 1905.

Fled apartments in Chicago: Adolph S. Ochs Papers, Box 32, Folder 36, Manuscripts and Archives Division, New York Public Library.

Rathom and Crawford: "Railway Press Bureau," *Huntington (IN) Herald*, Nov. 15, 1905; "Press Bureau Abandoned," *Winnipeg Tribune*, Nov. 15, 1905; "There Was No 'Collusion,'" *La Crosse (WI) Tribune*, Nov. 22, 1905; Editorial, *Evening Times-Republican* (Marshalltown, IA), Nov. 1, 1905; "Parry Faction Belongs to Railroads," *Chicago Tribune*, Oct. 27, 1905; Editorial, *People's Banner* (David City, NE), July 27, 1905; News brief, *Omaha Daily Bee*, July 3, 1905; "Railway Press Bureau Abandoned," *Evening Times-Republican*, Nov. 14, 1905; "Attacks Esch-Townsend Bill," *La Crosse Tribune*, Oct. 21, 1905; "Buying the Editorial Page," *Davenport (IA) Weekly Democrat and Leader*, Sept. 7, 1905; "Railway Press Dept." *Evening Star* (Washington, DC), Nov. 12, 1905.

Ray Stannard Baker: Carl Resek, ed., *The Progressives* (Indianapolis: Bobbs-Merrill Company, 1967), 157, 167, 172–73.

Paper became politically independent: Byrnes and Spilman, *The Providence Journal—150 Years*, 210–12.

An offer to become managing editor: Byrnes and Spilman, *The Providence Journal—150 Years*, 261–62.

Audience was small: N. W. Ayer & Son. *N. W. Ayer & Son's American Newspaper Annual and Directory* (Philadelphia, N. W. Ayer & Son, 1906), 795–96.

Groups settled in enclaves: Patrick T. Conley, *An Album of Rhode Island History, 1636–1986* (Virginia Beach, Donning Publishing Company, 1986). Kindly provided by Conley via email.

Competition was fierce: N. W. Ayer & Son. *N. W. Ayer & Son's American Newspaper Annual and Directory* (Philadelphia, N. W. Ayer & Son, 1915), 874–75, 1,165.

CHAPTER FOURTEEN

U-53 glided from a berth: Wellington Long, "The Cruise of the U-53," US Naval Institute *Proceedings*, Oct. 1966, 86–95; George Lowry, "Exploit of the U-53," *Proceedings*, Apr. 1961, 158–59.

The Deutschland: Francis Duncan, "*Deutschland*: Merchant Submarine," *Proceedings*, Apr. 1965, 68–75; "Facts about the Notable Voyage," *Baltimore Sun*, July 10, 1916; Johann Heinrich Graf von Bernstorff, *My Three Years in America* (New York: Charles Scribner's Sons, 1920), 226–29.

People crowded around the Journal: "Crowds Read Bulletins on Torpedoing of Ships," *Providence Journal*, Oct. 9, 1916.

Two civilian cryptographers: Barbara W. Tuchman, *The Zimmermann Telegram: America Enters the War, 1917–1918* (New York: Random House, 2014), 3–9.

Bernstorff arrived at about four o'clock: Robert Lansing, *War Memoirs of Robert Lansing* (Indianapolis: Bobbs-Merrill Company, 1935), 210–12.

Icebergs and fish: "Thanks to Belligerents," *Brooklyn Daily Eagle*, Feb. 2, 1917.

Prophetic and mysterious: "Germans Organized for Attack on America across Border," *Providence Journal*, Feb. 9, 1917.

Small but significant differences: Tuchman, *The Zimmermann Telegram*, 142, 144–45, 149.

Edwin Hood: Edwin M. Hood, obituary, *Tuscaloosa News*, Aug. 9, 1923.

Wilson had for so long resisted: Lansing, *War Memoirs of Robert Lansing*, 212.

Roosevelt wrote to Rathom: Franklin D. Roosevelt, letter to John Rathom, Apr. 21, 1917, Franklin D. Roosevelt Presidential Library and Museum, nondigitized collections, Papers as Assistant Secretary of the Navy.

CHAPTER FIFTEEN

A dinner and speaking program: National Archives, https://www.fold3.com/image/5200350; https://www.fold3.com/image/5214047; https://www.fold3.com/image/5224607.

Speech in Philadelphia: "Two US Officers Spies, Says Editor," *Philadelphia Inquirer*, Oct. 24, 1917.

Ad copy promised: Advertisement, *Chicago Daily Tribune*, Dec. 7, 1917.

Discreetly scribbled notes: National Archives, https://www.fold3.com/image/5224612.

Bad-mouthed the rest of America: "The Man Who Saw," *Orlando Evening Star*,
      24 Dec. 1917, page 6.

Wanted Rathom's thoughts: "Denounces Secretary of War," *Albuquerque Morning Journal*,
      Jan. 20, 1918; "War on Austria Wanted by Editor," *Chattanooga Daily Times*,
      Nov. 22, 1917.

Warned the people of Boston: "Says Boston is Full of Spies," *Boston Globe*, Nov. 22, 1917.

Wilson had set the tone: Transcript, Woodrow Wilson, Third Annual Message, Dec. 7,
      1915, https://millercenter.org/the-presidency/presidential-speeches
      /december-7-1915-third-annual-message.

Forced the registration: Daniel A. Gross, "The U.S. Confiscated Half a Billion Dollars
      in Private Property during WWI," *Smithsonian Magazine*, July 28, 2014,
      https://www.smithsonianmag.com/history/us-confiscated-half-billion-dollars
      -private-property-during-wwi-180952144/.

Karl Muck: Neil Swidey, "Sex, Lies and the National Anthem," *Boston Globe*, Nov. 2,
      2017; "Dr. Muck Arrested as an Enemy Alien," *New York Sun*, Mar. 26, 1918.

To cover Rathom's City Club speech: National Archives, https://www.fold3.com
      /image/5200566.

Arthur Page: Edward M. Block, "The Legacy of Public Relations Excellence behind the
      Name," https://page.org/site/historical-perspective.

An ominous letter: National Archives, https://www.fold3.com/image/5224431.

Strother: "French Strother Finds New York an Education in Real Life," *Fresno Morning
      Republican*, Aug. 6, 1905; "Life in New York," *Fresno Morning Republican*, July 10, 1904.

A very crestfallen mood: Nation Archives, https://www.fold3.com/image/5224449. The
      date on this memo is transcribed incorrectly; it should be December 19.

Secretly recorded their conversation: Transcript, National Archives, https://www.fold3.
      com/image/5223670.

Recorded the call: Transcript, National Archives, https://www.fold3.com/image
      /5224397.

Remarks of Mr. Rathom find echo: National Archives, https://www.fold3.com/image
      /5200604.

Ill-advised speech: "War Secretary Baker Pacifist, Editor Charges," *Democrat and
      Chronicle* (Rochester, NY), Jan. 20, 1918.

Jerked before the grand jury: National Archives, https://www.fold3.com/image/5224291.

Agent from New York was on the train: National Archives, https://www.fold3.com/image
      /5199927.

Gregory's terms were brutal: National Archives, https://www.fold3.com/image/5224180.

Wrote Rathom's confession: Bielaski memo to Gregory, Feb. 15, 1918, National Archives,
      https://www.fold3.com/image/5224275.

In Page's words: National Archives, https://www.fold3.com/image/5223989.

Bielaski brought French Strother: Bielaski memo to Gregory, Feb. 15, 1918.

At 8:30 p.m. at the Prince George: Bielaski memo to Gregory, Feb. 15, 1918.

Thick with sworn affidavits: National Archives, https://www.fold3.com/image/5200661.

CHAPTER SIXTEEN

Ervin Arnold: Sherry Zane, "'I Did It for the Uplift of Humanity and the Navy':
    Same-Sex Acts and the Origins of the National Security State, 1919–1921,"
    New England Quarterly 91, no. 2 (2018): 279–306, https://doi.org/10.1162
    /tneq_a_00670; Lawrence R. Murphy, *Perverts by Official Order* (New York:
    Harrington Park Press, 1988); Jonathan Katz, ed., *Government versus Homosexuals*
    (New York: Arno Press, 1975); John Loughery, *The Other Side of Silence: Men's
    Lives and Gay Identities: A Twentieth-Century History* (New York: Henry Holt,
    1998).

An undercover sting: Loughery, *The Other Side of Silence*, chap. 1.

Allow certain immoral acts: US Senate Committee on Naval Affairs, *Report Relative to
    Alleged Immoral Conditions and Practices at the Naval Training Station, Newport, RI*
    (Washington, DC: Government Printing Office, 1921), 4. Published in full in
    Katz, *Government versus Homosexual*.

Camouflaged in an ambulance: Zane, "'I Did It for the Uplift of Humanity and the
    Navy,'" 279.

Became known as Section A: Senate Committee on Naval Affairs, *Report Relative to
    Alleged Immoral Conditions and Practices*, 4.

116,516 died: Carol R. Byerly, "War Losses (USA)," International Encyclopedia of the
    First World War, Oct. 8, 2014, https://encyclopedia.1914-1918-online.net/article
    /war_losses_usa.

Internal scrub of its Rathom files: National Archives, https://www.fold3.com/image
    /5364639.

A speech to educators: "Editor Assails 'Red' Doctrines," *Brooklyn Citizen*, Feb. 19, 1919.

At the defendant's table: Murphy, *Perverts by Official Order*, 97–100, 121–24.

Blasted the Navy Department: "The Dirty Trail of Daniels," *Providence Journal*, Jan. 9,
    1920.

Designated three of its members: "Orders Investigation of Naval Vice Squad," *Argus-
    Leader* (Sioux Falls, SD), Mar. 2, 1920.

Prickly little conflict: "Roosevelt Denies Rathom's Charges," *New York Times*, Jan. 23,
    1920.

After forty-four ballots: Thomas Mallon, "How the Promise of Normalcy Won the 1920
    Election," *New Yorker*, Sept. 21, 2020; "Democrats Nominate Cox for President,"
    Indian Journal (Eufaula, OK), July 8, 1920; "By Acclimation," *Boston Post*, July 7,
    1920.

Daniels testified: "Secretary Daniels," *Modesto (CA) Morning Herald*, May 23, 1920.

Shot across his bow: "Declares Daniels Plots against Him," *Boston Globe*, May 28, 1920.

Praised Harding's character: "Rhode Island," *Hilo (HI) Daily Tribune*, Sept. 5, 1920.

The Hotel Palatine: Franklin D. Roosevelt, letter to Francis Caffey, Oct. 24, 1920,
    Franklin D. Roosevelt Presidential Library and Museum, nondigitized collections,
    Papers as Assistant Secretary of the Navy.

Low-wattage public quarrel: Geoffrey C. Ward, *A First Class Temperament: The
    Emergence of Franklin Roosevelt 1905–1928* (New York: Vintage Books, 1989),
    chaps. 12 and 13.

Had acquired evidence: John R. Rathom, letter to Roosevelt, Oct. 22, 1920, Franklin D. Roosevelt Presidential Library and Museum, nondigitized collections, Papers as Assistant Secretary of the Navy.

Roosevelt sent a blanket notice: Franklin D. Roosevelt, notice to editors, Oct. 24, 1920, Franklin D. Roosevelt Presidential Library and Museum, nondigitized collections, Papers as Assistant Secretary of the Navy.

He had another idea: Francis G. Caffey, note to Roosevelt, Oct. 25, 1920, Franklin D. Roosevelt Presidential Library and Museum, nondigitized collections, Papers as Assistant Secretary of the Navy.

Put out a public statement: "Editor's Confession of Falsely Claiming Credit for Anti-Spy Work Revealed," *St. Louis Post-Dispatch*, Oct. 31, 1920.

CHAPTER SEVENTEEN

My attention has been called: "The Confession of John R. Rathom," *Nation*, Nov. 17, 1920; "Big Spy System of Providence 'Journal' Myth," *New York Herald*, Oct. 28, 1920; Upton Sinclair commentary, *Appeal to Reason* (Girard, KS), Dec. 11, 1920; "Creatures of Propaganda," *Minneapolis Star*, Nov. 20, 1920.

Hardly too much to say: William Herbert Hobbs, *The World War and Its Consequences* (New York: G. P. Putnam's Sons, 1919), 202–3.

Post-confession mentions: Walter Millis, *Road to War: America 1914–1917* (Boston: Houghton Mifflin, 1935), 204.

Shared his feelings: John R. Rathom, letter to Adolf Ochs, Nov. 5, 1920, Adolph S. Ochs Papers, Box 32, Folder 36, Manuscripts and Archives Division, New York Public Library.

Three months after the election: Franklin D. Roosevelt, letter to Charles H. McCarthy, Feb. 10, 1921, Franklin D. Roosevelt Presidential Library and Museum, nondigitized collections, Papers as Assistant Secretary of the Navy.

Where the hair is short: McCarthy, Charles H. Letter to Franklin Roosevelt, 7 March 1921, Franklin D. Roosevelt Presidential Library and Museum, nondigitized collections, Papers as Assistant Secretary of the Navy .

Meeting of the American Defense Society: "Heckler Throws America Day Meeting in Uproar," *New York Tribune*, May 2, 1921; 'Irish Hyphens' Stirs Woman in Green Hat," *New York Herald*, May 2, 1921.

Released a scathing report: US Senate Committee on Naval Affairs, *Report Relative to Alleged Immoral Conditions and Practices at the Naval Training Station, Newport, RI* (Washington, DC: Government Printing Office, 1921).

Issued a long statement: Franklin D. Roosevelt, press release, July 18, 1921, Franklin D. Roosevelt Presidential Library and Museum, nondigitized collections, Papers as Assistant Secretary of the Navy.

Had been convicted of sodomy: Geoffrey C. Ward, *A First Class Temperament: The Emergence of Franklin Roosevelt 1905–1928* (New York: Vintage Books, 1989), chap. 12.

Roosevelt took some vacation: Amy Berish, "FDR and Polio," Franklin D. Roosevelt Presidential Library and Museum, https://www.fdrlibrary.org/polio.

An even harsher diagnosis: Garrett D. Byrnes and Charles H. Spilman, *The Providence Journal—150 Years* (Providence: Providence Journal Company, 1980), 299–301.

Florence penned Ochs a letter: Florence M. Campbell, letter to Adolf Ochs, Sept. 12, 1922, Adolph S. Ochs Papers, Box 32, Folder 36, Manuscripts and Archives Division, New York Public Library.

Sent Ochs a book of verse: John R. Rathom, letter to Ochs, July 28, 1922, Adolph S. Ochs Papers, Box 32, Folder 36, Manuscripts and Archives Division, New York Public Library.

Rathom's obituary: "John R. Rathom Dies after Long Illness," *New York Times*, Dec. 12, 1923; "John R. Rathom," editorial, *New York Times*, Dec. 12, 1923; "Famous Editor Is Dead in East," *Los Angles Daily Times*, Dec. 12, 1923.

Speak ill of the dead: "The Death of John R. Rathom," *Nation*, Dec. 26, 1923.

Appeared at Rathom's gravesite: Byrnes and Spilman, *The Providence Journal*, 300–301.

CHAPTER EIGHTEEN

Pulled the funeral carriage: "Funeral of the Late Judah Moss Solomon," *South Australian Register*, Aug. 31, 1880; "The Late Mr. Judah Moss Solomon," *South Australian Register*, Aug. 30, 1880; "Judah Moss Solomon," Find a Grave, https://www .findagrave.com/memorial/19210486/judah-moss-solomon; Jenny Cowen, *Descendants of Samuel Moss Solomon*, Australia, 2019; "Married. Solomon—Pulver," *South Australian Register*, Sept. 16, 1867.

Adelaide was a planned community: Pascoe, J.J., editor. *History of Adelaide and Vicinity*. Hussey Gillingham, Adelaide, South Australia, 1901.

Craggy-faced old man: Henry Jones, Photograph of Emanuel Solomon, ca. 1869, State Library of South Australia, https://www.catalog.slsa.sa.gov.au/record =b2049489~S1.

Clatter of iron keys: Trevor S. Cohen, "Solomon and Cashmore: Chain Migration and Early Jewish Settlement in Australia," *Journal of the Australian Jewish Historical Society* 15, no. 3 (2000): 315–66; E. S. Richards, "The Fall and Rise of the Brothers Solomon," *Journal of the Australian Jewish Historical Society* 8, no. 2 (1975), 1-22.

A growing social crisis: Jessica Brain, "British Convicts to Australia," Historic UK, https://www.historic-uk.com/HistoryUK/HistoryofBritain/British-Convicts-to -Australia/; Suemedha Sood, "Australia's Penal Colony Roots," BBC, Jan. 26, 2012, https://www.bbc.com/travel/article/20120126-travelwise-australias-penal -colony-roots; Sue Ballyn, "The British Invasion of Australia. Convicts: Exile and Dislocation," in *Lives in Migration: Rupture and Continuity* (Barcelona: Center for Australian and Transnational Studies, University of Barcelona, 2011), http://www .ub.edu/dpfilsa/2ballyn.pdf.

Schooled at Whinham College: "School Examinations—Whinham College," *Evening Journal* (Adelaide, Australia), Dec. 18, 1884; "School Examinations—Whinham College," *South Australian Register*, Dec. 16, 1882; "School Examinations—Whinham College," *Express and Telegraph* (Adelaide, Australia), Dec. 20, 1883.

The one-act farce: News item, *Express and Telegraph*, Dec. 8, 1884.

The gist of his toast: "The Old Colonists' Festival," *South Australian Register*, Jan. 2, 1872.

Worked as a news reporter: "Law Courts," *Northern Territory Times and Gazette*, Jan. 14, 1888. John Pulver Solomon testifying as a witness in an assault case gives his occupation as "a newspaper reporter."

Owned the Gazette: Trevor Cohen, "The Honourable Vaiben Louis Solomon, Biographical Notes," *Journal of the Australian Jewish Historical Society* 8, no. 3 (1977): 89–98.

Booked space on the Tsinau: "The Northern Territory," *Evening Journal* (Adelaide, Australia), Mar. 28, 1888.

Much of Rathom's biography was fake: Garrett D. Byrnes and Charles H. Spilman, *The Providence Journal—150 Years* (Providence: Providence Journal Company, 1980), 472–73.

Ocean liner Abyssinia: "From the Orient," *Vancouver Daily World*, Feb. 9, 1889.

He had decided [the fake Rathom parent names]: Byrnes and Spilman, *The Providence Journal*, 469.

A license to marry: British Columbia, Division of Vital Statistics, marriage registrations, 1888–1892.

CHAPTER NINETEEN

A classified advertisement: Advertisements, *South Australian Register*, Oct. 11, 1872.

In love with a Gentile: Trevor Cohen, "The Honourable Vaiben Louis Solomon, Biographical Notes," *Journal of the Australian Jewish Historical Society* 8, no. 3 (1977): 90, 92–93.

Melbourne Argus *wrote*: "From The United States," *Argus* (Melbourne, Australia), Sept. 1, 1877.

A consuming topic of debate: "A Sensation at Saratoga," *New York Times*, June 19, 1877; "Judge Hilton Explains and Defends the Course He Has Taken," *Detroit Free Press*, June 21, 1877; Jenna Weissman Joselit, "Imperfect Idyll: Remembering A Vacation That Made History," *Forward*, July 1, 2008, https://forward.com /culture/13687/imperfect-idyll-remembering-a-vacation-that-made-h-02117/.

Paid the real Horatio Alger: George S. Hellman, "Joseph Seligman, American Jew," *Publications of the American Jewish Historical Society* 41, no. 1 (1951): 27–40, www .jstor.org/stable/43059807.

No equivalent: E. S. Richards, "The Fall and Rise of the Brothers Solomon," *Journal of the Australian Jewish Historical Society* 8, no. 2 (1975): 10.

6,900 Jews on the continent: Charles Price, "Jewish Settlers in Australia, 1788–1961," *Journal of the Australian Jewish Historical Society* 5, no. 8 (1964), 357-411, Appendix 1.

Washington's 1790 letter: "George Washington and His Letter to the Jews of Newport," Touro Synagogue National Historic Site, https://www.tourosynagogue.org /history-learning/gw-letter.

Next several generations: John Higham, "Social Discrimination against Jews in America, 1830–1930," *Publications of the American Jewish Historical Society* vol. 47, no. 1 (1957): 1–33, www.jstor.org/stable/43059004.

General Order No. 11: Ron Chernow, *Grant* (New York: Penguin, 2017), chap. 11.

Rose another caricature: Higham, "Social Discrimination against Jews in America," 8-11.

Was born in 1819: "Seligman, Joseph," *National Cyclopedia of American Biography*
    (New York: James T. White & Co., 1893), 392–93; Hellman, "Joseph Seligman,
    American Jew," 28–34; Lee M. Friedman, *Jewish Pioneers and Patriots*
    (Philadelphia: Jewish Publication Society of America, 1942), 270–78.

Urged Lincoln to name Grant: Hellman, "Joseph Seligman, American Jew," 32.

The height of his career: Friedman, *Jewish Pioneers and Patriots*, 272.

Hilton told the Times: "A Sensation at Saratoga," *New York Times*, June 19, 1877.

Bad takes: Editorial, *Brooklyn Daily Eagle*, June 19, 1877.

Manhattan Beach Hotel: "Reviving a Prejudice," *New York Daily Herald*, July 22, 1879.

Crypto-Jews: "Crypto-Jews," Jewish Virtual Library, https://www.jewishvirtuallibrary
    .org/crypto-jews.

INDEX

A

absolute neutrality, 93–94

Abyssinian, 62–63, 282

Adelaide, Australia, 271, 285–286

Agent E-13, 51, 56–61, 139, 175, 181–186

Albert, Henrich, 87, 135–138, 147–152

Alexander I, 22

Alger, Horatio, 287

Allies, 22, 88, 93

American Defense Society, 229, 230, 262

American Federation of Labor, 140

American industry, 37, 114

American neutrality, 2, 5, 30, 35, 49–50, 56, 58; absolute, 93–94; sinking of *Falaba* and, 101–102; sinking of *Lusitania* and, 107–109; *U-53* attacks and, 205; violations of, 139–140

American Red Cross, 78

Ancona, 167–169

anti-immigrant fearmongering, 221–222

anti-Semitism, 287–295

Antonio Lopez, 110

Arabic, 108

Archibald, James Francis Jewell, 153–158

arms industry, 37, 114, 118

Armstrong, Collin, 82–83

Arnold, Ervin, 237–242, 244, 262

Arsenault, Henry, 11–12, 241

arsenic plot, 122, 127, 129–134

Artesani, Arthur L., 176–178

Asian-Americans, 222

Associated Press, 3, 126, 267

Astoria, Oregon, 72–74

Astorian, 72–73

Australia: Adelaide, 271, 285–286; Jewish community in, 285–288; penal colony in, 274–276; Solomon family in, 269–286

Austria-Hungary, 11, 17, 20, 21; Bohemia, 85; seizure of Bosnia by, 22–23; sinking of *Ancona* by, 167–169; start of World War I and, 29–30, 85

Austrian espionage, 158–159, 161–165

B

backdoor diplomacy, 105–107

Baker, George, 75

Baker, Ray Stannard, 193–194

balanced newswriting, 113

Bannon, Steve, 60

Barton, Clara, 78

Battle of Cantigny, 241

Battle of Puebla, 24

Battle of San Juan Hill, 80

Bauer, Hermann, 200

Belgium, 22, 30, 35, 52, 102

Bernhardi, Friedrich von, 36

Bernstorff, Johann Heinrich von, 49; Archibald and, 155–156; arms industry and, 114; on cruiser rules, 108; *Deutschland* and, 202; on Goricar story, 164–165; Huerta plot and, 143, 145; meeting with Lansing by, 207–208; propaganda campaign by, 54–55; Zimmermann telegram to, 206–207

Bethlehem Steel, 114

Bielaski, A. Bruce: biography of, 43–45; Goricar story and, 162–164; Horn and, 146–147; on Means, 181; in private practice, 242; Rathom and, 158–164, 174–178, 180, 186, 220, 223, 225–228, 231–235; *World's Work* and, 241

Bielaski, Alexander, 44

Black Americans, 79

Black Hand, 22, 23

blackmail: by Rathom, 66–67, 71–73; against Rathom, 231

black propaganda, 49–61, 192–194

"blank check," 29

Blommersdyk, 205
Boas, Abraham Tobias, 271
Boer War, 7
Bohemia, 84–85
Bohemian National Alliance, 87, 139,
    181, 256
Bolshevism, 243
bombs, 109–110, 117–118, 166
Bopp, Franz, 161
Bosnia, 18, 22–23, 27
Boston, Massachusetts, 197, 214–217
Boston Globe, 257
Boston Marathon attack, 189
Botkin, Cordelia, 126–129
Boy, Karl, 9
Boy-Ed, Karl, 49; backdoor diplomacy
    by, 105–107; biography of, 9–10;
    expulsion from U.S. of, 1–5, 12,
    114, 165–166; on Goricar story, 162;
    Huerta plot and, 120, 143–145; Means
    and, 56; Rathom and, 105–107, 165;
    Veracruz occupation and, 113
Bremen, 204
bribery, 44, 71, 74–75, 110, 135, 140, 164,
    178, 179–180, 185
Bridgeport Projectile Company, 37
Britain: Germany and, 22, 33–35; naval
    blockade by, 34–35, 37, 56, 109,
    201–202, 206; penal codes in, 274;
    pre-WWI, 20, 22; propaganda by,
    51–52; public opinion on, 92–93;
    shipping of convicts to Australia by,
    274–276; start of World War I and,
    30, 92; submarine blockade of, 98–99
British codebreakers, 206–207
Brown, T. E., 266
Bryan, William Jennings, 57, 101–102,
    108, 140
Buchanan, Frank, 118
Bulgaria, 22
Burea of Investigation: Bielaski as
    head of, 43, 44, 146; Gaunt and,
    158–159; German spies and, 220–221;
    investigation of Rathom by, 226–228,

235–236; Means sting and, 182–186;
    spying on Americans by, 221; tips
    to Rathom by, 159, 160, 175–178;
    Zwiedinek letter and, 180–181
Burke, Frank, 150–152
Burns, William J., 56
Byrnes, Garrett, 281

C

Cabrinovic, Nedeljko, 17–19, 23, 28, 29
Caffey, Francis G., 230, 251, 252–253
California, 74–75
Campbell, Florence Mildred, 7, 15–16,
    59, 121–134; affair with Rathom, 128–
    134; after Rathom's death, 267; arsenic
    plot of, 129–134; biography of, 123;
    in Chicago, 190–191, 192; meeting
    of Rathom by, 125; at Ocean House,
    123–124; public talks by, 124–125; on
    Rathom's illness, 265–266
Campbell, John A., 123
Campbell, Milton B., 123
Canada: attacks on, 37–38; Parliament
    Building fire, 170–175, 182–185;
    plots against, 185–186; Rathom's
    immigration to, 62–64; Rathom's trip
    to, 12–16; during World War II, 33
Canadian Pacific Railway, 38, 62
Canadian Press Association, 12, 15–16
Carranza, Venustiano, 115
Carter, Miranda, 21
Central Europe, 20
Central Powers, 8, 20, 21–22, 93
chemical weapons, 102
Chernow, Ron, 289
Chicago, 187–194
Chinese immigrants, 64
Chotek, Sophie. *See* Sophie, Duchess of
    Hohenberg
Christian Knudsen, 205
cigar bombs, 117–118
Cinco de Mayo, 24
Civil War, 289
Cobb, Frank I., 152

Cohen, Rachel, 277
Cohen, Trevor S., 272, 276, 286
Committee on Public Information, 221
Communists, 243
Conley, Patrick T., 197
contraband, 99
convicts, sent to Australia, 274–276
Coolidge, Calvin, 247, 260
Cooper, A. D. M., 123
Corbett, James J., 74
The Corbett-Fitzsimmons Title Fight, 74
Corbin, Austin, 293
counterespionage, 89, 94
COVID-19, 222
Cox, James M., 248, 249, 260
Cranston Citizen, 176, 177
Crim, John, 236
Crockford, Mary Harriet. *See* Rathom, Mary
Crowley, Aleister, 104
cruiser rules, 99, 100, 108
Crypto-Jews, 294–295
Cuba, 75–76, 79–81, 153–154
Czech nationalists, 86–87, 88
Czech Republic, 84–85

D
Daily Colonist, 63, 64, 66–68
Daniels, Josephus, 140, 232–233, 246, 248
Darrow, Clarence, 57
Davies, Frederick, 100
Davis, Gerald, 169
Delano, Anthony, 92
Department of Justice, 44, 175, 178, 180;
    Canadian Parliament fire and, 173,
    174; German spies and, 215; Means
    and, 181, 182, 186; new leadership
    of, 242; Rathom file in, 261–262;
    targeting of Rathom by, 222–232, 242;
    tips to, 159, 160. *See also* Bureau of
    Investigation
Derna, 91–92
Dernburg, Bernhard, 52–53, 102, 136
De Veulle, Jane, 70, 71
De Veulle, William, 70

Dimitrijević, Dragutin, 22
Doerries, Reinhard, 117
Dow, Daniel, 98
Dumba, Constantin, 155–156, 157
Dunn, Herbert O., 246
Dunning, John, 126–128
Dunning, Mary, 126–128
Durham County Gaol, 272

E
Earp, Wyatt, 74
Eckardt, Heinrich von, 207
Ed, Ida, 9
Edison, Thomas, 48
Einstein, Albert, 104
Elisabeth (Empress), 21
Ellis, L. H., 66
enemy aliens, 221–222
England. *See* Britain
Europe, before World War I, 19–23
Evening Bulletin, 195

F
Facebook, 119
fake news, 54
Falaba, 97, 100–102, 168
false flag ruse, 97–99, 168–169
Fatherland, 104–105, 114, 135, 166–167
Feilitzsch, Heribert von, 52, 54, 148
Ferdinand, Archduke Franz, 11, 21, 22;
    assassination of, 23–30, 85, 92, 198;
    attempt to assassinate, 17–19, 23; as
    heir to Austro-Hungarian throne,
    24–26; illness of, 25–26; marriage to
    Sophie of, 26–27; personality of, 26
First World War. *See* World War I
Fitzsimmons, Bob, 74
Florida, 77–78
Flynn, William, 150
Fox, May, 66, 71
Foy, Eddie, 189
France: attack on Mexico by, 24;
    pre-WWI, 20, 21–22; start of World
    War I and, 30, 35

Franz Josef I, 21, 26
Friedman, Lee M., 291
Friedrich der Grosse, 118
Fulton, C. G., 72, 73
Fulton, Charles, 72

G
Gaunt, Guy, 89–95, 113, 156, 158–159
gay sailors, 237–241. *See also* Section A sting
General Order No. 11, 289
George Town, 275–276
German-Americans, 221–222
German army, 154–155
German cyphers, 206
German espionage: documents relating to, 136, 138, 147–152; financing of, 135–136; *Providence Journal* and, 176–178, 217; stories of, 2–5, 12–16, 94–95, 215–220, 228–230; in U.S., 116–120, 215, 220, 223, 228–231
German immigrants, 93, 109, 289, 290
German Information Service, 52–53
Germans, in U.S., 33–38
German U-boats, 10, 97–109; blockade by, 98–99, 101, 102, 108, 167–169; sinking of *Ancona* by, 167–169; sinking of *Arabic* by, 108; sinking of *Falaba* by, 100–102; sinking of *Lusitania* by, 107–109; submarine warfare and, 200–201, 205–208; in U.S., 199–206
Germany: Britain and, 22, 33–35; merchant fleet of, 35; Mexico and, 116–120, 143–145, 207, 209–211; naval blockade of, 34–35, 37, 56, 109, 201–202, 206; pre-WWI, 20; propaganda by, 10, 46–61, 104–105; public opinion on, 93; start of World War I and, 30, 35–38, 92; U.S. diplomatic break with, 208–209; use of poison gas by, 102; U.S. relations with, 2; wireless transmissions by, 139–140; Zimmermann telegram and, 206–207, 210–211

Gibbons, Charles, 64–67, 72
Glass, Samuel Francis, 170–171
Gleaves, Albert, 204
Goldberg, Rube, 55
Gompers, Samuel, 140–141, 164
Goricar, Joseph, 161–165, 168
Grand, Sarah, 124
Grand Union Hotel, 290, 291–293
Grant, John, 65–66
Grant, Ulysses S., 32, 289, 291
gray propaganda, 53–56
Great Britain. *See* Britain
Gregory, Thomas Watt, 173, 174, 223–225, 227, 229, 231, 242, 248–249

H
Hale, William Bayard, 54, 147
Hall, Lewis H., 246
Harding, Warren G., 247, 249, 260
hate crimes, 222
Hearst, William Randolph, 76
Heart of Texas, 119
"hearts story," 14–15, 218, 236, 256
Herzegovina, 22–23
Higham, John, 289, 290
Hilton, Henry, 291–293
Hirsch, Charlotte Teller, 164
history: events of, 11–12; impact of, 28; writing, 188–190
HMS *Centurion*, 90–91, 92
Hobbs, William Herbert, 259
homosexuality, 237–241. *See also* Section A sting
Hong Kong, 280, 282, 283
Hood, Edwin, 210
Hope Diamond, 51
Horn, Carr G., 40
Horn, Werner: arrest of, 42–43; biography of, 38–39; bombing of train bridge by, 31–33, 39–43, 166; confession by, 43–45; escape plan of, 42; frostbite of, 41, 42; incarceration of, 43; Rathom reporting about, 146–147, 217–218, 255

Hotel Manhattan, 56, 119–120
Houghton, W. H., 150–151
Houston, Herbert, 234
Howick, Tom, 230
Hoyt, Edwin P., 50
Hudson, Erasmus, 240
Huerta, Victoriano, 2, 5, 13, 110–120;
    arrest of, 142, 143; fall of, 113;
    German spies and, 116–120; Mayo
    and, 112; Mexican Revolution and,
    111; in New York, 110–111, 113, 115–
    116; Rathom's story on, 142–147, 255;
    return to power by, 119, 120, 141–142;
    Wilson and, 111, 112, 113
Hughes, Charles, 223
hyphenism, 221–222, 262

I
immigrants, 191, 221–222, 289, 290
Industrial Revolution, 274
influenza pandemic, 242, 245
Internet Research Agency, 118–119
internment camps, 221–222
Irish-Americans, 93, 109, 221
Iroquois Theater fire, 187–190
Irvin, Will, 85
Isaacs, Jacob, 69
Isabella of Croy, Princess, 26
Iska, Frank, 178–181

J
Japan, 207
Japanese-Americans, 222
Jewish community: anti-Semitism and,
    287–295; in Australia, 285–288;
    Crypto-Jews, 294–295; in United
    States, 287–295
Jewish immigrants, 289, 290
Johnson, Niel M., 104
Judaism, 286

K
Kent, Samuel Neal, 243–247
Keyes, Henry, 246

King, Greg, 17
King, Maude, 51
King, William, 246
Kitchener, Horatio, 7, 86
Knight, Austin, 204
Koenig, Paul, 201–202
kompromat, 231–235, 242, 243, 247,
    248–249, 252–262, 265

L
Labor's National Peace Council, 118–119
Lansing, Robert, 102, 108, 109, 145, 165,
    185, 207–208, 210, 212
Larson, Erik, 102–103
Law, Bowman Brown, 173
League of Nations, 248
Lees, Isaiah, 130, 132
Leopold II, 25
libel charges, against Rathom, 72–73,
    252, 263–264
Lincoln, Abraham, 289, 291
Lindbergh baby, 51
Lindheim, Norvin, 166
Linotype machines, 48
Long, Wellington, 200
Loughery, John, 238, 240
Lovecraft, H. P., 267
Lovett, Robert, 264
Ludwig, Archduke Karl, 25
Lusitania, 150, 201, 233; false flag ruse
    by, 97–98; final voyage of, 103–105;
    sailings by, 102; sinking of, 107–109

M
machine-driven change, 102–103
MacMillan, Margaret, 20–21
Madero, Francisco, 111
Maine Central Railroad, 31–33, 39
Malone, Dudley Field, 57–60
Manhattan Beach Hotel, 293
marriage license, 283
Marshall, H. Snowden, 58, 174
Masaryk, Tomáš, 85–86
Masterson, Bat, 74, 191

Maximillian, Archduke, 24
Mayo, Henry T., 112
McAdoo, William, 150, 152
McCarthy, Charles H., 261–263
McCarthyism, 215
McIntosh, Burr, 81
McKinley, William, 7, 76, 102, 123
McLean, Evalyn Walsh, 51
Means, Frank, 59
Means, Gaston Bullock, 50–51, 56–61,
    95, 139, 141, 175, 181–186, 255
Mehmedbašić, Muhamed, 23, 27
merchant ships, 99
Mergenthaler, Ottmar, 48
Metcalf, Stephen O., 231, 249
Mexican-American War, 207
Mexican Revolution, 56, 111
Mexico, 5, 24; conflicts between U.S.
    and, 111–113, 119, 207; Germany's
    involvement in, 116–120, 143–145,
    207, 209–211; Huerta and, 110–120,
    141–142; problems in, 115–116; U.S.
    occupation of Veracruz in, 112–113
Michaelis & Ellsworth, 192, 193
Millis, Walter, 52, 259
Minneapolis Star, 258
Muck, Karl, 221–222
munitions industry, 30, 35, 37, 113, 114,
    118–119, 156, 161, 162, 164, 165, 173
murder, of Mary Dunning, 127–128
Murphy, Lawrence R., 245
Muslim Americans, 222

N
Nantucket Lightship, 204, 205
Nation, 258, 267
Naval Station Newport, 201, 237–241,
    245, 248–249, 262–264
Newcastle, 276
New Orleans, 77
Newport, Rhode Island, 237–239;
    navy scandal in, 237–241, 243–249,
    262–264
newspaper competition, 197

new woman, 124–125
New York Evening Mail, 55–56
New York Herald, 65, 256–257, 262, 283
New York Times, 4, 9, 50, 61, 141, 143,
    162, 259, 266–267
New York World, 4, 147, 148, 152, 257
Nineteenth Amendment, 124
Northern Territory Times and Gazette,
    279

O
obituary, of Rathom, 266–267
Ochs, Adolph, 9, 259, 265–266
Offley, William M., 159
Olivette, 79
Operation Perez, 55
oral sex sting, 239–241, 243–249
Orduna, 98
Oregon, 72–74
Osborne, Thomas Mott, 250–251
Ottawa, Canada, 170–173
Ottoman Empire, 22, 23

P
Pacific Ocean House, 122–125
Page, Arthur, 224, 234, 235
Page, Walter Hines, 210, 224
Palmer, A. Mitchell, 253
Panama Canal, 141
Papen, Franz von, 14, 36–38, 39, 45;
    Archibald and, 157; expulsion
    from U.S. of, 1–5, 114, 165–166;
    government spying on, 150; "hearts
    story" and, 218; Horn and, 146;
    Rintelen and, 117
Parker, Clarence, 264
Parliament Building fire, 170–175,
    182–185
passport-forging operation, 2, 36, 87, 89
Pearl Harbor, 265
penal colony, in Australia, 274–276
pencil bombs, 117–118
Pennington, Mary Elizabeth. See
    Dunning, Mary

Perissi, Harry, 175–176
Pike, C. W., 74–75
Pilgrim Publicity Association, 214
Pixley, E. B., 124
poison gas, 102
Portland Oregonian, 72–73
Portsmouth Naval Prison, 250–251
Potiorek, Oskar, 28, 29
presidential election: of 1896, 123; of 1916, 221, 223; of 1920, 247–249, 250, 260; of 2016, 54
press coverage. *See* U.S. press
Prest, Thomas, 274
Princip, Gavrilo, 23–24, 28–29
Prohibition, 242
propaganda: black, 53–54, 192–194; British, 51–52; counter, 94; German, 10, 49–61, 104–105; gray, 53–56; by railroad companies, 192–194; start of World War I and, 51–52; war, 10, 11, 49–61; white, 53
Providence, Rhode Island, 195–197
Providence Journal, 2–5, 12, 13, 166; circulation of, 47, 195; election of 1920 and, 249; *Evening Bulletin*, 47, 195; German spies at, 176–178; morning edition, 47; offices of, 47–49; Rathom as editor of, 2–5, 46–47, 94–95, 195, 197–198, 242–243; spy hunting and, 217; stories published by, 46–50, 58–61, 139–141, 161–165
Psalm 100, 294–295
Pulver, Adela, 277, 278
Pulver, Isaac, 277

R
racial stereotypes, 191
radio messages, 139–140
railroad bridge bombing, 31–33, 39–43, 146, 166
railroad companies, 192–194
Railway Press Bureau, 193–194
Rankin, Jeannette, 211
Rathom, John Revelstoke: Albert

story by, 149–150; *Ancona* story by, 168–169; anti-German advocacy by, 113–115; appearance of, 6, 76, 195; arrest of, 67; arsenic plot and, 130–134; assault charges against, 71; Austrian spy stories by, 158–159, 161–165; Bielaski and, 45, 158–161, 174–178, 180, 186, 220, 223, 225–228, 231–235; biography of, 7, 76–77; black propaganda by, 192–194; Boy-Ed and, 105–107, 165; burial of, 267–268; in Chicago, 187–194; at *Colonist*, 66–67; confession by, 231–235, 247–249, 252–262; contradictions in, 69; as correspondent during Spanish-American War, 75–83; creation of, 62–83; as crime reporter, 74–75; death of, 266–267; defeat of Central Powers and, 8, 94–95; downfall of, 8, 259–260; early career of, 64–69, 71–72; as editor of *Providence Journal*, 2–5, 46–47, 94–95, 195, 197–198, 242–243; extortion by, 66–67, 71–72, 73; fame of, 215, 219–220, 223, 233; FDR and, 238, 247, 249–253, 260–264; fearmongering by, 221–222; financial difficulties of, 192; Florence and, 123–134, 190–192; forgeries by, 65; Gaunt and, 94–95; German conspiracy stories by, 2, 4–5, 12–16, 114, 139–147, 209; German espionage stories by, 94–95, 215, 228–230; Goricar story by, 161–165; as government informant, 160; grand jury appearance by, 230–233; "hearts story" of, 14–15, 218, 236, 256; Horn story by, 146–147; Huerta story by, 120, 142–147, 255; identity of, 281–284; illness of, 265–266; on immigrants, 191; immigration to Canada by, 62–64; immigration to U.S. by, 72; as imposter, 5–8, 16, 71, 216, 236; influence of, 11, 50; Iroquois Theater fire story by, 187–190; Justice Department file on, 225, 236, 242,

261–262; libel charges against, 72–73, 252, 263–264; lies by, 16, 174, 215, 216, 223, 231, 233; marriage to Mary Crockford by, 70–71, 283; Means and, 175, 181–186, 255; move to Rhode Island by, 195; neutrality laws story by, 46–50, 58–61; obituary of, 266–267; in Oregon, 72–74; Papen and, 165; Parliament Building fire and, 173–175, 182–185; personal details of, 8–9; personality of, 6–7; poetry by, 73–74, 191; post-confession, 262; post-WWI, 242–243; as railroad company agent, 192–194; reasons for new identity of, 293–295; reporting by, 67–69; reputation of, 16, 64–65, 161, 178, 213; in San Francisco, 74–75, 121–122, 125–134; Section A sting and, 246–249; on sinking of *Falaba*, 101; sinking of *Lusitania* and, 107–109; "Some Inside History" talk by, 12–16; sources of, 139, 141, 143, 146–147, 158–161, 175, 181–182, 232, 255, 256; speaking tour of, 214–220, 223, 225, 229; as spy hunter, 215–220, 223, 229; stories for *World's Work*, 232–235, 241; targeting of, by Department of Justice, 222–232, 235–236, 242; trial of, 69–70; U.S. citizenship for, 195; on U.S. entrance into war, 212; Viereck and, 114–115, 166–167; Voska and, 94–95; Wilson and, 105–107, 142, 166–167, 231; yellow fever of, 81–83; Zwiedinek story by, 178–181

Rathom, Mary, 70–72, 74, 122, 125, 128–134, 190, 283

Record-Herald, 188, 191, 192

religious freedom, 288–289

Rhode Island, 195–197, 201

Richards, E. S., 287–288

Ridder, Herman, 145–146

Rintelen, Franz, 116–120, 143, 255

Rochemont, Louis de, 42–43

Romania, 22

Room 40, 206

Roosevelt, Franklin Delano: as assistant secretary of the navy, 202; libel charges by, 252, 263–264; Newport scandal and, 262–264; nomination as vice president, 248–249; polio diagnosis for, 264–265; political career of, 265; presidential election of 1920 and, 248–249, 260; Rathom and, 8, 212–213, 238, 247, 249–253, 260–264; sex crime operation and, 239–241

Roosevelt, Theodore, 77–78, 193–194, 229

Rose, Hans, 200–201, 203–206

Ross, George, 42–43

Rotterdam, 1, 3, 155, 156

Rough Riders, 77–78

Rudolf, Crown Prince, 25

Russia: pre-WWI, 20, 21; start of World War I and, 29–30, 35

Russian hackers, 118–119

Rutland, Suzanne D., 288

S

Sacramento Bee, 148

San Francisco, 74–75, 83, 121–122, 125–134

San Francisco Chronicle, 74–76, 79–80, 83, 121, 131, 165

Santa Cruz, California, 122–124

Sarajevo, 17–19, 27, 28

Saratoga, New York, 291

Saturday Evening Post, 53

Scheib, Elsie, 128–130, 133

Schlieffen, Alfred von, 35

Schwatka, Frederick, 7, 77

Scopes, John T., 57

Scopes Monkey Trial, 57

Second Battle of Ypres, 102

Second Boer War, 154

Secret Service, 150

Section A sting, 240–241, 243–250, 262–264

Seligman, Joseph, 287, 288, 290–293

Serbia, 22, 23, 29, 30

sex crime operation, 239–241, 243–250, 262–264

Shafter, William, 78, 79

Sheppard, Henry, 67, 69, 71, 72

Sinatra, Frank, 1

Sinclair, Upton, 257–258

social media, 11, 54, 119

Solomon, Emanuel, 271–277

Solomon, John Pulver, 270, 272, 277–285, 287, 293–295. *See also* Rathom, John Revelstoke

Solomon, Judah Moss, 269–271, 277–279, 285–286

Solomon, Samuel Moss, 273

Solomon, Vaiben, 271–277

Solomon, Vaiben Louis, 270, 279–280

"Some Inside History" (Rathom), 12–16

Sophie, Duchess of Hohenberg, 17, 18, 26–27, 29

Spanish-American War, 7, 75–83, 126, 153–154

Spilman, Charles, 281

Spring-Rice, Cecil, 88

Staats-Zeitung, 145–146

Stanley, Henry Morton, 283

Steed, Wickham, 86, 89

Stephano, 205

St. James Hotel, 118

Stonewall riots, 246

Strathdene, 205

Strother, French, 224–225, 232–235, 241

submarine blockade, 98–99, 101, 102, 108, 167–169

submarine warfare, 200–201, 205–208

"The Suicide" (Rathom), 73–74

Swan Point Cemetery, 267

Swilltown, 72

Sydney, Australia, 276

T

Taft, William Howard, 102, 229

Tague, Aubrey, 40–41

Takei, George, 222

Tampa, Florida, 77–78

Taussig, Joseph K., 250

terrorists, 23–24

Thompson, C. S., 230–231

Thrasher, Leon, 96–97, 100, 101, 102, 108

Titanic, 102

Tomory, Eugene von, 158–159

Touro Synagogue, 288

Trading with the Enemy Act, 181

Triple Entente, 22

Trump, Donald, 21, 54, 119, 293

Tsinau, 280

Tuchman, Barbara, 206

Turkey, 22

U

U-28, 100

U-53, 199–201, 203–206

U-boats. *See* German U-boats

United Muslims of America, 54, 119

United States: conflicts between Mexico and, 111–113, 119, 207; diplomatic break with Germany by, 208–209; entrance into war by, 8, 211–212; export of munitions to Allies by, 35–38; German diplomats in, 10, 35, 36; Germans in, 33–38, 93, 109, 289, 290; industrial capacity of, 37; Jewish community in, 287–295; neutrality of, 2, 5, 30, 35, 49–50, 56, 58, 93–94, 101–102, 107–109; public opinion in, 51–52, 109, 113; religious freedom in, 288–289; response to submarine warfare by, 208–209; U-boats dispatched to, 199–202, 203–206

U.S. banks, 141

U.S. Navy, 238–239; homosexuality in, 237–241; Section A sting, 243–249, 262–264

U.S. press: arsenic plot in, 130–132; coverage of Huerta plot in, 143–146; pro-German, 114–115; publication of Albert's papers by, 147–148, 152; on Rathom, 219–220; on Rathom's confession, 256–258; reaction to *Falaba*

sinking by, 101; on spies in U.S., 228–229; on *U-53*, 204, 205–206; war news in, 102. *See also specific papers*
USS *Maine*, 75–76, 79, 102
USS *Wheeling*, 123–124

V
Vanceboro railroad bridge bombing, 31–33, 39–43, 146, 166
Veracruz occupation, 112–113
Vesmir, 179–180, 181
Victoria, Canada, 63–65, 68–69, 71–72
Victoria Daily Times, 64
Viereck, George Sylvester, 104–105, 114–115, 135–137, 148, 150–152, 166–167
Voska, Emanuel, 84–89, 93–95, 113, 120, 139, 149; Archibald and, 155–158; Austrian spy story and, 158; Iska and, 181; Rathom and, 256
Voska, Villa, 87

W
Walker, Alastair, 99
Walker, James A., 124
Wall Street Journal, 114
war correspondents, 153–155
war propaganda, 10, 11, 49–61
Warren, Charles, 229
war supplies, stopping of, 32–38
war zone: neutral ships in, 99; ocean travel through, 103–104
Washington, Booker T., 191
Washington, George, 288–289
weapons makers, 114
Welland Canal, 37–38, 39, 166
Wendes, Dave, 91–92
West Point, 205
Whinham College, 278
white propaganda, 53
Wigzell, Mary, 285–286
Wilhelm I, 104
Wilhelm II, 20–21, 29, 199, 200
Williams, Roger, 196
Wilson, Edith, 211

Wilson, Woodrow, 1, 4, 30, 101, 117; declaration of war by, 211–212; diplomatic break with Germany by, 208–209; election of 1920 and, 247; fearmongering by, 221; Goricar story and, 162; Huerta and, 111, 112, 113; Kent trial and, 246; Mexico and, 119, 144; peace brokering by, 170–171, 209; Rathom and, 105–107, 142, 166–167, 231; Roosevelt and, 241; on sinking of *Ancona*, 168; sinking of *Lusitania* and, 107, 108; spy operations by, 150; on victory in WWI, 242
Wing, Yip, 71–72
wireless transmissions, 139–140
women's liberation movement, 124–125
Woolmans, Sue, 17
World Series, 203, 204
World's Work, 215–216, 224–227, 232–235, 241
World War I, 4; American neutrality during, 2, 5, 30, 35, 49–50, 56, 58, 93–94; casualties in, 10, 242; cause of, 11, 17–30; coverage of, 154–155; end of, 237, 242; European history before, 19–23; events of, 10–12; politics of, 93; public opinion on, 5, 10, 51–52, 109; Rathom's efforts in, 8; start of, 29–30; U.S. entrance into, 8, 211–212, 241; use of poison gas in, 102
World War II, 93, 222, 265
Wright, Ed, 65

Y
yellow fever, 78, 81–83
Young, John, 83

Z
Zeno, 87
Zimmermann, Arthur, 206–207
Zimmermann telegram, 206–207, 210–211
Zipf, Charles B., 243–245
Zwiedinek von Südenhorst, Erich Freiherr, 178–181